THE JOHANNINE THEOLOGY

By the Same Author.

THE PAULINE THEOLOGY. A Study of the Origin and Correlation of the Doctrinal Teachings of the Apostle Paul. Cr. 8vo. $2.00.

THE
JOHANNINE THEOLOGY

A STUDY OF THE

DOCTRINAL CONTENTS

OF

THE GOSPEL AND EPISTLES OF
THE APOSTLE JOHN

BY

GEORGE B. STEVENS, Ph.D., D.D.

PROFESSOR OF NEW TESTAMENT CRITICISM AND INTERPRETATION
IN YALE UNIVERSITY

Eugene, Oregon

Wipf and Stock Publishers
199 W 8th Ave, Suite 3
Eugene, OR 97401

The Johannine Theology
A Study of the Doctrinal Contents of the Gospel
and Epistles of the Apostle John
By Stevens, George B.
ISBN: 1-59752-186-8
Publication date 5/10/2005
Previously published by Charles Scribner's Sons, 1895

TO

TIMOTHY DWIGHT, D.D., LL.D.

PRESIDENT OF YALE UNIVERSITY

MY INSTRUCTOR AND MY PREDECESSOR IN THE CHAIR OF NEW TESTAMENT INTERPRETATION

I DEDICATE THIS VOLUME

AS A TOKEN OF GRATITUDE AND AFFECTION

PREFACE

THE aim of this volume is to present, in systematic form, the theological contents of the Gospel and Epistles of John. No account is here taken of the Apocalypse, since, whatever view be held respecting its authorship, it represents a type of teaching so peculiar in its form and matter that it should be treated separately. Accordingly, most writers on Biblical theology discuss its contents as a distinct subject, whether they ascribe it to the author of the Gospel and Epistles or not.

The purpose of my work also determines its scope. My plan did not require me to discuss the vexed literary questions connected with the writings which form the subject of my study. I ascribe these writings to the apostle John, but my task would not have been essentially different upon any other supposition respecting their authorship. The Gospel and Epistles which are commonly attributed to John present a certain distinctive type of Christian teaching, and this it has been my effort to interpret. I should have undertaken briefly to trace the history and describe the present state of criticism respecting the Fourth Gospel, had not this work been adequately done by others. I would refer the reader, in this connection, to two articles by Professors Schürer and Sanday, respectively, in the *Contemporary Review* for September and October, 1891. Schürer's article presents the negative, Sanday's the positive view respecting the apostolic authorship of the Gospel. The history of this controversy is reviewed at length, on the conservative side, by Archdeacon Watkins, in his Bampton Lectures for 1890, entitled *Modern Criticism considered in its Relation to the Fourth Gospel*. I would especially commend to the student the arguments for the apostolic authorship of the Fourth Gospel by Dr. Ezra Abbot,[1] Bishop Lightfoot,[2]

---

[1] *The Authorship of the Fourth Gospel: External Evidences*, published in Dr. Abbot's posthumous *Critical Essays*, Boston, 1888; also in a volume entitled *The Fourth Gospel* (Charles Scribner's Sons, New York, 1892), which contains one of the articles of Bishop Lightfoot referred to in the next note, and another by Dr. A. P. Peabody. These last two articles are on the internal evidence. Dr. Abbot's Essay is also published separately (Boston, 1880). It was originally printed in *The Unitarian Review* for February, March, and June, 1880. Statements of the argument, on the negative side, may be found in Keim's *Jesus of Nazara*, S. Davidson's *Introduction*, Holtzmann's *Einleitung* and *Hand-Commentar*, E. A. Abbott's article *Gospels* in the *Encyclopædia Britannica*, and Cone's *Gospel Criticism and Historical Christianity*.

[2] Two dissertations, one on the internal and the other on the external evidence, will be found in the late Bishop Lightfoot's *Biblical Essays* (London and New York, 1893). The former of these was originally published in *The Expositor* for January, February, and March, 1890, and was reprinted in the volume, *The Fourth Gospel*, referred to in the preceding note. The essay on the external evidence was printed from lecture-

and President Dwight.[1] Mr. R. H. Hutton's essay on *The Historical Problems of the Fourth Gospel* (in his *Theological Essays*) is an able review and refutation of Baur's objections to its genuineness.

The problem of authorship is not the only literary problem which the Fourth Gospel presents. For those who hold John to be its author there remains the interesting and important question as to its historical accuracy. Its account of the words and deeds of Jesus differs to such an extent in language and subject-matter from the account contained in the Synoptic Gospels, that candid scholarship cannot avoid the inquiry as to their relation and relative correctness. Are we to suppose that Jesus uttered *verbatim* the long discourses which John reports, and which are so different in style and matter from the Synoptic discourses? It can hardly be doubted that at least the *form* of these reports is more or less affected by the apostle's own thought and reflection. But this admission implies a subjective element in the Fourth Gospel. To define its limits with absolute precision is a task for which we have no adequate data. We can establish the substantial

---

notes and is found only in *Biblical Essays*. In this same volume are found important additions to the essay on the internal evidence as originally published. The two essays, with the additions, make nearly two hundred pages of the volume, and are of the highest value.

[1] *Introductory Suggestions with reference to the Internal Evidence*, appended to vol. i. of the American edition of Godet's *Commentary on the Gospel of John*, New York, 1886.

agreement in underlying ideas between John's version of the teaching of Jesus and that of the Synoptists. It would seem evident, however, that the apostle has given us this teaching in his own words, and in the shape and color which it had assumed through long reflection upon its contents and meaning. But whatever conclusion may be reached respecting these problems, it holds true that the Fourth Gospel represents in all its parts the Johannine theology. The question concerning the subjective element in John is a question for literary criticism rather than for Biblical theology. Since we have to deal exclusively with the contents of the book as a product of its author's mind, the validity of our results will not be dependent upon any views which may be entertained respecting the accuracy of his narratives.

In the preparation of this volume I have pursued substantially the same method as was employed in my treatise on the Pauline Theology.[1] I have sought to exhibit the salient features of the type of teaching with which I have dealt, and to show how the leading ideas stand related to one another and to the writer's method of thought. Since this method is intuitional rather than logical, it is more difficult than in the case of Paul to determine precisely the correlation of his ideas. It has seemed to

---

[1] THE PAULINE THEOLOGY, *a Study of the Origin and Correlation of the Doctrinal Teachings of the Apostle Paul.* Charles Scribner's Sons, New York, 1892.

me, however, that this task could be, in a good degree, accomplished by giving close attention to the peculiarities of John's thinking, and by taking as our guides a few fundamental and comprehensive ideas in which his whole theology seems to centre. In the first chapter on the peculiarities of John's theology I have sought to indicate how the scattered elements of doctrine in John may be traced up into the unity of certain great comprehensive conceptions. I have hoped by applying this method, to make clear the genetic connection of the writer's thoughts, and the real unity and simplicity of his teaching.

The Bibliography which is appended to the volume will guide the student to the most important recent literature of the subject. I have thought that it would prove useful, in addition, to prefix to each chapter a special account of the literature which might well be consulted in the further study of the various topics treated. I have made these references somewhat detailed by giving specific titles, number of pages, etc., in order that the student may form some judgment in advance respecting the nature and scope of the discussions. These various references to literature may also serve to indicate my own indebtedness to other writers on the theology of John. I have derived more or less assistance from almost all the authors to whose writings I have referred. My work has been chiefly done, however, on the basis of the text itself. I have been more aided by a few standard commentaries — especially those of Meyer, Westcott, Haupt, Weiss, and Plummer — than by any other books outside the Johannine writings themselves.

No treatise which purports to furnish a critical and systematic presentation of the theology of John has hitherto been composed in English. The works of Sears, Lias, and Peyton, which are cited in the Bibliography under the head of *Treatises on the Johannine Theology*, are either too limited in scope, or too apologetic or purely practical in aim, to be regarded as works on Biblical theology in any very strict sense. Nor is there any recent German work distinctly on the subject. The most recent and the most satisfactory one — at least, as respects method, scope, and thoroughness — is that of Weiss, published in 1862. It can hardly be doubted, therefore, that there is room in our theological literature for an exposition of the theology of John, which shall set forth the salient features of this great tpye of New Testament teaching. The Johannine conceptions of religious truth are destined to hold a larger place in theological thought than has usually been accorded to them. I shall be gratified if this volume serves in some measure to elucidate and emphasize some of those conceptions, to make more manifest their great depth and richness, and to illustrate their value for Christian thought and life.

G. B. S.

YALE UNIVERSITY,
Sept. 1, 1894.

CONTENTS

CHAPTER		PAGE
I.	THE PECULIARITIES OF JOHN'S THEOLOGY	1
II.	THE RELATION OF JOHN'S THEOLOGY TO THE OLD TESTAMENT	22
III.	THE IDEA OF GOD IN THE WRITINGS OF JOHN	46
IV.	THE DOCTRINE OF THE LOGOS	74
V.	THE UNION OF THE SON WITH THE FATHER	102
VI.	THE DOCTRINE OF SIN	127
VII.	THE WORK OF SALVATION	156
VIII.	THE DOCTRINE OF THE HOLY SPIRIT	189
IX.	THE APPROPRIATION OF SALVATION	218
X.	THE ORIGIN AND NATURE OF THE SPIRITUAL LIFE	241
XI.	THE DOCTRINE OF LOVE	266
XII.	THE DOCTRINE OF PRAYER	290
XIII.	THE DOCTRINE OF ETERNAL LIFE	312
XIV.	THE JOHANNINE ESCHATOLOGY	328
XV.	THE THEOLOGY OF JOHN AND OF PAUL COMPARED	355

BIBLIOGRAPHY 373
INDEX OF TEXTS 377
GENERAL INDEX 381

THE JOHANNINE THEOLOGY

CHAPTER I

THE PECULIARITIES OF JOHN'S THEOLOGY

Literature. — WESTCOTT: *The Gospel according to St. John*, Characteristics of the Gospel, pp. lxvi.-lxxvii.; WEISS: *Bibl. Theol.*, The Character of the Johannean Theology, ii. 315-320 (orig. 589-593); BEYSCHLAG: *Neutest. Theol.*, Eigenart des Lehrbegriffs, ii. 404-406; KÖSTLIN: *Johann. Lehrbegriff*, Allgemeiner Character des Johanneischen Lehrbegriffs, pp. 38-72; SEARS: *The Heart of Christ*, The Johannean Writings, their Congruity, Interior Relations, etc., pp. 64-90; GLOAG: *Introduction to the Johannine Writings*, The Theology of John, pp. 236-263; FARRAR: *The Early Days of Christianity*, chap. xxxiii., Characteristics of the Mind and Style of St. John (various editions); REUSS: *Hist. of Christ. Theol.*, etc., General Outline of the Theology of John, ii. 375-382 (orig. ii. 418-428); HAUPT: *The First Epistle of John*, Theological Principles of the Epistle, pp. 375-385 (orig. pp. 320-329); CONE: *The Gospel and its Earliest Interpretations*, etc., chap. v., The Johannine Transformation, pp. 267-317; HORTON: *Revelation and the Bible*, The Johannine Writings, pp. 369-402; NEANDER: *Planting and Training of the Christian Church*, The Doctrine of John, ii. 28-57 (Bohn ed.); E. CAIRD: *The Evolution of Religion*, The Gospel of St. John and the Idea of a Divine Humanity, ii. 217-243.

BIBLICAL theology undertakes to define the peculiarities of the various types of teaching which are found in Sacred Scripture. It aims to distinguish each type as sharply as possible from every other, in order to set the given writer's method of thought and style of argument in the strongest relief. This process does not prejudice the underlying unity of the different types, but by its sharp discriminations it enables us to define the nature and limitations of that unity. The fundamental unity in doctrine among the various Biblical books cannot be clearly discerned without a close study of each author separately, or of each group of books which naturally belong together.

No type of New Testament teaching has more of individuality than the Johannine; none has characteristics at once more marked and more difficult to define. The peculiarities of John's thought elude exact description. They are felt by all attentive readers, but they almost defy the effort to deduce from them the modes and laws of the writer's own thinking upon the great themes of religion.

I should place among the most prominent of John's peculiarities the tendency to group his thoughts around certain great central truths. Whatever may have been the actual order in which his ideas were unfolded in his mind, it is noticeable that in his presentation of them in the Gospel and in the First Epistle his thought moves out from certain formative and determining conceptions which he has of his subject. Whatever be the interpretation of the prologue, or the origin of its ideas, it is certain that it is designed to present the apostle's loftiest conception of the person of his Master and of his relation to mankind. The writer starts from this height of contemplation.

PECULIARITIES OF JOHN'S THEOLOGY

In a way somewhat analogous, the First Epistle opens with a reference to eternity, in which the content of the gospel message was stored up ready to come to the world in Christ. In both cases this secret of God which is to be disclosed to mankind is life or light. The Word was the bearer of life, "and the life was the light of men" (i. 4);[1] so also in the Epistle the import of the heavenly mystery which Jesus discloses is life (I. i. 2), and the "message" which he brought to the world is summed up in the truth that "God is light" (I. i. 5).

We thus see how the apostle has concentrated his thought upon a profound conception, which henceforth became for him the epitome of all that he had to teach. He grounds the work of Christ in his person. It is, in part, this order of thought which leads him to place his highest claims for the person of Christ at the opening of his Gospel. The incarnate life of Jesus is, to use one of Horace Bushnell's words, the "transactional" revelation of principles and forces which are essential and eternal in his very being. His bringing of life and light to men on his mission to earth was grounded in the larger and deeper truth that he had always been illumining the minds of men. All through the Old Testament

---

[1] Passages from the Fourth Gospel are referred to simply by chapter and verse, without any further designation, thus: viii. 42. To passages from the Epistles I have prefixed a numeral in large type, indicating the number of the Epistle from which the citation is made, thus: I. iv. 8: II. 4, etc.

period of revelation the true light of the Logos was shining into the lives, not of the Jews only, but of all men (i. 9, 10). This fact, again, was based on the essential nature of the Logos, who was with God in the beginning, and was God. But in the development of his thought John starts from this last and highest point. Thus, the specific Messianic mission of Jesus to earth is grounded in his universal relation to the world and man, and this relation, in turn, is grounded in his essential nature.

In accord with this mode of thought, we find that the action of God is always conceived of as springing from the divine nature. John is thus by pre-eminence the theologian in the original sense of that word. More explicitly than any other New Testament writer he sets his idea of God in relation to all his teaching. What God has done in revelation and redemption it was according to his nature to do. If God has loved the world, it is because he is love. If he has enlightened the world, it is because he is light. In revealing himself to men in Christ, he has expressed under a personal form his own thoughts, feelings, and will. The revelation does not consist primarily in announcements made about God; it consists rather in the coming to men of One who, in his own person and character, is a transcript of the divine nature. In John's interpretation of the revelation, it consists in what Jesus Christ is, in his power to say: "I and the Father are one" (x. 30); "He that hath seen me hath seen the Father" (xiv. 9). God has not merely

PECULIARITIES OF JOHN'S THEOLOGY

sent to mankind a message, but has come to the world in Christ, who embodies in his own person the Father's will and nature.

It is very clear that in the First Epistle, John deduces his whole teaching concerning the nature and demands of the Christian life from the idea of the ethical nature of God. Having said that the import of the gospel message is that God is light (I. i. 5), he proceeds to show that this holy purity of God must, on the one hand, make Christians see and feel that sin still clings to them, and, on the other, show them what is the true nature of the life which they profess. When we know that God is light we know that we are still sinful, but we also see the path which leads from all sin unto himself. In the light of God we see that he has provided for the forgiveness of our sins and for our fellowship with each other in Christian love. These ideas are unfolded by no formal process of reasoning; but they are not, on that account, less plainly developed from the truth that God is light (I. i. 5–ii. 6).

This truth also involves the principle and duty of love. Light and love are synonyms. He that loves is dwelling and walking in the light, while he who hates is in darkness. The nature of God as light or love determines the law and requirement of the Christian life (I. ii. 7–11). The same relation is defined even more explicitly in I. iv. 7–21, where the apostle shows that since God is love, the principle of love is the essential requirement of religion and the bond of all true brotherhood. Love is divine. It has its primal source in God. The love of God for us explains our endowment with capacity to love him in return, and this answering love of the heart to God carries with it the obligation to love our fellow-men, who are one with us by virtue of a common nature, and by being, like ourselves, the object of God's fatherly love. The tendency of John to refer all the duties and demands of religion to the moral nature of God as their source and norm, is nowhere better illustrated than in the passage : " Beloved, let us love one another: for love is of God ; and every one that loveth is begotten of God, and knoweth God. He that loveth not knoweth not God ; for God is love " (I. iv. 7, 8).

This peculiarity of thought, which centralizes ideas in their logical source or ground, is pervading and fundamental in the writings of John. It is partially described by the terms by which the Gospel and Epistles are commonly characterized, such as " spiritual," " intuitive," " contemplative." These and kindred designations have their truth in the fact that the apostle's mind penetrates to the heart of things, and dwells in rapt contemplation upon those deepest realities with which all true religion is mainly concerned. Religion is altogether a matter of personal relations. It is God-likeness, fellowship with Christ, sympathy with his spirit, fraternal helpfulness among men. John's treatment of the truths of religion is intensely ethical and spiritual. It deals wholly with

PECULIARITIES OF JOHN'S THEOLOGY

the relations between God and man, and with those of men to one another. It is characterized by an intense sense of God. It is contemplative, mystical, emotional, but not in the sense of being vague or shadowy. The most secure of all realities is God. The apostle is most certain as to what kind of a being, in his essential nature, God is, especially in his feeling toward the world. He knows that he is light, — pure, glorious, diffusive, beneficent, life-giving. He knows that he is love, — condescending, pitying, sympathetic, forgiving. These deep truths he has read in the life of Christ. Of all the disciples he most clearly penetrated to those divinest truths which lay at the root of every specific precept, parable, or miracle of the Saviour. To John the life, teaching, and death of Jesus are the language in which God has written out most plainly his deepest thoughts and feelings toward mankind. His conception of the life of Christ is well expressed in Tennyson's lines: —

> And so the Word had breath, and wrought
> With human hands the creed of creeds
> In loveliness of perfect deeds.

Just as the acts of God flow out of his nature, and the work of Christ is grounded on what he is, so the acts and choices of men are determined by what the men are in their fixed preferences and character. This correspondence between character and conduct John does not conceive after the manner of philosophical determinism; he treats it as the result of an ethical necessity. The Jews did not understand Jesus' speech because they could not hear his word (viii. 43). It was none the less true that they would not hear it. The moral inability to hear his word sprang out of their deep-set opposition in character and spirit to that which he taught. In such cases the ethical kinship of men is often denoted by saying that they are " of God " (viii. 42, 47 ; I. iii. 10 ; I. iv. 4, 6), or " of the devil " (I. iii. 8) ; " of the truth " (I. iii. 19), or "of the world " (I. ii. 15, 16 ; I. iv. 5), and the like. A man does the things which are consonant with the moral sphere of motive and interest to which he belongs, and in which he dwells and walks. To be of God, or to be born of God, is to live a life of which God is the determining power ; to be of the Evil One is to live a life of sin. He who is of the truth is described as belonging to it, so that it is his encompassing element, determining the whole quality and tendency of his being. The truth is in him ; he does not merely possess it ; it has its seat and home in him, and sways his life in all its aspirations and issues. He, on the other hand, who is of the world, lives a life of transitory pleasures, and all the expressions of his interest and desire are determined by motives of selfishness.

It naturally results from this mode of view that man is regarded as a unit in all his powers and actions. All the acts of a man involve his total personality. This is the reason why terms descriptive of acts and choices have with John so compre-

PECULIARITIES OF JOHN'S THEOLOGY

hensive a sense. To know the truth, for example, is to be free, and to have eternal life; but this does not mean, for the apostle, that the religious life is an intellectual affair, consisting in the mere possession of knowledge. To know the truth is to possess it as a determining power in one's life; to know God is to be in harmony and sympathy with his will. John's mode of thought is, in these respects, synthetic rather than analytic. He never separates mind and heart, will and emotion. In this he is true to life. The truths of religion make their appeal to the entire man. He who really knows God, in the apostle's sense of the word *know*, also obeys, trusts, and loves God. These various terms designate, no doubt, distinguishable phases of the religious life and spirit; but they cannot be separated, and should not be treated as if they could exist apart. The application of analytic thought to religion breaks it up into various departments, and often subdivides these, making the religious life an elaborate programme, and the conditions of salvation an extended series of exercises or *ordo salutis*. John's mode of thought is the opposite of all this. He simplifies and unifies acts and experiences which modern minds have learned sharply to discriminate, and even to treat apart.

It certainly can be justly said that, necessary as discrimination and analysis are in dealing with the truths of religion, the apostle's method of thought is that which corresponds best with normal and healthy religious life. His conception of religion is adverse to all narrowness and one-sidedness. As against the Gnostic over-emphasis of knowledge, he insisted that he only who *does* righteousness is righteous (I. iii. 7). The mere intellectual possession of truth cannot suffice; truth is not merely something to be known, but something to be done (iii. 21; I. i. 6). The Christian is to walk in the truth as his native element (II. 4; III. 3, 4); the truth dwells within him (viii. 44; I. ii. 4), controls and guides him; he belongs to it, and draws from it the strength and inspiration of his life (xviii. 37; I. ii. 21; I. iii. 19). Doctrine and life are inseparable. John never thinks of the truths of religion as dead, cold forms which one might hold without living the life which corresponds to them. Such a mere intellectual assent to truth would have for religion, in his view, no value or significance. Religion is life after the type which has been perfectly exemplified in Jesus Christ; but it is life in a full and rich, not in a narrow and limited, sense. It is a life that is abundant, a life which embraces the fullest activity and best development of the entire man. All powers and gifts should contribute to its enrichment. It should draw its supplies from the deepest sources, — abiding fellowship with God, and ethical likeness to him. Neither a barren intellectualism nor a dreamy and unpractical mysticism in religion could ever develop along the lines of teaching which John has marked out. All such excesses would be excluded by the very comprehensiveness and depth of his idea.

PECULIARITIES OF JOHN'S THEOLOGY 11

The mind of the apostle seems to see all things in their principles and essential ideas. This peculiarity of thought gives rise to a species of realism. All the forces of goodness are comprehended by him under some general idea, like light or truth, while all the forms of evil are summed up as darkness or falsehood. The whole course of history illustrates the conflict of these opposing powers or principles. The individual is allied to the one or to the other. The character and actions of men correspond to the principle which sways their lives. Individual acts spring out of the deep affinities of the soul. What men desire and choose is determined with a moral necessity by the governing idea of their lives. "Thus it happens," as Haupt has so aptly said, "that history appears to John not so much as a sum of individual free human acts, interwoven with one another, but rather is for him a great organism, — if one will not object to the word, — a process, the inner law of whose development is as much prescribed to it, and as naturally flows from it, as the plant springs from the seed. For everything individual stands inevitably and immediately, consciously or unconsciously, in the service of the idea. History is for John the outworking of the idea, the body which the idea assumes to itself; and this body is naturally conformed to the soul — that is, to the idea — which builds it for itself. History is the invisible translated into the visible." [1]

[1] *Der erste Brief des Johannes*, pp. 321, 322.

The apostle's habit of thinking in antitheses is an illustration of this peculiarity of his mind. Accordingly, his writings are characterized by a species of dualism, — not the metaphysical dualism which makes evil an essential and eternal principle of the universe, but a moral dualism which, as a matter of fact, finds illustration in human history from the beginning of the race. The moral history of mankind is the conflict of light and darkness, the shining of the true light in the world's darkness, and an appropriation, but slow and partial, of the light by the darkness.

Attention should here be directed to the way in which John conceives religion, as consisting in this immediate personal relation of the soul to God or to Christ. Religion is, above all things, fellowship with God, and this fellowship involves likeness to God. It is such an abiding in God, such a walking in his light, that the soul becomes possessed of something of the purity and love which dwell perfectly in God. The religious life begins with an impartation from God. To be born of God means to receive from him a communication of spiritual life whereby the soul is more and more transformed into Christlikeness. To the mind of John religion signifies the progressive attainment by man of his true type or idea, — not, indeed, by efforts of his own, but by his appropriation and use of that divine power which God freely bestows upon him. To be begotten of God is to be righteous, even as Christ is righteous (I. ii. 29). The Christlike life is the true life, and the only true life. Hence our author

PECULIARITIES OF JOHN'S THEOLOGY 13

insists with great energy that Christianity means pure character. "He that doeth righteousness is righteous, even as he [Christ] is righteous" (I. iii. 7). Between the Christian life and sin there is an absolute contrariety in principle. The Christian man is characteristically righteous, and while sin still cleaves to him (I. i. 8–10), he cannot live the life of habitual sin (ἁμαρτίαν οὐ ποιεῖ) (I. iii. 9). The Christian man has been cleansed; but as the traveller in Oriental lands needs, on coming in from the dusty street, to wash his feet, so the Christian needs to be purified from the sin which still cleaves to his life (xiii. 10). But supremely and characteristically sinful he cannot be; that would be a contradiction in terms. Hence, with his strong emphasis on the governing idea of the religious life, and with his intense sense of its characteristic quality, John does not hesitate to affirm: "Every one who abideth in him sinneth not" (οὐχ ἁμαρτάνει); "Every one who has been begotten from God does not do sin, because his seed abides in him, and he cannot sin, because he has been begotten of God" (I. iii. 6, 9).

Another peculiarity of the Johannine theology is seen in the way in which the apostle blends the religious life in this world with the eternal spiritual order. By his conception of eternal life as a present possession he unites this world with the world to come. To his mind the spiritual life is the heavenly life already begun. He comprehends the particular in the universal, and estimates all things in the light of eternity. Therefore the individual life that is formed upon the divine pattern belongs by its very nature to the world of abiding realities. Since it is the life of fellowship with God, it partakes of his own purity, and has in it the elements of true strength, endurance, and growth. The idea of eternal life which is found in the Fourth Gospel springs directly out of the Johannine mysticism. Whenever man receives the impartation of the Spirit of God and walks in fellowship with God, eternal life is begun. Heaven and earth are near together, and that which separates them is not death, but sin.

It will be apparent from the considerations which have thus far been presented that John has given us a purely ethical and spiritual conception of religion. The whole emphasis is laid upon the inner quality of the life. True worship is from the heart, and may be offered anywhere. Nothing is said of institutions, not even of the Church. No emphasis is laid upon sacraments. The establishment of the Lord's Supper is not recorded. The references to baptism are quite incidental, and are chiefly to John's baptism. The practice of baptism as a Christian rite receives no emphasis, unless the somewhat doubtful reference in iii. 5, "Except a man be born of water and the Spirit," etc., be referred to baptism; and, in that case, as Reuss remarks, "baptism is represented as a symbol of the spiritual birth, and not as the commemorative sign of an association."[1] It looks toward

[1] *Hist. Christ. Theol.* ii. 491 (orig. ii. 548).

union with Christ, and not toward union among believers in a community. The type of mind which our author illustrates, naturally concentrates its interest mainly upon the immediate relation of the soul to God. This is not done after the manner of a narrow subjective individualism. Duties to fellow-men are repeatedly emphasized. The person of Christ is not for John a mere ideal to be contemplated with devout rapture; the Master's life was the pattern of service. It was not, however, the outward aspects of his life, but the underlying motives and principles of it, which appealed most powerfully to the mind and heart of John. It was not the mere fact that he once performed an act of menial service in washing the disciples' feet; but it was the relation in which this service stood to the truth that he came forth from God and was going unto God (xiii. 3), to which John attaches such great significance. Indeed, the whole historic life of Christ seemed to him to be grounded in the eternal self-revealing impulse in God, and to express in terms of human life and experience the nature and thoughts of God which in all ages he had been making known in other ways to men (i. 4, 5, 9, 10).

Let us now raise the inquiry, What elements of Christian doctrine is the Johannine theology especially adapted to supply? It will hardly be questioned, I suppose, by any student of theology, that the Johannine type of thought has been far less influential than the Pauline type in shaping the great dogmatic sys-

16 THE JOHANNINE THEOLOGY

tems. The Christian doctrine of God has usually been developed from the legal conceptions of his nature and relations to men which underlie Paul's Jewish forms of thought. The dominant idea of John concerning the nature of God as light or love has not been the characteristic and central conception of the prevailing historic theologies. It has had its influence, but it has not occupied the commanding place which it occupied in the mind of the apostle John. Christian thought concerning God has continued through all the centuries predominantly Jewish, taking its color from the terms of Paul's polemic against Judaism, and growing more and more stereotyped in that form through the influence upon it of the severe logic of certain great minds of a strongly legal cast, such as Augustine, Calvin, and Grotius.

In direct connection with this legalistic tendency of thought concerning God stands the fact that the soteriology of the Church has been characteristically Pauline. The way of salvation has been expounded in rigid adherence to Paul's doctrine of juridical justification. The Pauline legal method of thought — rendered natural to his mind by his Jewish education, and made especially necessary by his conflicts with Judaizing errors — has, in great part, given the law to all Christian thinking on the subject. The conception of God's nature as consisting primarily and essentially of retributive justice, the idea of his absolute decrees, and the application of commercial and governmental analogies to the work of his grace

PECULIARITIES OF JOHN'S THEOLOGY

in redemption, flow directly out of the Jewish aspects of Paul's thought. It is aside from my present purpose to pursue the inquiry, how far this development of thought was justifiable and wholesome, and how far one-sided and misleading. The fact, however, can hardly be denied that the more mystical and purely ethical methods of thought which are illustrated in John have had but a sporadic influence in historic theology. I venture the opinion that theology would have been vastly deepened and enriched, had the profoundly spiritual thought of John permeated and shaped it in anything like the degree in which the polemics of Paul have done. Without detracting in the smallest measure from the great truths which Paulinism has contributed to Christian thought, it appears to me that there is much reason to desire that the spiritual mysticism of John may in time to come acquire its legitimate influence in Christian theology and life. The theology of John is consonant in spirit with that of Paul in its highest ranges; but it represents a mode of thought concerning God and his grace in salvation that is distinctly higher than the legalism of Paul, which he brought over from Judaism, and which supplied his weapons of war against his adversaries rather than furnished his favorite forms for the purely positive expression of the truths of his gospel. In any case, Paul's more legal mode of thought may well be supplemented by John's more spiritual mode; his argumentative handling of religious truth by

John's more direct and intuitive presentation of it, and his more analytic method by John's more synthetic method, which binds together all separate truths in the great all-comprehending truth that God is love.

It is not in the interest of Christian thinking chiefly, but in the interest of Christian life, that I would urge the value of the teaching and spirit of the Johannine writings. The tendency of an increased appreciation and application of John's methods of thought must be to lead to a better adjustment of doctrine and life. A one-sided adherence to the polemics of Paul — called out by the peculiar conditions of his age — has given to our Protestant theology a formally logical aspect which has often made religion too much a set of opinions, and too little a life of fellowship with God. This tendency has often set dogma above life, and theology above religion. It is certain that theology and religion are inseparable, and that they react upon each other; but religion is primary, theology secondary. Theology is the intellectual construction of the realities which in religion are known and experienced. Theology is theory, religion is life. Theology purports to be the intellectual equivalent — which must always be approximate only — of the realities of the religious life. The true method of thought respecting theology and religion is not to separate them, but to assign to each of them its true function. Our Lord's primary concern was religion, — that men should love and

PECULIARITIES OF JOHN'S THEOLOGY

trust God, and live in harmony with his requirements. But these primary truths of religion raise at once great theological questions: What is God's nature? What are his requirements, and how does he make them known to us? There can be no religion without theology, — unless religion can be divorced from thought, since theology begins with the simplest efforts of the mind to construe its religious ideas and experiences, and to interpret their significance, ground, and end. But for this very reason theology is secondary. It is religious thought, — reflection upon religious truth and experience, — and therefore quite distinct from religious life. Theology is to religion what a theory of knowledge is to our actual consciousness of ourselves and of the objects about us. No human being attains fully developed reason without some wonder, inquiry, or reflection concerning the way in which he knows himself and the world; but his thought respecting these perceptions — be it ever so simple or ever so profound — is clearly distinguishable from the actual living experience in which he knows himself and the world.

The apostle John has placed in the foreground of all his teaching the realities of the religious life, — God as love, man as needy, fellowship with God through likeness to Christ as eternal life. He had no occasion so to overlay these primal truths with arguments that they should present themselves to the mind primarily as matter for reasoning; he presents them rather to the heart, with the certainty that they will meet the conscious wants of mankind. His teaching summons men, first of all, to live the sort of life which Jesus Christ has revealed and illustrated. He seems to feel that in the living of that life lies the guaranty of essentially right ideas concerning God and man and duty. He seems willing to trust the religious life to give direction and shape to religious thought. He thus places at the centre what is by its very nature central. His method of treating religion — could it have had its legitimate effect in the Christian life of the world — would have tended strongly to the preservation of unity and harmony among Christians. The divisions of Christendom have arisen mainly from intellectual, and not from religious, differences. They have been differences which have not, in the main, touched the real essential unity in which believers stand through their common fellowship with Christ.[1]

---

[1] Compare the observations of E. H. Sears on this point in his treatise on the Fourth Gospel: "We cannot move toward the Christ without coming closer to each other. Leave him out and his unitizing Word, and let every man strike out for himself, and we tend to a crumbling individualism, to endless distraction and confusion. But those who acknowledge Jesus Christ as the supreme authority and guide, and enter more into his all-revealing mind, are making progress toward the harmonizing truths which he represents. However wide apart they may be at the start, their progress is ever on converging lines. Essential truth becomes more and more central and manifest, the non-essential falls away to its subordinate place, and orthodox and unorthodox move alike toward a higher

PECULIARITIES OF JOHN'S THEOLOGY

The assertion of Maurice that those who fraternize on any other basis than that of fellowship with Christ thereby deny the only true ground of Christian fellowship, is a just inference from John's conception of the unity of Christendom. This unity is real, despite all the efforts of men to destroy it by their conflicts of opinion and theory. It underlies their differences; and if the time shall ever come when Christianity is seen to be primarily not a dogma, but a life, it will reassert itself, and reduce to insignificance those superficial divisions among Christians which different modes of thought respecting metaphysics, polity, and ritual have created in the essentially indivisible Church of Christ. To the attainment of this end I believe the teachings and spirit of the apostle John are especially adapted to contribute.

and higher unity. It is not that any one sect is making a conquest of the others, but Jesus Christ is making a conquest of us all." — *The Heart of Christ*, p. 516.

CHAPTER II

THE RELATION OF JOHN'S THEOLOGY TO THE OLD TESTAMENT

Literature. — FRANKE: *Das Alte Testament bei Johannes;* WENDT: *Teaching of Jesus,* Attitude toward the Old Testament in the Johannine discourses, ii. 35-48 (orig. pp. 356-368); WEISS: *Der Johanneische Lehrbegriff,* Zweiter Abschnitt, Die Alttestamentlichen Grundlagen des johanneischen Lehrbegriffs, especially pp. 101-128; *Biblical Theology,* The preparatory revelation of God, ii. 384-392 (§ 152); O. HOLTZMANN: *Das Johannesevangelium,* Das Johannesevangelium und das Alte Testament, pp. 182-195; BEYSCHLAG: *Neutestamentliche Theologie,* Würdigung des Alten Testaments, i. 229-232; WESTCOTT: *The Gospel of St. John,* Introduction, Relation (of the Gospel) to the Old Testament, pp. lxvi-lxix; GODET: *Commentary,* The Relation of the Fourth Gospel to the Religion of the Old Testament, i. 127-134 (Am. Ed.).

FOR the apostle John, Christianity is the absolute religion. The Old Testament system was preparatory and provisional. It was, indeed, a divine system, but it was special in its nature. Underneath it, and operating through it, has ever been the essential gospel of the self-revealing Word. The religion of the Old Testament was a product of this self-revelation in its earlier stages, the purpose of which was to prepare the way for the personal manifestation and work of

JOHN'S THEOLOGY AND THE OLD TESTAMENT 23

the Logos. The Old Testament religion and Christianity are one, so far as their origin and aim are concerned; they differ as the temporary form differs from the permanent substance. "The law was given (ἐδόθη) by Moses;" it was a temporary, historic form which revelation assumed for a special purpose; but "grace and truth" — the full and final revelation of God's free love, the realization of the heavenly realities — "came (ἐγένετο) by Jesus Christ" (i. 17). The two words by which the introduction of the two systems is described suggest, respectively, their differing nature. The law-system is a temporary polity, embodying essential contents of divine truth, framed by a human agent; it is introduced, established, "given." The gospel is a system of spiritual truths and principles, or, rather, it is the work of God revealing himself in Christ, and through him reconciling the world unto himself; it is personal; it is inseparable from him who brings it to the world; it, therefore, becomes, transpires, "comes;" in the personal coming of Christ into humanity came God's grace and truth in their full manifestation.

In the epistles of John there are no quotations from the Old Testament, and no direct allusions to it. Although the Old Testament is quoted less frequently and less fully in the Fourth Gospel than in several other New Testament books, the points of contact between it and the Jewish religion and scriptures are numerous and significant. According to John, Jesus grounds his work and teaching distinctly upon an Old Testament basis. In the conversation with the Samaritan woman, he identifies himself with the Jews in respect to religion, and asserts that the Jewish people alone have a right knowledge of the object of worship: " *We* worship that which we know " (iv. 22). This statement he explains by declaring that salvation proceeds from the Jews ; that is, that the Messianic salvation which he brings is historically grounded in the religion of the Jewish people. They are the people of revelation. Their history has been, in a special sense, a preparation for the Messiah. Jesus, therefore, assumes both the reality of Old Testament revelation, and the inseparable connection of his own work with that revelation as its completion. The same relation is plainly implied in the prologue : " He came unto his own (τὰ ἴδια), and they that were his own (οἱ ἴδιοι) received him not " (i. 11). The Jewish people as a whole were the true and proper possession of Christ, because all through their history God had been preparing for his coming and work. The refusal, therefore, of those who of right belonged to him to accept him, involved a great failure on their part to realize the purpose of God in their history.

The necessity that Old Testament prophecy should be fulfilled, is as explicitly asserted in the Fourth Gospel as it is in the First, or in the Epistles of Paul (*cf.* xv. 25 ; xvii. 12). " The scripture cannot be broken " (x. 35) ; that is, cannot be deprived of its validity. Both the unity and the inspiration of Old

Testament Scripture are pre-supposed in this assertion. According to John, Jesus frequently refers to events in Old Testament history, and builds in his teaching upon their significance. The lifting up of his body upon the cross, and its saving benefits, are compared to Moses' lifting up the brazen serpent in the wilderness (iii. 14; *cf.* Num. xxi. 8). He appeals (vi. 45) to the prophetic word: " And all thy children shall be taught of the Lord " (Is. liv. 13) — freely quoted from the Septuagint — as describing the spiritual enlightenment of the people in the Messianic time, and affirms that it is those in whom this description is fulfilled — the spiritually susceptible and teachable — who are accepting him as the Messiah. Sometimes reference seems to be made to the import of Old Testament teaching in general where no single passage is exclusively in mind. Such an instance is found in the words, " He that believeth on me, as the scripture hath said, out of his belly shall flow rivers of living water " (vii. 38). The thought of the passage is, that the divine grace which the believer receives, shall not remain shut up within him, but shall communicate itself to others. This communication is metaphorically described as the flowing forth from him of a stream of living water, and this result is said to be according to Old Testament Scripture. Some have supposed the reference to be to an apocryphal writing, others have referred to the smiting of the rock in the wilderness; but the preferable view is that the general import of Scripture respecting the fulness of blessing in the Messianic age is here indicated, in view, especially, of such passages as employ the figure of a stream or spring in describing that blessing (*e. g.* Is. xliv. 3; lv. 1; lviii. 11).

There are several instances in which the apostle sees close and definite relations between particular words of Old Testament prophecy and specific circumstances in the life of Jesus. In the unbelief of the Jews he sees fulfilled the words of Isaiah: "Lord, who hath believed our report?" (Is. liii. 1), where the prophet speaks of the disbelief by the heathen and the ungodly of his description of Jehovah's righteous servant (xii. 38). Again, he explains (xii. 39, 40) that the Jews could not believe on Jesus because Isaiah had said, "He [God] hath blinded their eyes," etc. (Is. vi. 9, 10), a passage in which the prophet is bidden to declare to his hearers their incapacity for spiritual instruction, and, indeed,—in accordance with a peculiar Hebrew mode of thought,—himself to effect this result as Jehovah's representative. The apostle concludes: "These things said Isaiah, because he saw his glory; and he spake of him" (xii. 41). Our author, in accord with the methods of interpretation current in his age, sometimes applies language to the events of Jesus' ministry or experiences which in its original connection referred to circumstances of the prophet's own time, and even grounds the necessity of the event upon the supposed prediction of it. The language of the Psalmist, where he speaks of his enemies hating him without a cause (Ps. lxix. 4), must have its fulfilment, says the apostle, in the treatment which Jesus received from the Jews (xv. 25). In the narrative of the crucifixion are found several examples. The soldiers cast lots for Christ's garments (xix. 24) in order to fulfil — not consciously, but in the divine purpose — the words: "They parted my garments among them, and upon my vesture did they cast lots" (Ps. xxii. 18), where, so far as an examination of the psalm itself shows, the garments were those of the writer, which he describes as stripped off by his fierce enemies. Again, the legs of Jesus were not broken after the crucifixion, "that the scripture might be fulfilled, A bone of him shall not be broken" (xix. 36). This language, in its substance, occurs in Ex. xii. 46 and in Num. ix. 12, where the method of cooking and eating the paschal lamb is prescribed. One of the requirements was that the animal must be cooked entire, and eaten without being dismembered. If this requirement be here referred to, then the meaning is, that in the case of Jesus, who is the antitypical paschal lamb, the same requirement must find fulfilment. It is possible, however, that the reference is to Ps. xxxiv. 20: "He keepeth all his bones: Not one of them is broken," — a passage in which Jehovah's protection of the righteous man is celebrated. In either case, it will be noticed how definite is the relation which the apostle presupposes between these passages and the particular events in the history of Jesus, — a connection so definite that the events must occur in order to fulfil the Old Testament words.

28 THE JOHANNINE THEOLOGY

One further example from the history of the passion may be noted. In xix. 37 the language of Zechariah (xii. 10), " They shall look upon me [or to me] whom they have pierced," is applied to the piercing of Jesus' side by the spear of the Roman soldier. The evangelist departs from both the Hebrew and the Septuagint in substituting the phrase " on him " (εἰς ὅν) for " on [or to] me" (אֵלַי; Septuagint, πρός με), following, probably, in so doing, some manuscript or version of his time. The prophetic passage is a difficult one, and Old Testament scholars are not agreed either as to its translation or interpretation. Some would render : " They " (the people of Jerusalem) " shall look to me " (Jehovah) " in respect to him (אֵת אֲשֶׁר) whom they have pierced " (slain); that is, they shall turn penitently to Jehovah for comfort and forgiveness on account of their brethren of Judah who were slain in war with foreign enemies, in consequence of enmity between Jerusalem and the country districts.[1] More commonly the passage is rendered as in our versions. On this view the relative pronoun in the passage (אֲשֶׁר) is regarded as in apposition with the personal pronoun, and the preposition of the original (אֵת) is explained as marking the following relative more plainly as an accusative, since otherwise it might mean, " who pierced [me]." [2] The general sense of this passage, then, as commonly understood is : In consequence of the " spirit of grace

---

[1] So Toy, *Quotations in the New Testament*, pp. 92, 93.
[2] So Keil and Delitzsch, *Minor Prophets, in loco*.

JOHN'S THEOLOGY AND THE OLD TESTAMENT 29

and of supplication" which Jehovah will pour out upon them, the inhabitants of Jerusalem will regard him whom they have pierced (Jehovah) by their sins with bitter sorrow and penitent grief. The apostle seems to regard the language as referring directly to the Messiah, and as literally fulfilled in the act of the Roman soldier.

It is clear that, in the case of the quotations last cited, criticism must distinguish between their original sense and application, and the reference which is assigned them by the apostle. In accord with the mode of viewing Messianic prophecy which was current among the Jews, and which was inherited from them by the first Christians, the primary reference of individual passages is often disregarded; and if the words find a parallel in some incident in the history of Jesus, they are freely applied to it, and even held to necessitate that particular circumstance. While it is to be admitted that the New Testament writers often apply passages without reference to their historic sense, and in the belief that they primarily related to the particular circumstances which are in hand, two important considerations are to be remembered. The first is that this excess — if I may so call it — in the application of particular passages to specific events springs out of their profound and true sense of the prophetic and Messianic import of Old Testament history. The second point is that, while exegesis cannot always justify the identification of the immediate reference in quotations with the situation to which they are applied, it is seldom difficult to discern a deeper point of connection, a relation of principle between the two, which shows that it is not alone the form of individual prophetic passages with which the writer's mind is concerned, but that he penetrates to the prophetic significance of Jehovah's relation to the theocratic people, and regards that relation as the type of that which shall at length be constituted between Jehovah, on the one hand, and the incarnate Redeemer and his kingdom, on the other. The problem which is involved in the use of Old Testament passages by the New Testament writers can neither be solved by making their application of texts give the law to Old Testament interpretation, nor by the supposition of a double sense in prophecy, but only by admitting, on the one hand, the limitations which verbal exegesis, universal in their time, imposed upon their minds, and by maintaining, on the other, the principle of typical parallelism, — the view that the religious truths and ideals of prophecy furnish parallels and illustrations of the various stages and aspects of the final revelation of God in the person and work of Jesus Christ.

The discourses in the Fourth Gospel are very explicit in their recognition of the Messianic import of the Old Testament. In his discussion with the Jews, Jesus takes common ground with them so far as the foundation of the Messianic hope in the Old Testament is concerned (v. 45–47). You appeal to Moses, he says, on whom you have set your hope; to Moses

JOHN'S THEOLOGY AND THE OLD TESTAMENT

you shall go. If you did really believe him, in the true import of the system which he founded, you would thereby be led to accept me as the Messiah, "for he wrote of me" (v. 46). Here, too, the reference is to the general Messianic import of the Pentateuch and to the prophetic nature of its types, although, possibly, Deut. xviii. 15 may be especially thought of: "The Lord thy God will raise up unto thee a prophet from the midst of thee, of thy brethren, like unto me; unto him ye shall hearken." What is of importance, for our present purpose, is that Jesus treats the teaching of Moses as so related to his own mission that a true belief, involving a right spiritual apprehension of what is taught in the Mosaic law, would logically conduce to an acceptance of his Messiahship. To the same effect, according to the most probable interpretation of the passage, is the assertion of Jesus in v. 37: "And the Father which sent me, he hath borne witness of me. Ye have neither heard his voice at any time, nor seen his form." The witness which the Father has borne to him is most naturally understood to be that which is contained in Sacred Scripture, since in the next verse (38) he refers to the "word" of God, and especially because in verse 39 he refers to the Scriptures, and asserts that they bear testimony to himself. The reference to the Mosaic books at the end of the discourse (verses 45–47) confirms this view. The Jews are reproached, in language somewhat anthropomorphic, with failure to hear the voice of God which speaks in their own Scriptures, and to see the form of God — a figurative designation of his true nature — which is there disclosed. In the words that follow, Jesus repeats the idea, which is here presented under the figure of moral deafness and blindness, in terms which are designed to emphasize the lack on the part of the Jews of the essential, inward possession of the truths contained in the Old Testament, which would, if dwelling in them, have disposed them to believe on him.[1]

In a way somewhat similar to that in which he refers to Moses does he appeal to Abraham as a witness to his Messiahship. The Jews resent his claims because they seem to them to involve the absurd idea that Jesus is greater than Abraham. Jesus replies that Abraham, who was a friend of the truth, rejoiced in hope of seeing (ἵνα ἴδῃ) "his day," the realization of the Messianic ideal, "and he saw it" — in Paradise he beheld the fulfilment of the Messianic promise — "and was glad" (viii. 56). The exultation of Abraham in anticipation of witnessing the appearance of the Messiah and the joyful realization of this hope in the world beyond, require the supposition of the Messianic significance of God's covenant with him (*cf.* Gen. xv. 1–6), and present a striking point of contact between the Johannine discourses and the Old Testament.

The references of Jesus to the facts of Old Testament history and life as points of departure for his

[1] *Cf.* Wendt, *Teaching of Jesus*, ii. 40–44 (orig. pp. 360–365).

JOHN'S THEOLOGY AND THE OLD TESTAMENT

own teaching, often reveal his mode of viewing the institutions of the old covenant. Thus he speaks of Moses as giving the Jews circumcision, but explains that the rite was not original with Moses, but was a primitive patriarchal custom whose observance Moses re-enacted (vii. 22). He calls the temple his "Father's house" (ii. 16), and by his indignant expulsion from it of those who profaned it by buying and selling animals for sacrifice, and by exchanging for profit the various kinds of money which strangers brought to the feast, he reminded the disciples of the Psalmist's avowal (Ps. lxix. 9) of his consuming zeal for God's house (ii. 17). In argument with the Pharisees, Jesus takes his stand upon the maxim of the law (Deut. xvii. 6; xix. 15) that "the witness of two men is true" (viii. 17), and claims that he has even a stronger attestation for his Messiahship than this principle requires. He has his own consciousness of his Messianic calling, and, in addition to this, the testimony of the Father to his Messiahship. This testimony is variously understood to refer to the witness of God which is contained in Scripture, to that borne by the divine voice from heaven, to the attestation which God gave to Jesus through the power conferred upon him to work miracles, and to the sense of the Father's approval which was given in Jesus' own consciousness. In any case, his attitude toward the Old Testament maxim remains unchanged. Our Lord also assumes the Old Testament standpoint in designating the judges of the theocratic people as *gods*

(x. 34, 35). In consideration of the dignity of their stations as the representatives of Jehovah in the nation, the Psalmist addresses them as gods (אֱלֹהִים), notwithstanding their personal unrighteousness (Ps. lxxxii. 6; *cf.* xlv. 6; Ex. xxii. 28). The argument in the passage in question is, that if the judges of Israel, as the dispensers of justice and the bearers of the Divine Word, may be called *Elohim*, or (as in the Septuagint) θεοί, with how much better right may he, whom the Father has consecrated to a work far higher than theirs, claim the title "Son of God" (x. 36).[1]

To the general view which we have presented of the relation, according to the Johannine discourses, of Jesus to the Old Testament, it is sometimes objected [2] that, in some of the passages in question, he speaks of the Old Testament as *their law,* as if he did not recognize it as authoritative: "In your law

[1] The argument turns on the superiority of his dignity and person as compared with those of the judges and rulers. If they were called *Elohim* without blasphemy, surely he may be called "Son of God" without blasphemy. It is very doubtful whether (with Meyer and Westcott) we are to suppose a further contrast to be intended between their designation "gods" and his "Son of God," on the view that he claimed only a *humbler* title than that which the law applied to them. In this case the argument would depend upon a *double* contrast, thus: The judges and rulers were called *gods;* one who is *greater* than they may surely claim the *lesser* title "Son of God." Most interpreters do not recognize this supposed second contrast.

[2] For example, by Messner, *Lehre der Apostel,* p. 345.

JOHN'S THEOLOGY AND THE OLD TESTAMENT

it is written, that the witness of two men is true" (viii. 17; *cf*. x. 34; xv. 25). But it is to be noticed that Jesus uses this expression, "your law," in an *argumentum ad hominem* with the Jews. His mode of argument is: Your law upon which you lay such stress, which you prize as your chief authority, but so inadequately comprehend and apply, is quite capable of being turned against you, and in my favor. Your law requires two witnesses to prove a case; I furnish them, and one of them is God. Your law calls the judges of Israel gods; I, who came forth from the Father, have only claimed the title Son of God. It is obvious that the emphasis of these expressions does not lie upon the idea that the law is *theirs* and in no sense *his*, but upon the idea that they, in their false view, consider it theirs in the sense that it is unfavorable to him, and justifies their opposition to him, whereas he shows how the reverse is the case. The use which he makes of the Old Testament passages in the cases where he refers to them as "your law" shows that he too builds upon their authority, and, so far, takes common ground with the Jews in respect to the Old Testament. The objective way in which the gospel constantly refers to "the Jews" has been thought to indicate a writer who stood outside the sphere of Judaism. But this peculiarity is naturally accounted for, partly by the fact that the writer, although a Jew, had long resided in a Roman province, and had long been identified with Gentile Christianity, and especially by the fact that the Jews are almost always thus spoken of as the determined opponents of Jesus. It is not the writer's relation to "the Jews," but their relation to Jesus, which his mode of reference to them is intended to indicate.

The words in the allegory of the Door of the Sheepfold, "All that came before me are thieves and robbers" (x. 8), have often been appealed to, on the supposition that they refer to Moses and the prophets, as evidence that the gospel was the work of a Gnostic of the second century. But in view of the estimate elsewhere placed upon the Old Testament in the passages which we have reviewed (*cf.* iv. 22; v. 37, 45; vii. 19), it is impossible to justify this supposition. The reference must be, either to false Messiahs who had claimed to be "doors of the sheep," that is, teachers and guides to the people,[1] or, as is more commonly held, to the members of the Jewish hierarchy, who had been increasing their influence as religious leaders previous to the appearance of Jesus as the "door" to the fold. On this view the present tense — "*are* thieves and robbers " — has force, as depicting the existing antagonism which Jesus is experiencing from these would-be leaders of God's people. In either case, the passage cannot be legitimately used as illustrating an anti-Judaistic tendency in the Fourth

---

[1] So Wendt, *Teaching of Jesus*, ii. 46, 47 (orig. pp. 366, 367), following many earlier interpreters. The principal objection to this interpretation is that historical proof of the appearance of false Messiahs before Christ's day is wanting.

JOHN'S THEOLOGY AND THE OLD TESTAMENT

Gospel, inconsistent with that found elsewhere, or inconsistent with the Johannine authorship.

It is important to observe, however, that while Jesus is at one with his contemporaries in recognizing the authority of the Old Testament, he often stands in sharp contrast with them in respect to the understanding and application of it. By no incident is this difference more clearly illustrated than by the discussion which arose between him and the Jews over the healing of the infirm man at the pool of Bethesda. The Jews regarded the action of Jesus in curing the man as a violation of the Old Testament Sabbath law (v. 16). Jesus replies, in substance, that their whole idea of the Sabbath law moves in the sphere of the letter; that they have not grasped the conception of the utility of the Sabbath, and of its subservience to human well-being. They have proceeded as if the rest of God after creation, on which the law based the sabbatic institution, meant inactivity on his part, and involved his refraining from lending man his sympathy and aid, and from actively promoting his true interests. On this false view was based the idea of the necessity of man's complete inactivity on the Sabbath, precluding even the right to relieve human suffering. Jesus affirms that the premises on which their whole conception of the Sabbath rests are false. God is intensely active in helping and blessing men. He "works" from the beginning "even until now" (v. 17). He is unceasing and untiring in his efforts to promote human welfare. There can, therefore, be no reason, grounded in the nature or action of God, why works of benevolence should cease on the Sabbath. In doing good on the Sabbath day Jesus is therefore but doing "what he seeth the Father doing" (v. 19). In this narrative we find a striking illustration of the way in which Jesus was accustomed to correct the religious and moral errors of his time by exposing the false idea of God upon which they rested, and by substituting for it a true conception.

Whether or not the words of Jesus, "Destroy this temple, and in three days I will raise it up" (ii. 19), should be cited in illustration of his attitude toward Old Testament institutions, depends in some degree upon the view taken of John's explanation of the words, "He spake of the temple of his body" (ii. 21). Meyer adopts the opinion that the evangelist has given the intended meaning of Jesus' words, which were designed to "throw out a seed of thought for the future which could not take root at the time." This author seeks, however, to give the language a reference to the literal temple also, by supposing that in speaking the words in the temple court, Jesus points to the temple, in which he "sees the sacred type of his body;" and, by identifying, without explanation, the type and the antitype, he announces "in a pictorial riddle" his resurrection.[1] Others have recognized more explicitly than does Meyer a double sense in the words, "Destroy this temple." The

[1] *Commentary, in loco.*

supposition is made that by "this temple" he means the Jews' sacred house, but that a reference to his resurrection can still be veiled under his words, since he knows that it is in his own person, and specifically by his death, that the destruction of the Jewish religious system, represented in the temple, will be consummated. The meaning therefore is: Destroy, as you are bent upon doing, your temple; overthrow, as your present conduct surely will, your religious system; I will reconstruct it according to its true, divine idea through my death and resurrection. On the view just mentioned, it may be held either that Jesus intended the double sense which is found in his words, — in which case the theory would be substantially the same as Meyer's, — or, that he directly referred only to the literal temple, but that, since the reconstruction predicted was actually to be accomplished by his resurrection, the evangelist's explanation of what was involved in his words is a just one.

If it is once admitted that the apostle's explanation of Jesus' words was derived from the subsequent events of his death and resurrection, and did not rest upon any clear reference or exposition of Jesus at the time, criticism is left free to regard this explanation as more or less natural, according to its estimate of its appropriateness. The way is thus opened to the theory that John's interpretation of the words, "Destroy this temple," etc., is the result of his own reflection, in the light of subsequent events, upon later teachings of Jesus concerning the temple-worship and the abrogation of the Jewish religious system through its fulfilment in the gospel. If the definite reference to "three days" seems to forbid this supposition, it is answered, on the other side, that these are probably the very words which gave rise to the evangelist's interpretation; and that while they naturally suggested to his mind, in the light of facts which occurred afterwards, the idea that Jesus spoke of his resurrection after three days, they are really capable of quite another interpretation. "Three days" is a proverbial expression for a short time. The prophet Hosea, describing the healing of the wounds of the nation by Jehovah, says : "After two days will he revive us: on the third day he will raise us up, and we shall live before him" (Hos. vi. 2). This view, it is said, accords with an incident which is preserved in the Synoptic tradition of Jesus' trial. The false witnesses declared: "We have heard him say, I will destroy this temple that is made with hands, and in three days I will build another made without hands" (Mk. xiv. 58; Matt. xxvi. 61). These were, indeed, false witnesses, and the falseness of their testimony is apparent in their ascribing to Jesus the assertion that *he* would destroy the temple, whereas he distinctly asserts that it is *they* who are to do this (λύσατε, John ii. 19). But neither this false statement nor any perversion of his meaning which their testimony may be naturally supposed to contain, can disprove the view that some word of Jesus about rebuilding the temple in three days had been preserved (*cf.* Acts vi. 13, 14). In view of these considerations, and on account of the difficulties of the "double-sense" theory, many scholars adopt the opinion that in saying that he would rebuild "*this* temple" in three days, Jesus means that he will in the shortest possible time reconstruct the system of worship, which the Jews are destroying, according to its true idea. This is the "sign" which he will give, and which will show that he is the Messiah of the nation. They treat him as the destroyer of their religious institutions; he tells them that it is they themselves who persist in overthrowing their own religion. He, on the contrary, conserves its ideal, essential doctrines, and will re-establish it on the secure foundations of imperishable spiritual truth. That which he will establish is the Church, the spiritual temple of God; but he can still call it "this temple," because he regards his kingdom as organically connected with the Jewish theocracy, and, so far, historically identical with it.[1]

It is not necessary for our purpose to decide confidently which of these theories is to be preferred. I can only say of Meyer's view that, if a "riddle" is to be found in the passage, it seems much more natural to ascribe the making of it to the writer of the gospel than to Jesus. On either of the other views which I have sketched, the passage is important in its bearing upon the attitude of Jesus toward

[1] So Weiss, *Life of Christ*, ii. 12–17. Wendt, *Teaching of Jesus*, ii. 37 (orig. pp. 356, 357).

the Old Testament. It illustrates his strong sense of the continuity of divine revelation, culminating in himself. He comes to establish no different religion from that of the Jewish people. His work is a reconstruction of their demolished temple. The divine ideal which the Jewish religion contemplates, can be realized only in his truth and kingdom. But his words illustrate, at the same time, the wide separation between him and the actual religion of his contemporaries. He must build what they are destroying. He ironically bids them go on with the work of destruction, to which they are devoted. They are blind to the true meaning of their own history, false to the divine ideal which is contained in their own Scriptures and embodied in their institutions. He has come to disclose the real import and goal of this history, to reveal and to embody in himself this ideal; but with his conception of the Messianic work they have no sympathy, and of the proofs which he gives of being the Chosen of God they have no appreciation.

These two truths are brought out side by side in other narratives. To the Samaritan woman he affirms: "We [Jews] worship that which we know: for salvation is from the Jews" (iv. 22); and, at the same time, he contrasts his conception of God as spirit (iv. 24) with the current Jewish idea "that in Jerusalem is the place where men ought to worship" (iv. 20), as well as with the tenet of the Samaritans. The import of his teaching is: The Jewish people have, indeed, preserved the true idea of God as compared with that of other peoples, but this idea has been greatly lowered and narrowed. The Jewish people know the true God, but they do not know him adequately. Their conception must be greatly elevated and ennobled before it can be the basis of a true spiritual worship. To bring this fuller knowledge, I am come. The hour has already arrived (verse 23) for worthier thoughts of God and of his worship than those which prevail even among the chosen people.

In no passage is the independence of Jesus, and his elevation above the religious life and scriptural knowledge of his contemporaries, more forcibly presented than in the words : " Ye search the scriptures because ye think that in them ye have eternal life ; and these are they which bear witness of me; and ye will not come to me, that ye may have life " (v. 39, 40). It appears to me certain that the Revised Version has rightly rendered ἐραυνᾶτε (verse 39) as indicative, " ye search," instead of as an imperative, as our older version renders, " search." The surrounding verbs in the context are indicative (οὐκ ἔχετε, verse 38 ; οὐ θέλετε, verse 40) ; the causal clause which follows, " because ye *think*," etc., gives a natural reason for the fact that they search the Scriptures, but not for an exhortation to them to search them; and the drift of the passage as a whole shows that Jesus is rebuking their profitless study of Scripture. They search the writings (τὰς γραφάς), but in a manner so superficial and prejudiced, and with so little discernment of their import, that they do not find God's true word (τὸν λόγον αὐτοῦ, verse 38) therein. Jesus certainly does not mean, in so speaking, to place a light estimate upon the study of the Old Testament Scriptures, or to intimate that the way of eternal life may not be found in them, but only to assert that their study as conducted by his Jewish opponents cannot yield this result, and especially to affirm that a true understanding of Sacred Scripture would conduct to the acceptance of himself as the Messiah. In saying, "These are they which bear witness of me" (verse 39), he shows that his work stands in inseparable connection with the Old Testament, and that he attaches the highest importance to its authentication of his mission. Jesus does not, therefore, rebuke the Jewish zeal for the Scriptures, in itself considered, but he deprecates the narrowness, selfishness, and blindness of mind which have misdirected that zeal, turned it into a superficial adherence to the letter, and subjected the language of Scripture to strained and unnatural interpretation in support of current traditions.

That which is most striking and important in the attitude of Jesus toward the Old Testament, as represented in the Fourth Gospel, is the confidence with which he asserts — as against the Messianic ideas of his time — the correspondence of his person and work to the prophetic ideal. He brushes aside the superficial verbal exegesis of his contemporaries, which found in the Messiah of the prophets only a second

David who should subdue Israel's enemies and rule the nation in power and pomp, and asserts that such is not the real prophetic ideal of Messiah's character and work. The Messiah in whom that ideal is realized, and who can accomplish that moral renewal and bestow that spiritual life for lack of which the nation is perishing, belongs to a higher order, — the order of the spirit and of holiness. That true Messiah is himself. Whether the Jewish people will receive him or not, is for them the question of destiny.

CHAPTER III

THE IDEA OF GOD IN THE WRITINGS OF JOHN

Literature. — BEYSCHLAG: *Neutest. Theol.*, Die Gottesidee, i. 220, 221; WENDT: *Teaching of Jesus*, Conception of God in the Johannine Discourses, i. 203-206 (orig. pp. 154-157); WEISS: *Johann. Lehrb.*, Der Begriff der Erkenntniss Gottes, pp. 11-18; REUSS: *Hist. Christ. Theol.*, Of the Essential Nature of God, ii. 383-388 (orig. pp. 428-435); LECHLER: *Apostolic and Post-Apostolic Times*, Of God, ii. 181-183 (orig. pp. 458-461); BAUR: *Neutest. Theol.*, Das Wesen Gottes als reine Geistigkeit und als absolute Thätigkeit, pp. 354-356; LIAS: *Doctrinal System of St. John*, The Nature and Attributes of God, pp. 16-32; WESTCOTT: *The Epistles of St. John*, The Fatherhood of God, pp. 27-34; St. John's Conception of Love, pp. 130-133; KÖSTLIN: *Johann. Lehrb.*, Lehre von Gott, 73-113.

THE study of the idea of God as presented in the writings of John should proceed from that word of Jesus to the Samaritan woman: " God is spirit " (iv. 24). Both our English versions here render πνεῦμα "*a* spirit"; but the sense which is given by the translation "God is a spirit" is less appropriate, since the context shows that it is not the personality but the nature of God which the words are intended to describe. In contrast to the inadequate idea of the Samaritans, and even to the current popular notion of the Jews, that God must be worshipped in one particular place, as if his presence were local, Jesus sets his thought that God may be truly worshipped anywhere. As spirit, he is above all limitations of time and space. The conditions of true worship are, that it shall be rendered "in spirit," — that is, that the highest affections of the worshipper shall be consecrated to God, — and that it shall be "in truth," — that is, shall proceed from a true and worthy idea of the divine nature. Moreover, it accords better with a mode of thought frequently found in John's writings to understand πνεῦμα ὁ θεός as a generic description of the divine nature. Analogous expressions are: "God is light" (I. i. 5) and "God is love" (I. iv. 8). The statements of verse 23 as to the nature and conditions of true worship, accord best with the idea that, in the sentence under consideration, Jesus is presenting the true idea of the spiritual nature of God which a genuine worship, proceeding from the heart, presupposes and requires. The argument therefore is: The genuine worshippers — as opposed to those who suppose that God must be worshipped on Mount Gerizim or in Jerusalem — will render him a purely spiritual service, a service which alone accords with what he *is*, for his nature is spiritual. It should also be noticed that the emphatic position of πνεῦμα in the sentence shows that this word is the pivot of the whole argument, and accords perfectly with the interpretation of its meaning which we have given.

This passage presents the most abstract and generic

idea of God which is to be found in the Johannine writings. God is, in his essence, spirit. He is not restricted in respect to the time or place of his manifestation. There is no time when the sincere worshipper may not find him; there is no place where he will not manifest himself to the trustful and obedient heart. This idea of the spirituality of God is not, as is sometimes supposed, placed in contrast to the Old Testament idea of God, for there we meet with the view — most impressively presented — that God is not limited to earthly dwelling-places, nor even to the highest heavens (1 Kings, viii. 27). Nor is the idea of Jesus opposed to the Samaritan theology as such; but it stands in contrast to the practically imperfect apprehension of God's transcendence and omnipresence which was implied in such questions as that of the Samaritan woman as to where men ought to worship. The statement of Jesus, " God is spirit," communicated no new conception of the divine nature; it only gave strong, fresh emphasis to a truth which was very inadequately apprehended and applied in religious thought and life, and furnished a basis for showing how essential is a true idea of God to a worship which shall be at once rational and sincere.

Closely connected with the conception of God as spirit stands the idea that he is invisible. " No man hath seen God at any time " (i. 18). He reveals himself to men not by making to their senses an immediate presentation of himself, but by manifesting his

THE IDEA OF GOD IN WRITINGS OF JOHN 49

will and nature to them in the person of the only begotten Son, who ever stands in most intimate fellowship with himself, and who therefore has an immediate intuition of the mind of the Father. This Son, who is in the bosom of the Father, hath declared God to men (i. 18). It is obvious that in this passage the contrast is drawn between God as hidden to the senses of man and as revealed in his grace and truth through Jesus Christ. In I. iv. 12, where God is spoken of as invisible and yet as dwelling in men, the idea is that, although he cannot be discerned by the senses or known by the natural understanding of man, he reveals himself as love to those who themselves have the disposition of love, and who therefore have an affinity of life with him. In so far as man is morally like God, is he capable of receiving the knowledge of God. "If we love one another, God abideth in us, and his love is perfected in us" (I. iv. 12).

Both the ways in which the invisible God is thus said to reveal himself stand directly connected with the conception of God as spirit. As spirit he reveals himself to the senses of men only mediately through the incarnation of the Son, who so perfectly embodies in his own person the Father's will and nature that he can say, "He that hath seen me hath seen the Father" (xiv. 9). So also does the other form of revelation by which the invisible God becomes known accord with the divine nature as spirit. God reveals himself as love to the inner life of man, where the conditions of a spiritual apprehension of him are fulfilled. Since God is a spiritual being, he can only reveal himself to man as a spiritual being, and upon the fulfilment of spiritual conditions. As spirit, God is apprehended by man only by the development of a capacity for what is spiritual. Thus, the very nature of God as spirit determines the method and conditions of his direct manifestations of himself to the soul. Only through moral likeness to himself can God be truly apprehended and known.

The words recorded in v. 37, "Ye have neither heard his voice at any time, nor seen his form," seem, when taken by themselves, to be a denial of the possibility that God can be perceived by the senses. The context, however, makes it apparent that this is not their purpose. The words are intended to assert that the Jews by reason of their moral obduracy and spiritual blindness have failed to apprehend those revelations of God which he has made in their own history. The assertion which immediately follows (v. 38), "And ye have not his word abiding in you," makes it clear that the sentence just referred to is a rebuke of their insusceptibility. They have not heard in any such way as to appreciate the voice of God, which has spoken to them through their own prophets, nor seen God's self-manifestation, which he has made in their own Scriptures, which they search to so little purpose (v. 39).

The spiritual, invisible God is presented in the writings of John as "the true God" (ὁ ἀληθινὸς θεός,

I. v. 20), the One who in reality corresponds perfectly to the idea of God. All other so-called gods are but idols; the God who is revealed in Jesus Christ is God alone. Hence he is called "the only God" (ὁ μόνος θεός, v. 44); and, again, eternal life is defined as consisting in the knowledge of the only true God (τὸν μόνον ἀληθινὸν θεόν, xvii. 3), and of him whom God did send, Jesus Christ. The Johannine doctrine of God, so far as we have traced it, may be summed up in the statement that in contrast to all anthropomorphic ideas of God he is presented in these writings as the invisible, absolute Spirit, and in contrast to all polytheistic conceptions he is affirmed to be the one and only Being who corresponds to the true idea of Deity.

The terms which have thus far been considered, especially the definition of God as spirit, are chiefly descriptive of those divine attributes which in theology are called immanent. These attributes represent qualities which belong to the metaphysical nature of the Deity. They are intended to describe what God is in himself. But God is not presented to us in the Johannine writings in this aspect of his being alone. He is not thought of as self-contained, or as dwelling within himself in separation from the world and man. On the contrary, the main emphasis is laid upon the relations which God sustains to his creatures, and upon the way in which he manifests himself to them in mercy and love. Speaking in the language of theology, we should say that the writings of John dwell most upon those attributes of God which are called ethical or transitive. As we found that the statement "God is spirit" formulated more precisely than any other the conception of what God in his metaphysical nature is, so we shall find that the Johannine idea of God's moral nature — of his disposition and mode of action toward his creatures — is best summed up in the words, "God is love" (I. iv. 8, 16).

This proposition in both places where it occurs in the First Epistle, has a practical and not a dogmatic purpose. John exhorts his readers to love one another, on the ground that love is of God, that is, has its seat or dwelling-place in the being of God (I. iv. 7). He whose life is ruled by this divine principle is born of God, and knows God. He has received from God a divine impartation of spiritual life, and has entered into that fellowship with God which his likeness to God makes possible. Conversely, he who does not love cannot be in fellowship with God, for "God is love" (I. iv. 8). Better than any other single word love describes God's moral nature in its forth-putting of interest and sympathy toward his creatures. It designates God as existing and acting in relations. It implies not only the existence of an object of love, but the idea of a self-impartation to that object. Love is, in its very nature, the disposition to impart blessing to its object.

Love implies the existence of goodness in the subject of it and the impartation of good to its object.

The statement of the apostle, therefore, means much more than that God *has* love. He *is* love, that is, he is the absolutely good Being, for love is the essence of goodness. Love, the impulse to bless and to impart his own goodness, makes him what he is. Were he less than perfect love at any moment or in any degree, he would not be God. Love is a name for his moral perfection. In other words, the assertion of the apostle indicates that love is not a mere temper or inclination which it is optional with God to exercise or not to exercise toward the beings whom he has made. It is absolutely essential and constituent in God's being. Love is not a mere determination of the divine will, as if it were said that God were full of love; it is a name for his ethical nature in its essential and changeless character. The affirmation of the apostle appears to me to exclude the position of some theologians, that God may at will suspend the operation of his love.[1] To do this would be, in the apostle's use of terms, to relinquish moral perfection, to cease to exercise toward his creatures those feelings of interest and sympathy which are fundamental in the ethical character of God. If love is held to be

[1] *Cf.*, *e. g.*, Strong, *Philosophy and Religion*, p. 196: "Love is an attribute which, like omnipotence, God may exercise or not exercise, as he will."

Shedd, *Theological Essays*, p. 285: "We can say, 'God may be merciful or not, as he pleases,'" etc.

Patton, *Princeton Review*, Jan. 1878: "God is bound to be just; he is not bound to be generous. The measure of God's benevolence is a matter of option."

an optional quality of God's action, it must be much more narrowly defined than John has conceived it. It must be understood not in the sense of universal benevolence, the exercise of which God cannot be conceived as withholding without impairing the very idea of God, but in the narrow sense of complaisance or favor, — terms which denote feelings whose exercise is conditioned upon the attitude of God's creatures toward him. The position that God ever does or ever could cease to be generous, merciful, and loving is a perilous admission for theology, involving, as it does, the alternative that either naked justice alone is essential to moral perfection, or that God can be conceived as choosing to become something less than perfect. Neither of these positions seems to me to be reconcilable with the teaching of John. In the effort which theology has often made to enthrone justice as the one essential and necessary attribute of God,[1] it is compelled to ground the remaining attributes in his *will* alone. This view involves the denial that all God's perfections are grounded in his essence, and confuses the idea of his ethical completeness by assigning a different basis to justice from that which is assigned to other attributes. We shall recur to this subject in a later chapter.

As in the passage just considered (I. iv. 8) the affirm-

---

[1] *Cf.* Shedd, *op. cit.*, p. 285: "Whatever else God may be or may not be, he must be just. It is not optional with him to exercise this attribute or not to exercise it, as it is in the instance of that class of attributes which are antithetic to it."

ation " God is love " is made the ground of the negative statement that only he that loveth can be begotten of God, so in the second passage (I. iv. 16) the same statement is made the support of the corresponding positive assertion that "He that abideth in love abideth in God, and God abideth in him." Since God's nature is love, he who loves has entered into fellowship with God, and abides in him.

This most general statement concerning God's nature as love is illustrated by several concrete examples. Three objects of the love of God are specified. The first of these is his Son, Jesus Christ: "The Father loveth the Son, and hath given all things into his hand" (iii. 35). Similarly in xvii. 24 Jesus speaks of the Father as loving him before the foundation of the world. This love of the Father for the Son is treated, in the connection, as a type of the love which God bestows upon Christ's disciples.

Again, when Jesus has occasion to defend himself against the objections of the Jews on the ground that he did works of healing on the Sabbath, he urges that in so doing he is but working along the lines of the Father's activity: "My Father worketh even until now, and I work" (v. 17). "For," he continues, "the Father loveth the Son, and showeth him all things that himself doeth" (v. 20). Again, the love of the Father to the Son is grounded upon the willingness of the Son to lay down his life for the world:

"Therefore doth the Father love me, because I lay down my life, that I may take it again" (x. 17). Jesus also makes the love of the Father to himself the type and measure of his own love to his disciples: "Even as the Father hath loved me, I also have loved you" (xv. 9).

The love of God is most fully illustrated in the Gospel of John by this love of the Father to the Son. The language of the apostle which describes it presupposes the existence between Jesus and the Father of a unique, pretemporal relation. With good reason, therefore, has theology appealed to these passages as illustrating the idea that love must find within the divine Being himself an eternal object for its exercise. If God is the absolute Being, and the universe is not eternal but dependent upon his will, then must the essential nature of God as love find its object and exercise within God himself. This could not be the case if God were absolutely solitary; on the other hand, the conception of love requires the view that there is within his essence some kind of a manifoldness and intercommunion of life. The very nature of love as the outgoing, self-imparting impulse in God, suggests, and even seems to require, some conception of the divine Being which includes the idea of the interrelation of subject and object. Many theologians, therefore, from Augustine onward, have sought to deduce the concept of the Trinity from the nature of God as love, or, at least, to illustrate from the idea of love the necessity of a Trinitarian conception of the divine nature.[1]

The second object of the divine love which the apostle mentions is the world: "God so loved the world that he gave his only begotten Son," etc. (iii. 16), and in the First Epistle John refers to the divine love as shown by the fact that God has made him and his readers "children of God" (iii. 1). The love of God to undeserving men is the basis of salvation. This love antedates and underlies all human love. The love of God for men was the motive which prompted the sending of Christ to save them, and this love should both quicken our gratitude to God and beget in us a corresponding love to one another (I. iv. 9–11). The love of Christians for one another has its ground and spring in the love of God to men. It is because God's nature is love, and because he makes men the sharers of his spirit, that men are impelled to love God and their brethren. Love among men is the

[1] *Cf.* Sartorius, *The Doctrine of the Divine Love*, p. 8, *sq.* It is obvious that this line of argument is greatly weakened by that type of theological thought to which we have adverted, which grounds love in the divine will, and makes it a disposition subject to the divine choice. The essentialness and centrality of love in God are justly insisted upon by Sartorius as the presupposition of his whole argument in deducing the notion of the Trinity from the idea of love. "The attributes of the divine nature," he says, "are explained and combined in too poor and human a relation of reflection, if they are not perceived to be one in all-comprehending love, which, as free as necessary in its action, is not so much an attribute which God *has*, as the nature which he *is*; for God *is* love." *Op. cit.* p. 8.

answering echo of the love of God for them. "We love, because he first loved us" (I. iv. 19).

In the third place, believers are said to be the objects of God's love. This idea is presented in the passage already alluded to (xvii. 23), where a parallel is drawn between the love which the Father has for the Son and that which he has for the disciples of Jesus. The passages which describe God's love to men justify the theological distinction that, while God loves all men with the love of benevolence, he loves only the trustful and obedient with the love of complacency. In the former sense the world is the object of God's love; yet Jesus says, "If a man love me, he will keep my word: and my Father will love him," etc. (xiv. 23), — meaning, of course, with the love of approval, as is shown by the assurance that with such both he and the Father will make their abode (*ib.*). Elsewhere the love of God for the disciples of Jesus is grounded upon their love to their Master and their acceptance of him as the Messiah: "The Father himself loveth you, because ye have loved me, and have believed that I came forth from the Father" (xvi. 27). This love of the Father for believers can only be that closer sympathy and fellowship which faith makes possible, and which cannot exist where love is not appreciated and reciprocated.

Such are the elements of the teaching respecting the divine love in the writings of John. God is presented in this teaching as the great Giver. In his love is grounded the gift of his Son for the world's

THE IDEA OF GOD IN WRITINGS OF JOHN 59

salvation, and all the gifts of grace with which he has blessed the world through him. According to this teaching God is near to us. His transcendence is, indeed, affirmed and emphasized, but it is an ethical transcendence which is grounded in his holiness. It is not a transcendence which implies remoteness or absence from the world; nor is it founded upon the idea of a purely legal relation between God and man, which requires man to approach God through sacred rites and meritorious works. The theology of John represents God as accessible to every loving and obedient heart. Man may enter into fellowship of life with God on conditions which are simple and purely spiritual.

Nor is God merely accessible. Love, which is the essence of his ethical nature, is an active, energetic, self-revealing principle. God constantly seeks to make men the recipients of influences of grace and blessing. The divine love is always pouring itself forth upon the world, and is the perpetual motive and inspiration of all the impulses of religion in man.

There are several forms in which, in the writings of John, this self-revealing impulse of God's nature is emphasized. The most general of these is that in which God is depicted as the Source and Giver of *life* to men: "As the Father hath life in himself, even so gave he to the Son to have life in himself" (v. 26). Many theologians have understood this giving of life to the Son as referring to his "eternal generation" from the Father; but the context shows decisively that the reference is to the spiritual or eternal life which is imparted to believers. The whole passage (v. 19-27) is best regarded as a description of the life-giving work of Jesus, in which it is shown that this work is grounded in the purpose and nature of God. The quickening of the spiritually dead (verse 25) is wrought by Christ, because when the Father sent him into the world he gave him (note the aorist, ἔδωκεν) the right and power to communicate divine life, or salvation, to men. It is according to the nature of God as the absolutely living One (ὁ ζῶν πατήρ, vi. 57) to bestow life. God imparts this spiritual life to the world through the Son, who, by reason of his unique and essential relation to the Father, is said to live "because of the Father" (διὰ τὸν πατέρα, vi. 57), that is, because the Father is the absolute Source of life. We may note in passing that while these passages do not refer to what is called the "eternal generation" of the Son, they do imply both a pretemporal existence of the Son and a metaphysical union of the Son with the Father.

The representation of God as light (I. i. 5) is especially significant in this connection. Haupt defines the distinction between the idea of God as light and the idea of him as love to be that the former designates the metaphysical being of God, — the totality of the divine perfections, — while the latter designates his ethical activity. "The former is the immanent, the latter the transitive, side of the divine nature."[1]

[1] *Commentary*, on 1 John iv. 8.

It is very doubtful whether this distinction can be strictly applied. The figure of light, both in itself and in its use, is especially adapted to define the principle or impulse of self-revelation and self-impartation in God. In the First Epistle light is little more than a figurative designation for life, as the context of the passage (I. i. 5) shows. God has brought life to the world through his Son (I. i. 1–4). To do this was according to his nature, which is light, and in which is no darkness (I. i. 5). God is perfect and self-imparting holiness. As light, he blesses men, banishes from their lives the darkness of sin, and makes them participants in his own purity. The two ideas of life and light are placed in closest relations in the Gospel (viii. 12) : "He that followeth me shall not walk in the darkness, but shall have the light of life" (τὸ φῶς τῆς ζωῆς), — that is, he shall possess within himself the saving power which confers life upon men; he shall be a mediate source of the light of truth to others.

We find a similar use of the figure of light in the prologue of the Gospel. There the life that dwells in the Logos is described as "the light of men" (i. 4). The word represents the self-manifesting quality of the divine life. This heavenly light shines in the darkness of the world's ignorance and sin. Through the activity of the Logos this true light "lighteth every man, coming into the world" (i. 9). This passage (especially if ἐρχόμενον be construed with ἄνθρωπον and not with ὅ)[1] presents the Logos as the principle of self-revelation in God whereby God has in all ages made himself known to men. The theology of John therefore teaches explicitly, in its own peculiar terms, the universality of divine revelation.

The gracious, saving activity of God is strikingly presented in the words of Jesus, which are found in connection with the narrative of the healing of the impotent man at the pool of Bethesda on a Sabbath (v. 2–18). The Jews objected both to the performance of the cure (verse 16) and to the man's carrying his bed on the Sabbath day (verse 10). "But Jesus answered them, My Father worketh even until now, and I work" (verse 17). Activity in the line of blessing to his creatures is accordant with the very nature of God; his benevolence knows no Sabbath. In serving and blessing men Jesus is but doing what he sees the Father continually doing (verses 19, 20). The right of Jesus to work miracles of grace on the Sabbath is based upon the perfect harmony of such action with the perpetual working of the Father, — the ceaseless outflow of his boundless goodness in streams of blessing to the world.

The benevolent or self-imparting aspect of God's nature is much more frequently emphasized in the Johannine writings than is his holiness or self-affirmation. References to the latter are not, however,

[1] As in our older English version: "That was the true Light, which lighteth every man that cometh into the world."

entirely wanting. In one passage only in the Gospel is the word δίκαιος applied to God: "O *righteous* Father, the world knew thee not, but I knew thee," etc. (xvii. 25). The idea of God's righteousness here appears to be that it is the quality which prevents him from passing the same judgment upon Christ's disciples which he passes upon the sinful world. Upon this equitableness of God, Jesus bases his confidence in asking that special blessings be conferred upon his disciples. The thought is similar in xvii. 11, where the Father is designated as ἅγιος. As the One who is absolutely good — wholly separate from all that is sinful and wrong — God is besought to guard from evil those whom he has given to his Son. In both these cases the holiness of God is conceived of, not as a forensic or retributive quality, but as God's moral self-consistency, his justice to his own equity.

The retributive action of God toward sin is, however, abundantly recognized in the Gospel of John. God is described as subjecting the world to a continuous process of judgment. Although the coming of Christ into the world had salvation and not judgment for its object (iii. 17; viii. 15; xii. 47), yet a process of judgment is inevitably involved in his saving work. When Jesus says (ix. 39), "For judgment (εἰς κρίμα) came I into this world," he seems to contradict such statements as, "God sent not the Son into the world to judge (ἵνα κρίνῃ) the world" (iii. 17), and, "I judge no man" (viii. 15); but a careful consideration of the context shows that the judgment for which (in ix. 39) he says he came, does not stand in contrast to the world's salvation, but is a judicial hardening of the self-righteous who rejected him and his mission. He must, in the very act of presenting himself to men, bring to them the penalty of their obduracy in case they reject him. He comes to them to call them to repentance; but if they deem themselves to be just and to need no repentance, his coming then necessarily involves, according to the law of the divine order, an increase of their blindness. This was the case with the Jews. They said, "We see; we have no need of thy light or guidance." He can therefore only pronounce the judgment — and it belongs to his mission to do this — that in case of those who are of this spirit, their sin — the sin of wilful, moral obduracy and spiritual pride — abides (ἡ ἁμαρτία ὑμῶν μένει, ix. 41). The judgment which Jesus disclaims is the world's judgment as opposed to its salvation; the judgment which he pronounces is that which is unavoidably involved in the attitude which men take toward the truth (iii. 19-21). In this view of the matter Jesus is represented as judging men (v. 30; viii. 16), and even as appointed to perform this function (v. 22), in so far, that is, as the attitude of men toward the revelation of God's grace which has come to them in human form (v. 27) involves a test of their obedience to God. In accepting or rejecting Christ they honor or dishonor God himself (v. 23), and are thereby judged.

Twice in the First Epistle (I. i. 9; ii. 29) God is

described as righteous (δίκαιος), and, in both cases, in a sense closely akin to that which we have found in the Gospel. "If we confess our sins, he is faithful and righteous to forgive us our sins," etc. (I. i. 9). The correlation of the word righteous with the word faithful (πιστός), as well as the entire context, shows that righteousness here is that quality of God which would certainly lead him to forgive those who repent. It would be inconsistent in God — contrary to his promises and to his nature — not to forgive the penitent, and to exert upon his life the purifying influences of his grace.

In the remaining passage, the term righteous has a broader meaning, and designates the moral perfection of God in general, as the type and ideal of all goodness in man: "If ye know that he [God] is righteous, ye know that every one also that doeth righteousness is begotten of him" (I. ii. 29). Since God is essentially righteous, those who are begotten of him must also be righteous. A similar thought is presented in I. iii. 7, but in the reverse order. Here, instead of deducing from the divine righteousness the truth that those who live righteously are begotten of God, the apostle starts from the human side, and affirms that he who lives a righteous life is thereby shown to be like the pure and spotless Son of God.

The question now arises: How, according to John, do men arrive at the knowledge of God? Underlying all that is said on this subject is the idea that this knowledge presupposes a likeness between its subject and its object. Man can know God only as he becomes like God. "Every one that loveth . . . knoweth God . . . for God is love" (I. iv. 7, 8). It is obvious that by knowledge the apostle here means much more than the intellectual apprehension or possession of truth. The knowledge of God is pre-eminently an ethical affair, and implies in the possessor of it a kinship of life with God. The Johannine usage abundantly illustrates this conception of knowledge. The sinful world did not know the heavenly light of the Logos which was shining in its darkness (i. 10). The Jews in their spiritual blindness have not known God (viii. 55); "but I know him," said Jesus, "and keep his word" (*ib.*). Whatever be the precise meaning of the phrase "eternal life," and the relation between it and the knowledge of God, in the passage, "This is life eternal, that they should know thee the only true God," etc. (xvii. 3), I do not see how the objection of Weiss[1] to the "deeper sense" of the word *know* can be sustained. He asserts that "exegetical tradition" unwarrantably makes the word *know* in this passage mean practically the same as *love*. But what does Weiss himself make it mean? He admits that it denotes no mere theoretic, but an intuitive and contemplative knowledge, and that it is a peculiarity of John's thinking to conceive of the whole spiritual being of man as a unit in its action. He acknowledges that "a way leads direct from this knowledge to *willing*,"[2] but insists that the view of

[1] *Der Johanneische Lehrbegriff*, § 2.   [2] *Ib.* page 13.

Messner that the knowledge of God here includes an action of the will, is to be rejected. The separation which Weiss maintains between the cognitive and the voluntary elements in the knowledge of God is certainly formal rather than real. We cannot exclude the mystical element from John's conception of the knowledge of God. Even if the view which excludes from the knowledge of God the element of fellowship with God and of likeness to him, could be maintained in the case of the passage under review, it would certainly prove inapplicable in the First Epistle, where the knowledge of God is so blended with the idea of being begotten of God as to make it clear that this knowledge is grounded in a new direction of the will and affections (I. iv. 7).

The view which I have presented is confirmed by such passages as that in which the knowledge of the life which Christ has brought to the world is based on fellowship with the Father and with his Son Jesus Christ (I. i. 2, 3), and that in which the certainty of possessing the knowledge of God is conditioned upon the keeping of his commandments (I. ii. 3). In I. iii. 2 the assurance of becoming like Christ in the heavenly world is based upon the fact that we shall see him as he is.[1] While the form of thought in this passage is peculiar, — since likeness is here condi-

---

[1] I prefer, with Haupt, Rothe, Westcott, and Holtzmann, to refer the pronouns in this verse to Christ. Lücke, Huther, and Plummer refer them to God. It must be admitted, however, that the point remains a doubtful one.

tioned upon knowledge or sight, and not knowledge upon likeness, — this passage, equally with the others, illustrates the fundamental Johannine idea of an inseparable connection between a true knowledge of God and moral likeness to him. Finally, in answer to the question, How is God known? we would quote the following passage: "He that hath my commandments, and keepeth them, he it is that loveth me: and he that loveth me shall be loved of my Father, and I will love him and manifest myself to him. Judas (not Iscariot) saith unto him, Lord, what is come to pass that thou wilt manifest thyself unto us and not unto the world? Jesus answered and said unto him, If a man love me, he will keep my word: and my Father will love him and we will come unto him, and make our abode with him" (xiv. 21-23).

The attributes of God are not particularly dwelt upon in the writings of John except so far as they are involved in the conception of God as spirit, light, and love. The omniscience of God is, however, asserted in one passage: "Hereby shall we know that we are of the truth, and shall assure our heart before him, whereinsoever our heart condemn us; because God is greater than our heart and knoweth all things" (I. iii. 19, 20). Interpreters are divided upon the question whether God's omniscience is here thought of as the basis of severity or of leniency in his judgment of men's faults. On the former view the passage means: We shall persuade ($\pi\epsilon\iota\sigma o\mu\epsilon\nu$) our hearts that in whatsoever we condemn ourselves, God condemns

THE IDEA OF GOD IN WRITINGS OF JOHN 69

us yet more severely, because he is greater (in strictness) than our heart, and knoweth all things; that is, if our hearts detect and condemn our sins, he in his omniscience sees them yet more clearly, and condemns them yet more severely.[1] For the linguistic considerations which bear upon the question I must refer to the critical commentaries.[2]

It is necessary, in order to get the natural force of the passage, to read it in the light of the preceding argument. In verse 18 the apostle exhorts his readers to cultivate sincere love; for by so doing, he says, we shall prove ourselves to belong to the truth (19 a). The sentence which now follows, "and shall assure our heart before him" (καὶ ἔμπροσθεν αὐτοῦ πείσομεν τὴν καρδίαν ἡμῶν, 19 b), is co-ordinate with the statement, "We know that we are of the truth;" that is, it expresses the idea of a comforting assurance which, like the certainty of possessing the truth, arises from genuine love. It seems impossible to place the two parts of verse 19 in contrast. They together express the comfort which springs out of love. Now the second part of verse 20 gives the reason for this comfort, namely, "God is greater than our heart, and knoweth all things." But if greatness in severity or judgment were meant, this could not be a ground of comfort. The thought therefore is: Those who truly love God and men thereby know that they belong to the truth, and have this comfort, — that the

[1] So, *e. g.*, Lücke, Neander, DeWette, Ebrard.
[2] See, especially, Huther, Haupt, and Westcott.

faults for which their own hearts condemn them, God will freely forgive, since he is greater in mercy than their own conscience is. He knows all things, — the right moral direction and sincere intentions of him who belongs to the truth, the weakness of his nature, and the strength of his temptations, — and he pardons the faults which still inhere in the child of God more freely than the man's own conscience condones them. The presupposition of the whole argument is that the life of the persons in question is ruled by love, and that they are therefore sincerely penitent for their sins and desirous to forsake them.[1]

In the Johannine discourses Jesus frequently speaks of God as his Father, and refers to the intimate fellowship which exists between the Father and himself (i. 18; iii. 35; v. 17 *sq.*). But God is also the Father in his relation to men generally. "The true worshippers shall worship the Father in spirit and truth" (iv. 23). Especially in his assurances to his disciples that their prayers in his name will be answered, does Jesus speak of God as the Father: "If ye shall ask anything of the Father, he will give it you in my name" (xvi. 23; *cf.* xv. 16). In the Epistles also God is frequently spoken of as the Father, without further definition (I. ii. 1; iii. 1; II. 3, 4). God, then, is the Father of all men. Does it therefore follow that all men are his children? Are the two terms strictly correlated? There are two passages which must be

[1] This interpretation, in substance, is adopted by Haupt, Westcott, Huther, and Dwight.

appealed to in answer: "As many as received him, to them gave he the right (ἐξουσίαν) to become children of God (τέκνα θεοῦ γενέσθαι), even to them that believe on his name" (i. 12). Here, certainly, men are said to receive, on condition of faith in Christ, the right or privilege of becoming sons of God, — a statement which clearly implies that they were not such before. In the following verse (13) the apostle explains that men become children of God by a spiritual renewal or transformation. Men are not naturally children of God in the sense of the terms of this passage; in other words, the natural relation in which all men alike stand to God as his creatures or offspring is not designated as sonship. That term is reserved to express the relation of likeness, fellowship, and loving obedience into which men enter by faith. It is true that all men are ideally sons of God, — that is, it is their true destiny, and they have the capacity, to become such. But they actually enter upon the possession of this divine privilege only through an inward transformation.

The other passage to which reference must be made is I. iii. 1: "Behold what manner of love the Father hath bestowed upon us, that we should be called children of God (τέκνα θεοῦ): and such we are." The writer is addressing his fellow-Christians. This condition of sonship to God he describes as the result of a spiritual begetting, the reality of which is attested by the doing of righteousness (I. iii. 9, 10). Sonship to God, therefore, in the sense of the passage, is conditioned upon being begotten of God, that is, upon the renewal of the natural man by regeneration.

We may, then, state the conclusion to which these passages lead us in this paradoxical form: God *is* the Father of men, but men *become* sons of God.[1] Between God the Creator and man the creature the ideal relation is one of unity and harmony. But this ideal relation does not, as matter of fact, exist. Man has impaired it by sin. God continues good and gracious to man; he always corresponds to the perfect idea of what he should be; he is the Father still; but man has forfeited his moral sonship to God, involving fellowship and likeness, by disobedience. In this sense God can be called the Father of men because he always remains *actually* in his relations to men what he is *ideally;* whereas men must *become* sons of God because they are not *actually* what they are ideally; it is on their side that the ideal relation has been impaired; on their side, therefore, must it be restored. Only as men renounce their sins and become obedient and like to God, do they become, in an ethical sense, his sons. The language of John especially emphasizes the idea of growth in likeness and fellowship with God by the use of the word *child* (τέκνον) rather than *son* (υἱός). The latter word — characteristic of Paul — emphasizes the dignity of the believer's position, while the former emphasizes more the close relation of fellowship with God into which the believer has entered, — a

[1] *Cf.* Wendt, *Teaching of Jesus*, i. 194.

THE IDEA OF GOD IN WRITINGS OF JOHN

relation in which lies the guaranty of his continuous progress in all that is Godlike. This distinction is well defined by Haupt: "According to Paul, we secure, for Christ's sake, the *right* of a child (*Kindesrecht*); according to John, we secure, through Christ, the *nature* of a child" (*Kindeswesen*).[1]

How evident it is that the idea of God which is found in the writings of John is one which accords with the demands of the religious life. Those aspects of the divine character are presented which are essential to practical religious thought, and inspiring to religious confidence and joy. We do not meet in these writings the God of abstract philosophical speculation, — the vague, absentee Deity of Gnosticism, — but the Father of our spirits and the God of all tender mercies. The God whom this apostle knows and proclaims is the living God, who perpetually reveals his goodness to men, and who comes to the world in the fulness of his grace and truth in the person of his Son Jesus Christ.

[1] *Commentary*, on I. iii. 1.

CHAPTER IV

THE DOCTRINE OF THE LOGOS

Literature. — LÜCKE: *Commentar über das Evangelium des Johannes*, Der Prolog, pp. 249-294, and 365-378, translated in the Christian Examiner for 1849, pp. 165-189 and 412-432; WEISS: *Der Johanneische Lehrbegriff*, Die sogenannte johanneische Logoslehre, pp. 239-251; *Bibl. Theol.* The Christology, ii. 325-347; REUSS: *Hist. Christ. Theol.*, Of the Essential Nature of the Word, ii. 389-399 (orig. ii. 435-447); BAUR: *Neutest. Theol.*, Der Logos als das göttliches Offenbarungsorgan, pp. 356-359; LIAS: *Doctr. Syst. of St. John*, Doctrine of the Logos and the Person of Christ, pp. 33-64; SIEGFRIED: *Philo von Alexandria*, Die Lehre vom Logos, pp. 219-229, and Das Johannesevangelium, pp. 317-321; FROMMANN: *Der Johann. Lehrb.*, passim (F. treats the whole theology of John from the standpoint of the Logos-doctrine); LIPSIUS: art. Alexandrinische Religionsphilosophie in Schenkel's *Bibel-Lexicon*; SCHÜRER: *Hist. Jewish People*, Philo, the Jewish Philosopher, iii. 321-381; GLOAG: *Introduction to the Johannine Writings*, Dissertation on the Logos, pp. 167-189; SMITH's *Bible Dictionary*, arts. on The Wisdom of Solomon, and The Word (For ample references to the literature of the subject see especially the latter article; also SCHÜRER and GLOAG, *op. cit.*); SANDAY: *The Authorship and Historical Character of the Fourth Gospel*, The Prologue, pp. 5-20; HARNACK: Ueber das Verhältniss des Prologs des vierten Evangeliums zum ganzen Werk, in the *Zeitschrift für Theologie und Kirche*, 2 Jahrg., 3 Heft, 1892; SALMOND: article Logos in the *Encyclopædia Britannica*; WEIZSÄCKER: *Das apos. Zeitalter*, Die Logoslehre, pp. 549-558; LIDDON: *The Divinity of*

THE DOCTRINE OF THE LOGOS

our Lord, Lect. II. Anticipations of Christ's Divinity in the Old Testament, pp. 45-99, and Lect. V. The Doctrine of Christ's Divinity in the Writings of St. John, pp. 209-278. For full discussions of the Logos-doctrine in Philo and in Greek Philosophy I refer to the following works: JAMES DRUMMOND: *Philo Judæus, or, Jewish Alexandrian Philosophy in its Development and Completion*, London, 1888; E. ZELLER: *Die Philosophie der Griechen, u. s. w.*, 3 Theil, 2 Abtheilung, pp. 338-418; M. HEINZE: *Die Lehre vom Logos in der Griechischen Philosophie*, Oldenburg, 1872, pp. 204-297. For the critical exposition of the language of the prologue I would refer especially to the Commentaries of Lücke, Meyer, Westcott, and Godet.

THE most characteristic single doctrine which is found in the writings of John is the doctrine of the Logos or Word. He uses this term to denote the pre-existent Son of God who became incarnate in Jesus. It is evident from the fact that the apostle does not explain the word or seek to justify its use by argument, that it was a term of current speech which he assumes that his readers will understand. But to modern ears the term *Word* has a strange sound as a designation for Christ, and the force of John's use of it can only become apparent by an investigation of its historical meaning.

Baur and his school, who ascribed the Gospel to a Christian Gnostic who wrote about the middle of the second century, held that the idea of the Logos was derived from the Gnostic systems;[1] but all the considerations which have been adduced since Baur's time in

---

[1] See, *e. g.*, BAUR: *Neutest. Theol.*, p. 361 *sq.*; PFLEIDERER: *Urchristenthum*, p. 698.

76 THE JOHANNINE THEOLOGY

favor of an earlier date for the Gospel unite to render this supposition improbable. The Logos-idea is indeed found in the systems of Basilides and Valentinus, but it is only a minor element in a complex series of æons or emanations. The Logos in these systems has a different character and an inferior significance compared with those which it bears in the Fourth Gospel.

It is still a debatable question whether the primary source of John's Logos-doctrine was Jewish or Alexandrian, — whether we are to look chiefly to the Old Testament or to Philo for its explanation. The latter has long been, and doubtless is still the prevailing view.[1] But it is to be noticed that even if we attribute John's use of the term Logos to the direct or indirect influence of Philo, we do not thereby disprove the Old Testament origin of the conception. Two main streams of thought met and mingled in the Alexandrian philosophy, — one Hellenic, emanating from Plato and the Stoics, the other Jewish, emanating from the Old Testament and the later Jewish theology. Philo was a devout Jew, and the basis of his philosophy of religion was the Old Testament. With the Jewish religion he sought to blend ideas derived from the Greek philosophy, on the assumption that this philosophy was also the product of a real divine inspiration. The result was a conglom-

[1] So, for example, Meyer, Lücke, Reuss, Beyschlag, Weizsäcker, Harnack; *per contra*, Luthardt, Weiss, Liddon, Godet, Plummer.

THE DOCTRINE OF THE LOGOS 77

erate system, incoherent and self-contradictory in many of its parts, but still resting, in the belief of its author, upon an Old Testament basis.

In order clearly to indicate the bearings of the question at issue, it is necessary briefly to illustrate the ideas from the Old Testament, and those from Philo, which stand connected with the Johannine use of the term Logos.

In the Old Testament we frequently meet with the phrase "word of Jehovah" as a symbol of the power of God or of the energizing of his will.

> "By the word of the Lord were the heavens made;
> And all the host of them by the breath of the mouth.
>
> . . . .
>
> For *he spake*, and it was done;
> He commanded, and it stood fast" (Ps. xxxiii. 6, 9).

These expressions are based upon the idea of God's creative *fiat*, as it appears, for example, in the cosmogony in Genesis: "And *God said*, Let there be," etc. In some passages, "the word of God" is poetically described as an energetic agent which is active in accomplishing the divine purposes; as when, in a description of God's action in nature, it is said: "He sendeth out his *commandment* upon earth; His *word* runneth very swiftly" (Ps. cxlvii. 15), or as when, through the prophet, Jehovah declares that his *word* shall accomplish that which he pleases (Is. lv. 10, 11).

With the use of God's *word* as a symbol of his power, is closely connected the use of it as a name for the revelation of his will, applied especially to his messages to men through the prophets. Isaiah " saw the word [of Jehovah] concerning Judah and Jerusalem (Is. ii. 1). " The word of the Lord came " is the formula with which most of the prophetic books are prefaced.

Some of the passages already quoted illustrate a tendency to personify *the word*. This tendency is still more noticeable where attributes of God are predicated of his word, as when it is affirmed to be right (Ps. xxxiii. 4), enduring (Ps. cxix. 89), and powerful (Jer. xxiii. 29). These personifications are, of course, poetical, but they illustrate the beginnings of a mode of thought which is carried much further in the uses of the terms *word* and *wisdom* which we have yet to notice, and which throws light upon the genesis and significance of the Johannine Logos-doctrine.

In the Book of Job and in Proverbs we find a personification of *wisdom*. In Job the term is a poetical designation for the gracious purpose of God which he is working out in human experience. Hence in the theodicy of the book it is only the righteous man who knows and shares in this wisdom. This divine wisdom is the great secret of life (Job xxviii., *passim*). It is more securely hidden from men than are the metals in the earth (1–6); the wild birds and beasts have not found in the rocks and mountains its hiding place (7, 8); the costliest jewels cannot equal it in value (15–19); only God "knoweth the place thereof" (23).

THE DOCTRINE OF THE LOGOS 79

" Whence then cometh wisdom ?
And where is the place of understanding ?

. . . .

Behold, the fear of the Lord, that is wisdom ;
And to depart from evil is understanding " (20, 28).

More strikingly still is wisdom personified in the Book of Proverbs (chs. viii., ix.). She is the cardinal virtue who stands on the street-corners and at the city gates, and invites men to walk in her ways (viii. 1–4). God created, or prepared her, before the world was made (22–29), and she was at his side as the artist who shares the Creator's plans; she was " daily his delight, rejoicing always before him " (30) ; she therefore exhorts men to listen to her instruction and assures those who do so of life, blessedness, and the favor of Heaven (32–36).

It will be seen that the conception represented by the *word of God* in Hebrew thought relates more to the divine activity; that represented by *wisdom* relates more to the divine attributes. Both terms are means of expressing the idea of the living, self-revealing God. The manifestations of Jehovah's power, especially in nature, are the operations of his *word ;* the revelation of his ethical nature and of the moral requirements which God makes of men, is the voice of his *wisdom*.

The next step in the development of thought which we are tracing is found in the Apocryphal books, " Ecclesiasticus " or " Jesus, the Son of Sirach," and " The Wisdom of Solomon." Both these books belong to the second century before Christ, and represent — especially the Book of Wisdom — a development of Biblical ideas under the influence of Greek speculation. "Ecclesiasticus" is clearly an imitation of the canonical Book of Proverbs. Its fullest descriptions of wisdom are found in chapters i. and xxiv. The ideas closely resemble those of Proverbs viii. which we have noticed. A few examples are here adduced : —

> "All wisdom cometh from the Lord,
> And is with him forever.
>
> . . . .
>
> Wisdom was created before all things,
> And prudent understanding from everlasting.
>
> . . . .
>
> He created her, and saw her, and made her known,
> And poured her out upon all his works.
>
> . . . .
>
> The root of wisdom is to fear the Lord,
> And the branches thereof are long life" (i. 1, 4, 9, 20).

In chapter xxiv. is found a much more highly colored description of wisdom in the form of a soliloquy which represents the most characteristic thought of the book. We quote a few verses : —

> "I came forth from the mouth of the Most High,
> And covered the earth as a mist.
> I dwelt in the heights,
> And my throne was on a cloudy pillar.
> I alone compassed the arch of heaven,
> And walked about in the depth of abysses.
> In the waves of the sea, and in all the earth,

THE DOCTRINE OF THE LOGOS

And in every people and nation, I got a possession.
With all these I sought rest;
And in whose inheritance should I abide?
Then the Creator of all things gave me a commandment,
And he that made me caused my tabernacle to rest,
And said, Let thy dwelling be in Jacob,
And thine inheritance in Israel.
He created me from the beginning, before the world,
And I shall never fail.
In the holy tabernacle I served before him;
And so was I established in Sion " (xxiv. 3-10).

It is evident that we have here a poetic description of God's self-revelation under an objective and personal form. The intention of the passage is not to hypostatize wisdom, but only to personify, for rhetorical effect, the manifestation of God's attributes which is made in the government of the world, and especially in the Old Testament law.

In the Book of Wisdom the development of thought is carried one step farther. Its author was evidently an Alexandrian Jew who sought to combine Greek speculation with the Jewish religion, and who may therefore be regarded as one of the forerunners of that peculiar philosophy of religion which is best represented in Philo. Solomon is the speaker. In chapters vii. and viii., he gives a description of wisdom, " who she is, and how she arose" (vi. 22). She is " the artificer of all things " (vii. 21), a subtle, all-permeating principle (vii. 24), " is initiated into the mysteries of the knowledge of God, and is a chooser of his works " (viii. 4). " She is a breath of the power of God, and a pure effluence from the glory of the Almighty; therefore no defiling thing falls into her; for she is a reflection of the everlasting light (ἀπαύγασμα φωτὸς ἀϊδίου; cf. ἀπαύγασμα τῆς δόξης κ. τ. λ., Heb. i. 3), and an unspotted mirror of the efficiency of God, and image of his goodness. And though but one, she can do all things; and though remaining in herself, she maketh all things new; and from generation to generation entering into holy souls, she equippeth friends of God, and prophets. For God loveth none but him that dwelleth with wisdom. For she is more beautiful than the sun, and above every position of stars; being compared with the light, she is found superior" (vii. 25-29).

It is impossible to determine with certainty how far this ascription of personal qualities and activities to wisdom is to be regarded as merely poetic or figurative. The description of wisdom as a holy spirit of light and an active agent of God in the world seems to form a connecting link between the poetical personifications in the canonical Wisdom-books and the Logos-doctrine of Philo, the chief features of which we shall presently notice.

Attention should here be directed to the personification of the *word* (Memra) of Jehovah which is found in the Targums or Aramaic paraphrases of the Old Testament books.[1] These Targums were in current use among the Jews in the apostolic age, and John

[1] See Weber, *Die Lehren des Talmud*, Das Memra Jehova's, pp. 174-179.

THE DOCTRINE OF THE LOGOS 83

was probably acquainted with their phraseology. They personified the *word* of God and ascribed to it divine power in order more completely to separate God from the world. Especially were the anthropomorphic acts of God referred to the Memra. Instead of Adam and Eve hearing the *voice* of the Lord in the garden (Gen. iii. 8), they are said to have heard the voice of the *word* of the Lord, and the like. This *word* is described by the Rabbis as proceeding out of the mouth of God and becoming an active potency, a personal hypostasis, whom the angels serve in executing the divine will. God dwells in and works through the Memra; he stands for the popular thought in the place of Jehovah, and the providential and redemptive acts of God are freely ascribed to him. The Memra of the paraphrasts presents a striking analogy to the Logos of the Jewish Alexandrian philosopher Philo (fl. 40–50 A. D.).

Philo's system is a complex of Jewish, Greek, and Oriental elements. As a Jew he believed in the God of the Old Testament, but under the influence of philosophy he was led to the most abstract conception of his nature. God was absolutely removed from the world and could have no contact with it. Between the pure Spirit and the sensible world there could be no communication. This gulf between the transcendent Deity and the lower world Philo sought to bridge by his doctrine of intermediate powers or ideas. The sum or epitome of these various agencies is the Logos. This term Philo probably adopted from the Old Testament, but the content and use of it were determined by that gnosis which had its principal sources in the Platonic doctrine of ideas and in the Stoic doctrine of causes or powers.

The term Logos, as denoting the archetypal idea, was fitted to express both the immanent reason of God and also the principle of revelation in the divine nature. The Logos, considered as immanent reason, corresponding to unuttered thought (λόγος ἐνδιάθετος) in man, is as transcendent and incomprehensible as God himself; but in its other aspect as an active, forth-putting power, corresponding to uttered thought (λόγος προφορικός) in man, the Logos is the medium of God's self-communication by which he reveals himself in creation and providence. This uttered Word is the agent through whom God created the world and is continually active within it. In him is summed up all divine wisdom and goodness. He is the first-born son of God, the highest angel, the second God (ὁ δεύτερος θεός).

Whether Philo regards the Logos as strictly a person distinct from God is a disputed question. The difficulty of deciding it with certainty arises from the shifting and inconsistent meanings in which he employs the term. Much of his language can, no doubt, be explained as poetical, and in no case can a clear and consistent conception be derived from his expressions. But after all due allowance is made for vague and figurative language, there remains, I think, decisive evidence that his descriptions of the Logos can denote nothing less than a real person, an hypostasis distinct from God. Since the Logos is defined to be "the

THE DOCTRINE OF THE LOGOS 85

second God" in a figurative sense (ἐν καταχρήσει), is begotten of the Father, and therefore dependent for his existence upon him, the monotheism of Philo would not be undermined by the ascription of personality to the Logos.

Such are the elements of the Logos-doctrine in its various stages of development. It is rooted in the soil of the Old Testament. But, although it stands in direct connection with the Old Testament personification of God's power under the term *word* and the personification of his ethical attributes under the term *wisdom*, it is hardly conceivable that the Logos-idea should have taken the form which it has assumed in Philo except through contact with Greek speculation. The doctrine of ideas as the archetypal essences of all things and kindred forms of thought, and the conception of God's metaphysical absoluteness, are the two elements of Greek thought which gave shape to the idea of the Logos which Philo had derived from the Old Testament. The Logos-doctrine was a means of showing how the transcendent God might still come into relation with the world and man. The later Jewish theology, which more and more removed God from active contact with the world, solved the same problem by its doctrine of angels who were the agents of God in all his acts. We have occasional traces of this tendency to ascribe God's action to the mediation of angels in the New Testament.[1]

[1] Acts vii. 35; Heb. ii. 2; and, especially, Gal. iii. 19, where the giving of the law is ascribed to the mediation of angels, — an

It is evident from what has been said that the Logos-idea must have been a familiar one when the apostle John wrote. Wisdom literature had been current for two centuries or more, and the elaborate system of Philo was wrought out forty or fifty years before the Fourth Gospel was written. The apostle did not adopt the word Logos because he was himself inventing some recondite system of speculation concerning the person of Christ. He adopted it as a term of current philosophical speech in order by its use to adapt his idea of Christ's pre-existence and divinity to the minds of his Greek readers. In his use of it we need not suppose that it retains precisely the same associations and contents which it had in the speculations of the time. On the contrary, it bears quite a new character as employed by John. "The personification of the divine word in the Old Testament is poetical, in Philo metaphysical, in St. John historical."[1] The use of the term is an illustration of the natural tendency of Christian thought to avail itself of the philosophical conceptions and phraseology which prevail at any given time. Other examples are found in Paul's use, in the Epistles of the Imprisonment, of terms derived from an incipient Gnosticism, especially πλήρωμα, and the wide adoption in the

---

idea not found in the narrative of the giving of the law. It is probably found, however, in the original of Deut. xxxiii. 2, and is clearly expressed by the Septuagint rendering of that passage (ἄγγελοι μετ' αὐτοῦ).

[1] Plummer, *Cambridge Gk. Test.* Notes on John i. 1.

THE DOCTRINE OF THE LOGOS

theological language of our time of phraseology derived from the theory of evolution. It is as if John had said to his readers: You are familiar with the speculations which have long been rife respecting the means whereby God reveals himself, — the doctrine of an intermediate agent through whom he communicates his light and life to men. The true answer to the question regarding this mediator is, that it is our Lord Jesus Christ. He is God's agent in revelation; he is the bond which unites heaven and earth.

The development of the Logos-doctrine which we have briefly traced indicates the answer to the question as to the origin of the idea in the writings of John. It cannot be explained without reference to Philo. Whether John had ever read the writings of Philo we do not know. Whether he was directly familiar with Philo's system we have no means of deciding. But that he was familiar with that type of speculation concerning the Logos whose chief representative is found in Philo seems certain, and some direct knowledge of Philo's system is highly probable. Be that as it may, we cannot naturally explain his use of the term Logos without supposing him and his readers to have been somewhat familiar with Alexandrian thought. But it is none the less true that John's Logos-doctrine is rooted in the Old Testament, partly because he was himself familiar with the Jewish ideas of the *word* and *wisdom*, and partly because in Philo's system the conception of the *word* is an elaboration of these ideas under forms of thought derived from Greek philosophy. The dispute whether John's Logos-doctrine is Jewish or Alexandrian draws the lines too closely. It is both, for the Alexandrian philosophy of religion was largely Jewish. Both the effort to find the occasion and ground of John's doctrine in the Old Testament alone,[1] and the failure to take account of the Old Testament basis of the doctrine,[2] are alike unwarranted. The fact is that the philosophy of Philo, which developed and applied the Old Testament idea, was the medium through which that idea became available for the apostle's purpose, and so passed into his writings.

Let us now turn to the prologue of the Gospel, i. 1–18, and see in what way and for what purpose John employs the Logos-idea. From such an examination we shall be able to determine the points of likeness and of difference between John's Logos-doctrine and that of Philo, and to define the purpose of the doctrine in its relation to the Gospel as a whole.

The prologue begins with the idea of the *eternity* of the Logos (ἐν ἀρχῇ ἦν ὁ λόγος, i. 1). This idea is repeated in verse 2 (οὗτος ἦν ἐν ἀρχῇ πρὸς τὸν θεόν), and is confirmed by the expression of Jesus in xvii. 5, where he speaks of the glory which he had with the Father "before the world was" (πρὸ τοῦ τὸν κόσμον εἶναι). To the same effect is his statement, "Before Abraham *was born*, I am (πρὶν Ἀβραὰμ γενέσθαι ἐγὼ

---

[1] See, *e. g.*, Weiss, *Der Johann. Lehrb.*, pp. 244, 245.
[2] See, *e. g.*, Weizsäcker, *Das apostol. Zeitalter*, p. 551.

THE DOCTRINE OF THE LOGOS

εἰμί, viii. 58; *cf*. Ps. xc. 2). In the opening words of the First Epistle (I. i. 1) we find a parallel to the begining of the prologue, where the saving grace which came to the world in Christ is designated as "that which was from the beginning" (ὃ ἦν ἀπ' ἀρχῆς).

It has been held by many that these statements amount only to an assertion of the relative pre-existence of the Logos, and are not equivalent to an affirmation of his eternity.[1] The opening words of the prologue present, no doubt, an allusion and a parallel to the opening words of Genesis. Reuss therefore affirms that "if we infer from these words the eternity of the Word, we must infer also from the beginning of Genesis the eternity of the world." But, supposing that in both cases the word "beginning" denotes the beginning of time, there remains the important difference that in Genesis that which is placed at the beginning is an *act* (creation), while in John that which is placed at the beginning is the *existence* of the Word. The Word *was* at the beginning; he existed before the world came into being. It is true that John does not employ the words *eternal* or *eternity* in the connection, but we hold that this idea is involved in the logical relation between the terms *was* and *in the beginning*. When John speaks of that which comes into existence he uses both a different word and a different tense (πάντα δι' αὐτοῦ ἐγένετο, κ. τ. λ., i. 3). All things *came into being*, but in the beginning of things he *was*. Without assign-

[1] See, *e. g.*, Reuss, *op. cit.*, ii. 391, 392 (orig. ii. 438, 439).

ing to ἀρχή — with some of the older interpreters — the meaning *eternity*, we think that the idea is involved in the passages which we have noticed, as well as demanded by other assertions of the apostle concerning the Word.[1]

John's next proposition concerning the Logos is that he existed in intimate fellowship with God (καὶ ὁ λόγος ἦν πρὸς τὸν θεόν, i. 1). The force of the preposition πρός may be partially indicated by the very unidiomatic English rendering: "The Word was *toward* God." The preposition expresses more than παρά would do (*cf.* xvii. 5.). It emphasizes a direction or tendency of life. The moral movement of his life is centred in God, and ever goes out toward God. The bond of this essential fellowship is love, since the Father loved the Son "before the foundation of the world" (xvii. 24). A similar thought is probably intended in the words, "which is in the bosom of the Father" (ὁ ὢν εἰς τὸν κόλπον τοῦ πατρός, i. 18). Some interpreters understand these words to be spoken from the standpoint of the writer at the time, and therefore to refer to the *exaltation* of Jesus.[2] But the point of the passage is to show how the Son is fitted to reveal God to mankind, and it is his essential and eternal relation to the Father which would constitute the ground of that fitness. The *declaration* of the Father referred

[1] "For 'before the world was,' a philosophical writer would have said 'from eternity.'" Beyschlag, *Neutest. Theol.*, ii. 427.

[2] So Meyer, *Commentary, in loco* ; Weiss, *Johann. Lehrb.*, p. 239.

THE DOCTRINE OF THE LOGOS

to in ἐξηγήσατο, is that which the Son has made in his incarnation. His fitness to make that revelation must therefore be logically grounded in his pre-incarnate relation to the Father (τὸν θεόν) to which alone can the words ὁ ὢν εἰς τὸν κόλπον naturally refer.[1] Here, too, the use of the preposition (εἰς), indicating motion or direction, should be observed, suggesting an "active and living relation" (Godet) between the Son and the Father.

To the assertion of the pre-existence of the Logos and of his abiding fellowship with God, John now adds: "and the Word was God (καὶ θεὸς ἦν ὁ λόγος, i. 1). Θεός is here emphatically prefixed because the stress of the thought lies upon the *divine nature* of the Logos, and is without the article because John will not absolutely identify ὁ λόγος and ὁ θεός. To do this would be to contradict the previous sentence where a distinction is presupposed between ὁ λόγος and ὁ θεός (the Father). John here uses ὁ θεός to denote specifically the Father — the central seat and fountain of divinity — and θεός to denote the category of divine nature or essence in which the Son, equally with the Father, partakes. He thus affirms a distinction of persons, but an identity of essence, between the Logos and the Father. That this is the import of the apostle's words is generally admitted by candid interpreters, whatever adjustment they may make of the fact with theological speculation.

[1] So Lücke, De Wette, Godet, Westcott (*Commentaries, in loco*).

Writers who, like Ritschl[1] and Beyschlag,[2] suppose the Logos to denote a principle or impulse in God, or a pretemporal purpose of God to reveal himself in a person, appeal in support of their views rather to what they regard as the practical, non-speculative purpose of the prologue than to the simple, immediate import of the words. Lücke's objections to the usual interpretation are untenable.[3] He says, for example, that, if θεὸς ἦν ὁ λόγος was intended to emphasize the *unity* of essence as an offset to the *distinction* of persons implied in ὁ λόγος ἦν πρὸς τὸν θεόν, an adversative particle (ἀλλά or δέ), and not the simple connective καί, would have been required. To this the answer is, in part, that it is the commonest peculiarity of John's style to string sentences together, in Hebraistic fashion, by the simple connective, and, further, that the apostle's thought does not require him to set these statements in contrast, but in unity. His assertion that the common view would necessitate the article with θεός to correspond to πρὸς τὸν θεόν, overlooks the natural and intentional difference between ὁ θεός and θεός. This author weakens θεός to the sense of Philo's phrase ὁ δεύτερος θεός which he applied to the Logos by accommodation. Lücke's conclusion is that the sense is nearly the same as if John had defined the Logos as θεῖος, and that the words θεὸς ἦν ὁ λόγος do not add a new thought to

[1] *Rechtfertigung und Versöhnung*, iii. 378 *sq.*
[2] *Neutest. Theol.*, ii. 427.
[3] *Commentary, in loco.*

THE DOCTRINE OF THE LOGOS 93

the two previously expressed, but only further define and explain the relation denoted by $\pi\rho os\ \tau\grave{o}\nu\ \theta\epsilon\acute{o}\nu$. This interpretation unwarrantably allows the natural force of John's words to be overborne by the assumption of a close resemblance between John's idea of the Logos and that of Philo.

The creation of the world is ascribed to the Logos ($\pi\acute{a}\nu\tau a\ \delta\iota'\ a\vec{v}\tau o\hat{v}\ \dot{\epsilon}\gamma\acute{\epsilon}\nu\epsilon\tau o,\ \kappa.\ \tau.\ \lambda.$, i. 3, 10). It will be noticed that it is a mediate function ($\delta\iota\acute{a}$) in creation which is here designated. Nothing came into being apart from him ($\chi\omega\rho\grave{\iota}s\ a\vec{v}\tau o\hat{v}$). In this respect the theology of John accords with the representations of other New Testament writers, for example, with that of Paul: "In him ($\dot{\epsilon}\nu\ a\vec{v}\tau\hat{\wp}$) were all things created," etc.; "All things have been created through him ($\delta\iota'\ a\vec{v}\tau o\hat{v}$) and unto him ($\epsilon\grave{\iota}s\ a\vec{v}\tau\acute{o}\nu$); and he is before all things and in him all things consist" (Col. i. 16, 17). In Hebrews also the writer speaks of the Son "through whom ($\delta\iota'\ o\hat{v}$) God made the worlds," and who "upholds all things by the word of his power" (i. 2, 3). God is the Creator in the absolute sense, but the Logos is the co-efficient agent of God in creating, sustaining, and governing the world. It is thus a matter of interest to observe that John, as well as Paul, has the idea of "the cosmic significance of Christ," — an idea which sustains an important relation to his doctrines of revelation and redemption.

The fifth and final thought of the introductory passage (i. 1-5), which may be called the prologue in the narrower sense, is that the Logos is the giver of life or dispenser of light to men (i. 4, 5). The Logos is the agent of divine revelation, — the mediator of spiritual life to mankind universally. He is the seat and source of life, which he communicates to men. This life is defined under the figure of light in order to emphasize its diffusive and beneficent character and power. This light has been pouring itself forth upon the sinful and unreceptive world in all ages.

The remainder of the prologue may be regarded as an illustration and amplification of this thought, drawn from the historical manifestation of the Logos in Jesus Christ. From the sixth verse onward the writer makes the incarnation and life of Jesus his ruling thought. John the Baptist — the last representative of the old covenant and the herald of the new — testified that Jesus was the true divine light of the world (6-9). As participating in the world's creation he has an abiding relation to it. He was perpetually active ($\mathring{\eta}\nu$) in the world as the revealer of God, but the world received not his revelation (10). At length he came ($\mathring{\eta}\lambda\theta\epsilon\nu$) in his incarnation to his own proper possession ($\epsilon\mathit{i}\varsigma$ $\tau\grave{\alpha}$ $\mathit{i}\delta\iota\alpha$), the Jewish nation, but those who were, in the divine destination, his own people ($o\mathit{i}$ $\mathit{i}\delta\iota o\iota$), acting in their free self-determination, rejected him (11). Such as did receive him, however, entered by faith in him into a new world of blessedness in loving fellowship with the Father (12, 13). The main thoughts which are here indicated respecting divine revelation are: (1) Revelation is universal; the light of the

THE DOCTRINE OF THE LOGOS

eternal Logos shines in the world's darkness, seeking to bless and save men. (2) It is the sinfulness of men which blinds their minds to the true knowledge of God and prevents them from realizing the blessedness of fellowship with God. (3) In the incarnation of the Logos a special revelation was made to the Jews, in whose whole history God had been seeking to prepare the way for the reception of the Messiah when he should come. (4) While as a nation the Jews, who thus, in a peculiar sense, belonged to Christ, rejected him, he was accepted by others on conditions purely spiritual; and these have attained the end contemplated in all revelation, — loving obedience and fellowship with God.

The final section of the prologue (14–18) introduces no strictly new thoughts. John affirms that the Logos became incarnate ($\dot{o}$ $\lambda\acute{o}\gamma o \varsigma$ $\sigma\grave{a}\rho\xi$ $\dot{\epsilon}\gamma\acute{\epsilon}\nu\epsilon\tau o$, 14), and that he dwelt in humanity as in a tabernacle ($\dot{\epsilon}\sigma\kappa\acute{\eta}\nu\omega\sigma\epsilon\nu$ $\dot{\epsilon}\nu$ $\dot{\eta}\mu\hat{\iota}\nu$, 14). The word $\sigma\acute{a}\rho\xi$ denotes human nature, and not a human body ($\sigma\hat{\omega}\mu a$) merely. The verb $\dot{\epsilon}\gamma\acute{\epsilon}\nu\epsilon\tau o$ cannot, in view of John's whole doctrine, be understood to mean that the Logos changed his nature and became human in the sense of ceasing to be divine. The sentence $\dot{o}$ $\lambda\acute{o}\gamma o \varsigma$ $\sigma\grave{a}\rho\xi$ $\dot{\epsilon}\gamma\acute{\epsilon}\nu\epsilon\tau o$ expresses with pregnant brevity the idea of his assumption of human nature by union with which the divine-human personality is constituted. We must understand this formula in the light of the explanatory words: "and tabernacled among us" (i. 14), and of expressions like $\dot{\epsilon}\nu$ $\sigma a\rho\kappa\grave{\iota}$ $\ddot{\epsilon}\rho\chi\epsilon\sigma\theta a\iota$ (I. iv. 2; II. 7) as denoting the mysterious unity of divinity with humanity in the person of Jesus Christ. In his person, "full of grace and truth" (14), the glory of God — his holy perfections — stood revealed to men. Again the Baptist's testimony is quoted: Although Jesus came after me in time he has taken rank before me in the dignity of his work (ἔμπροσθέν μου γέγονεν, 15), because he existed before me (πρῶτός μου ἦν, 15). We became sharers, continues the apostle, in the plenitude of divine blessing which came to the world in Christ, and, in consequence, one gift of grace has succeeded another (χάριν ἀντὶ χάριτος, 16). He closes by hinting at the greater fulness of revelation through the incarnation in comparison with that made in Old Testament times. The revelation made through Moses — from which the activity of the Logos must not be supposed to have been absent — was a revelation of law which, in the nature of the case, could make only a very partial manifestation of God. Commandments and prohibitions are extrinsic to God, and furnish, at best, but partial disclosures of his will and nature. But in Christ revelation became personal. God came close to men in a life which revealed the very heart of God to them, and, while he still remained hidden to the senses, he was declared in his essence and disposition by the Son, who in his essential life is in perpetual and perfect fellowship with the Father.

A comparison of the Logos-idea, as thus developed, with that of Philo, will reveal similarities of form with striking and essential differences of content. The Logos of John, like that of Philo, is the mediator

THE DOCTRINE OF THE LOGOS

between the absolute God and the world, but the motive for the mediation in the two systems is fundamentally different. In Philo the motive lies in a certain philosophical view of the world and of God. The world is gross and evil, and the transcendent God can hold no direct relations with it. God comes into relation with the world only mediately through the Logos. Thus the motive for the Logos-doctrine in Philo is found in a metaphysical view of the universe. With John the motive is historical. The fact of divine revelation in Jesus Christ is the logical starting-point of the Johannine theology. For John, God is also transcendent, but his transcendence is ethical, not metaphysical. For him the world is separated from God, but this separation is due, not to the constitution of the world, but to its sinfulness. Philo's system rests upon a metaphysical dualism inherent in the universe; John's doctrine proceeds upon the idea of an ethical dualism, incidental to the system and arising from human sin. The Logos-doctrine is not adopted and shaped by John — as by Philo — as a means of solving the difficulties inherent in a certain philosophy, but is adopted as a convenient and useful method of presenting the fact that the pre-existent Son of God became incarnate in Jesus Christ. John in the prologue seeks to present to his readers, under the terms of a doctrine which was current among them, two truths concerning Jesus: (1) the fact of his saving historical work, whose blessing he had himself experienced; and (2) the fact of his personal pre-existence and essential unity with the Father, to which Jesus had testified in his teaching concerning himself.

Again, in John we have what is not found in Philo, — a clear and consistent personification of the Logos. In Philo the use of the word oscillates between the two common meanings of the term, *reason* and *word*. The Logos, considered as the immanent reason of God, is a name for an element or phase of the personality of the absolute Being, while the Logos, in the sense of the uttered Word of God, is treated as a distinct hypostasis. These two quite different senses of the term are not clearly distinguished. The word is thus involved in vague and shifting senses. Moreover, the relation of Philo's philosophy to Old Testament and later Jewish thought, enhances the uncertainty of its meaning. Many of Philo's titles for the Logos, — the Wisdom of God, the Son of God, the Archangel, the Man of God, etc., — seem to be reproductions of Jewish conceptions which may be understood figuratively or poetically. But in John the identification of the Logos with the person of Jesus Christ, and the clear assertion of his pretemporal existence and of his deity, make it impossible, without exegetical arbitrariness, to interpret his language in a mere ideal or poetical sense.

From what has been said of the differing motives of the Logos-doctrine in John and in Philo, it is evident that the idea of the incarnation of the Logos would be radically inconsistent with Philo's whole system. The divine Logos could form no union with

THE DOCTRINE OF THE LOGOS 99

weak and corruptible human nature. The words ὁ λόγος σὰρξ ἐγένετο, (i. 14) mark a fundamental difference between John's doctrine and Philo's. There are no presuppositions in the apostle's thought which constitute a barrier to the idea of a union of divinity with humanity. In fact he has had personal knowledge of such a union in the person of his Master, in whom the divine life has been manifested (I. i. 1, 2). John's doctrine is grounded thus, not in abstract speculation, but in observation and experience. His fellowship with his Master and his knowledge of his teaching and claims are the grounds on which he builds his doctrine of the nature, incarnation, and historical function of the Logos.

While we thus recognize a historic relation between Alexandrian speculation as represented in Philo, and John's Logos-doctrine,[1] we think the differences much more fundamental than the resemblances. If this is the case, it raises a strong presumption against the opinion[2] that the Logos-idea is the starting-point and controlling thought of the Fourth Gospel. In this view it is regarded as the aim of the Gospel to exhibit the various stages of a conflict between light and darkness (i. 4, 5, 7, 9; iii. 19–21; viii. 12; ix. 5; xii. 35, 36, 46). The Gospel is a highly wrought description of the meeting of opposing powers which

[1] The resemblances in phraseology and idea are exhibited in detail in Siegfried's *Philo von Alexandria*, pp. 317–321.

[2] See, *e. g.*, Weizsäcker, *Das apostol. Zeitalter*, p. 553; O. Holtzmann, *Das Johannesevangelium*, pp. 78, 79.

are represented by the Logos and the sinful world respectively. This abstract, philosophical conception which the writer adopted when he appropriated to his use the term Logos determines his whole representation of the life of Jesus, and gives to it a distinctively speculative cast. Philo furnished the fourth evangelist, concludes Oscar Holtzmann, with " an essentially new conception of Christianity." [1]

The phenomena of the Gospel do not appear to me to sustain this view. The term Logos, as a personal designation, does not occur outside of the prologue, and even there is treated historically, rather than philosophically. The Logos is not presented as an abstract principle, but as the pretemporal form of the person Jesus Christ. Light and darkness in the prologue, and in the Gospel elsewhere, are not abstract metaphysical conceptions, but ethical conceptions. Darkness is sin, and light is goodness. These terms are symbols of ethical realities, the use of which accords with the writer's peculiar mode of thought respecting the nature of God and of man, and which abound in the First Epistle (i. 5, 7 ; ii. 8–10) where the Logos-doctrine is not developed and, in the view of many, is not even referred to (see I. i. 1, περὶ τοῦ λόγου τῆς ζωῆς). The writer's own account of his purpose in composing the Gospel is: " These (signs) are written, that ye may believe that Jesus is the Christ, the Son of God; and that believing ye may have life in his name " (xx. 31). His purpose was strictly historical

[1] *Op. cit.*, p. 79.

THE DOCTRINE OF THE LOGOS

and practical. The saving good that has come to the world is found in the person and work of Jesus, who declared himself to have existed in essential union with God before his human appearance. To emphasize this pre-existence and union with God, and to present the thought that, as the eternal Son, Jesus was the medium of divine revelation in all ages, John employs the term Logos.

Harnack concludes his discussion of the relation of the prologue to the Gospel as a whole, in these words:

"The prologue of the Gospel is not the key to the understanding of the Gospel, but it prepares the Hellenistic readers therefor. The writer seizes upon a known quantity, the Logos, works it over and transforms it — implicitly combating false Christologies — in order to substitute for it Jesus Christ, the μονογενὴς θεός, that is, in order to disclose it as being this same Jesus Christ. From the moment when this is done, the Logos-idea is allowed to fall away. The author continues his narrative now only concerning Jesus, in order to establish the faith that he is the Messiah, the Son of God. This belief has for its principal element the recognition that Jesus originates from God and from heaven; but the author is far removed from the purpose of securing this recognition from cosmological and philosophical considerations. Upon the basis of his testimony, and because he has brought full knowledge of God and life — absolutely heavenly, divine benefits — does Jesus prove himself, according to the evangelist, to be the Messiah, the Son of God."[1]

[1] *Op. cit.*, pp. 230, 231. I do not intend by this citation to indicate my accord with Harnack's general estimate of the Logos-idea in the Fourth Gospel.

CHAPTER V

THE UNION OF THE SON WITH THE FATHER

Literature. — WEISS : *Johann. Lehrb.*, Die Einheit des Sohnes mit dem Vater, u. s. w., pp. 203–219, and *Bibl. Theol.*, The Christology, §§ 143–145; WENDT: *The Teaching of Jesus*, The Relation of Jesus to God, and Pre-existence of Jesus according to the Johannine Discourses, ii. 151–178 (orig., pp. 450–472); FROMMANN: *Johann. Lehrb.*, Sohn Gottes, pp. 409–418; BEYSCHLAG: *Neutest. Theol.*, Der Eingeborene, ii. 409–420; H. P. LIDDON: *The Divinity of our Lord and Saviour Jesus Christ*, Lecture V., The Doctrine of Christ's Divinity in the Writings of St. John, pp. 209–278.

SOME of the most important considerations which bear upon the present subject have come under our notice in the study of the Logos-idea. It remains to examine the apostle's teaching as a whole in the light of the Christology of the prologue, in order to determine whether or not the ideas there found are pervading and fundamental in the Johannine view of Christ's person. This inquiry will involve chiefly a study of the terms *the Son of God* and *the only begotten Son*, and an examination of those passages which refer to the pre-existence of the Son and to his relation to the Father.

The title *the Son of God*, or its shortened form *the Son*, is applied to Jesus about thirty times in the

UNION OF THE SON WITH THE FATHER

Gospel, and more than twenty times in the Epistles of John. In a few passages the title is modified by the word *only-begotten* ($μονογενής$) (i. 14, 18; iii. 16, 18; I. iv. 9). It is necessary to determine, if possible, what this title signifies. The principal problem is, whether the term *Son* refers merely to an ethical union of Christ with God, or also denotes or implies a metaphysical union; whether it simply describes Christ as the chosen object of the divine love, or also designates him as standing in essential and eternal union with the Father in respect to his nature.

No one can read the passages in the Gospel of John where Jesus speaks of his filial relation to God without receiving the impression that this relation is regarded as something unique, — that he is declared to be the Son of God in some pre-eminent sense. Take, in illustration, such passages as these: "The Father loveth the Son, and hath given all things into his hand" (iii. 35). "Not that any man hath seen the Father, save he which is from God, he hath seen the Father" (vi. 46). "I and the Father are one" (x. 30). "I am in the Father, and the Father in me" (xiv. 11). The question now arises whether this unique relation to which these passages refer is solely ethical, that is, a relation of loving fellowship, and thus the same in kind with that in which all men as "sons of God" stand to God, or whether a relationship of essence is also involved. Weiss has adopted the former view in respect to the meaning of *Son*. In his opinion the term *Son of God* describes

Jesus "as the object of the divine love, upon whom the good pleasure of God rests."[1] This author, however, holds, in general, that the pre-existence of Christ and the metaphysical union of essence between Christ and God are taught in the writings of John.[2] But he maintains that these ideas are not involved in the title *Son of God*, which is an Old Testament metaphor derived from human relations, and with which is sometimes joined the designation "only-begotten" in order to emphasize "the closest relation of love" existing between the Father and the Son.[3] But this author holds that on the question "whether this [sonship] reaches back into eternity and depends upon an original relationship of essence on the part of the Son to the Father, the self-testimony of Jesus could give no disclosure."[4] Other recent writers seek, in connection with this view of the sonship of Jesus, to rule out from the Fourth Gospel the idea of a personal pre-existence of the Son.[5]

The title *Son of God* was not in current use among the Jews as a designation for the Messiah. It is,

[1] *Bibl. Theol.*, § 17, *b*.

[2] Weiss admits that "the Johannean self-testimony of Jesus decisively goes beyond that of the Synoptists," and holds that passages like xvii. 5 and viii. 58 denote "an existence which excludes all becoming," and point to "a pre-historical existence with the Father." *Ib*. 144, *a*.

[3] *Ib*. § 145, *a*.

[4] *Ib*. § 17, *c*, note 3.

[5] For example, Beyschlag, *Neutest. Theol.*, ii. 412 *sq*. and 417 *sq*.; Wendt, *Teaching of Jesus*, ii. 151 *sq*. (orig. p. 450 *sq*).

indeed, found in the Book of Enoch (cv. 2), and in the Fourth Book of Esdras (vii. 28 *sq.*; xiii. 37 *sq.*; xiv. 9), where Jehovah is represented as calling the Messiah his Son; but these passages are only reminiscences of the Old Testament conception of Israel, and especially of Israel's king, as God's Son. From extra-Biblical sources we derive no light upon the meaning of the title as applied to the Messiah. It is probable that our Lord's application of the term to himself stands historically connected with the Old Testament representations to which we have just referred. In 2 Sam. vii. 14 we read: "I will be his (David's) father, and he shall be my son;" and in Hosea xi. 1: "When Israel was a child, then I loved him, and called my son out of Egypt." As the ideal theocratic Son of God, the antitypical King of Israel, Jesus applies to himself the term *Son* in order to designate the unique relation in which he stands to God. The name stands closely connected with the title *Messiah*, but is not strictly synonymous with it. In Peter's confession they are united: "Thou art the Christ, the Son of the living God" (Matt. xvi. 16). In like manner the titles are several times coupled together by others, as by the high priest (Matt. xxvi. 63), by Martha (John xi. 27) and by the apostle John (xx. 31). But these passages do not prove more than that sonship to God was an attribute of the Messiah and a prerequisite of his work. The Messianic title of Jesus remains Χριστός. The title *Son of God* designates the personal, rather than the official, character and relations of Jesus. It refers not so much to the work to which he has been appointed as to the relation to God which that work presupposes. The Messianic work of Jesus is grounded in his sonship to God.

It is necessary, now, to examine the more significant passages from the Gospel in which this term is used, in order to determine what peculiarities of the person of Christ it is intended to describe. The first question to which an answer must be sought is, whether the name *Son*, as applied to Christ, refers only to his historic life on earth, or also points, directly or inferentially, to a pretemporal existence and thus to an eternal relation on his part to the Father.

Christ is twice referred to in the prologue as the only begotten Son (i. 14, 18). In the first of these passages it is uncertain whether he is directly called "the only begotten from the Father" (A. V., R. V.), or is only compared to a father's only begotten son. The absence of the article from the words *only-begotten* and *Father* (ὡς μονογενοῦς παρὰ πατρός) favors the rendering: "An only begotten from a father" (R. V. marg.). On this view the words designate Jesus as the One on whom God concentrates his special love and favor, as an earthly father would concentrate his love upon an only son. So far, the view which regards the sonship in question as an ethical relation seems to meet the requirements of this passage. But the glory ($\delta\acute{o}\xi a$) which has been manifested is certainly regarded, as the whole import of the prologue shows, as belonging to this Son and as inhering in his person, before its manifestation in his incarnate form of being. He does not *become* a Son by his incarnation, as men by faith become children of God (i. 12). He brought to manifestation in his incarnation "the glory which he had" with the Father "before the world was" (xvii. 5).

The bearing upon our subject of the second of these passages (i. 18), "No man hath seen God at any time; the only begotten Son, which is in the bosom of the Father, he hath declared him," is partly dependent upon its interpretation. If the participle ὤν is referred to the time when the author is writing,[1] the passage would then be an assertion of the exaltation of the Son into closest fellowship with the Father, but would contain no reference to his pre-existence, and would therefore have no bearing upon the question whether the idea of pre-existence was here associated with the phrase "the only begotten Son." On the other hand, if this participle be given the force of an imperfect,[2] the passage would assert that the only begotten Son was, in his pre-incarnate life, in closest fellowship with the Father, and that he had left this position in order to reveal God to men. On a third interpretation, which seems to me preferable, the participle ὤν is a timeless present, and the passage would designate the only begotten Son as in a continuous, abiding fellowship of life with the

[1] So Meyer, Weiss.   [2] So Luthardt, Gess.

Father. He is, even in his earthly life, in the bosom of the Father, even as the Son of man is said to be " in heaven " (iii. 13) because heaven is the sphere to which he belongs.[1] On either of these last two views the term " only-begotten Son " carries with it the idea of personal pre-existence and clearly implies a unique relation of Jesus to God.

Upon the reading μονογενὴς θεός (God only begotten) in i. 18, which is now widely adopted among scholars, instead of ὁ μονογενὴς υἱός, our passage would still have an important bearing upon the general subject of John's conception of our Lord's person, but not upon the special question now under consideration, whether *Son of God* involves only an ethical, or, in addition, an essential relation of Jesus Christ to God. For these two readings the evidence is — all things considered — very evenly balanced.[2] While the preponderance of external testimony may be regarded as favoring μονογενὴς θεός, considerations of internal probability reinforce in no small degree the evidence for the other text. The expression *God only begotten* occurs nowhere else, and, while the fact that the Logos is called θεός in the pro-

[1] So Tholuck, Westcott.

[2] For a very full exhibit of the evidence on both sides, see Dr. Ezra Abbot, *On the reading "only begotten God,"* in his *Critical Essays*, p. 241 *sq.*; also briefer summaries, with references to the literature of the subject, in Westcott and Hort's Greek Testament, vol. ii., and in Westcott's Commentary. Dr. Abbot favors the reading ὁ μονογενὴς υἱός; Drs. Westcott and Hort adopt μονογενὴς θεός.

logue weakens in some degree the presumption against this reading, it is possible that the words καὶ θεὸς ἦν ὁ λόγος may serve to explain how the usual expression ὁ μονογενὴς υἱός might the more readily be changed by copyists into (ὁ) μονογενὴς θεός. Since, therefore, we have to do in this passage both with a doubtful text and with an uncertain interpretation, our conclusion must be a cautious one, but we think the probabilities favor the view that this passage designates the only begotten Son as standing in close, perpetual intimacy with the Father. If so, then the two passages reviewed would, taken together, describe the glory of the pre-existent Son dwelling in abiding union with the Father. But what the nature of this glory and of this union is, may still be regarded as undefined.

The great majority of the passages where *the Son* is spoken of are indecisive and cannot be shown to involve, in themselves, more than the ethical relation of Jesus to God. When, for example, it is said that "the Father loveth the Son, and hath given all things into his hand" etc. (iii. 35), the nature of the relation is not explicitly defined. In the connection, however, we find the coming of the Son from heaven referred to and the statement that he is "above all" (iii. 31). While it cannot justly be claimed that the term *Son* is used in such passages in the hypostatic sense, it must be admitted that there is coupled with it the idea of his pre-existence and of his pre-eminence as representing the authority of God. In the two remaining passages from the Fourth Gospel where Christ is called "the only begotten Son" (iii. 16, 18), it is not clear that the phrase refers to a metaphysical relation of essence. Yet the sending of "the only begotten Son" is said to be the means by which God saves the world; faith in him is declared to be the condition of having eternal life, and to refuse him is to expose one's self to the divine judgment. It seems to me, therefore, that the question of Christ's relation to God as represented in John cannot be pivoted upon the phrase *the Son of God* by itself, but must be studied in the light of the associations which that term carries with it.

The Jews understood Jesus to claim for himself a unique sonship to God, and sought to kill him partly because he "called God his own Father (πατέρα ἴδιον), making himself equal with God" (v. 18). He did not, indeed, make himself equal with God in the sense in which they understood him to do so, for "he answered and said to them, Verily, verily, I say unto you, the Son can do nothing of himself, but what he seeth the Father doing" (v. 19); and elsewhere (xiv. 28), when speaking of his return to the Father, he says that this return will involve a gain for his disciples, "because the Father is greater" than he; that is, because in the renewed fellowship with the Father who is the source of his authority for his mission, he will be able to work with even greater efficiency toward the ends of his kingdom. In reply to the criticism of the

Jews noticed above, Jesus explains the nature and conditions of his work. In this explanation we find, as we should expect, not a definition of his person, but a defence of his authority. He explains that he, as the object of the Father's special love, has been made the giver of life (v. 20, 21) and the dispenser of judgment (22), and that it is God's will that "all may honor the Son, even as they honor the Father" (23), and then, from the bestowment of spiritual life the thought shades over into the idea that in the Son lie the power and authority to quicken men at the resurrection: "The hour cometh, in which all that are in the tombs shall hear his voice, and shall come forth" (28). Granting that the word *Son* refers in this whole passage only to the ethical relation of Jesus to God, — that is, to him as the chosen object of divine love and the bearer of divine authority, — we have still to deal with the question whether the whole claim of Jesus to be the author of salvation and the judge of the world, does not presuppose the consciousness of a relation to God specifically different from that which any other human being sustains.

In his teaching concerning himself as the bread of life (vi. 22-65) it was certainly not the purpose of Jesus to comment on the nature of his relation to God except so far as was necessary in order to assert his claim as the bearer of salvation. Yet in the course of this teaching he affirms that he bestows eternal life, and that faith in him is the one required "work of God" (27-29). He claims to represent on earth the mind and will of God, and to be the One who will raise men from the dead at the last day (38, 40). When the Jews murmur at these claims, he asserts in reply that he stands so related to God that those who really know God are led by this knowledge to receive him, and that his is a fellowship with God which is absolutely unique: "Not that any man hath seen the Father, save he which is from God, he hath seen the Father" (vi. 46; *cf.* Matt. xi. 27; Luke x. 22). When every fair concession to those who maintain the ethical import of these passages is made, there still remains the capital fact that Jesus makes claims for himself which would be preposterous in any other; that he declares that he comes forth from God and represents God in a sense altogether unique, and that he is the bearer in himself of divine life, and the judge of the world. It becomes more and more evident as the decisive passages are passed in review that the Johannine doctrine of Christ's person is dependent in but a very small degree on the question whether the term *Son* has always an ethical sense, or sometimes also a metaphysical import. But this question, as forming an element in the larger problem, must be further considered.

There are several passages which show that it is not the sending of Jesus Christ into the world which constitutes him Son of God, but that he *is* the Son who is sent into the world, and that his sonship to

God therefore involves his relation to the Father previous to his incarnation; for example: "God so loved the world, that he gave his only begotten Son," etc. (iii. 16). He is the Son of God previous to his coming into the world, whatever that relation may include. To the same purport is the next verse: "God sent not the Son into the world to judge the world," etc. (iii. 17). In some passages where the term *Son* is not employed, the same idea is brought out even more explicitly: "And now, O Father, glorify thou me with thine own self ($παρὰ σεαυτῷ$, at thy side) with the glory which I had with thee before the world was" (xvii. 5). "Verily, verily, I say unto you, before Abraham was born, I am" (viii. 58). While these passages do not in themselves bear directly upon the import of the title *Son of God*, they do tend, in connection with passages which speak of God's sending the Son, to establish the conclusion that the sonship of Christ to God presupposes and includes a pretemporal and eternal relation between him and the Father.

It is doubtless true that the ethical aspect of Jesus' relation to God and of the mission given him by the Father, is what is most prominently brought forward in the passages which speak of his sonship. This is what the practical and historical character of the Gospel should lead us to expect. The Gospel is not a treatise on the metaphysical nature of Christ, but an account of the way in which he revealed God. His perfect harmony with the Father's will, and his consequent fitness to accomplish the work of man's salvation, are naturally made especially prominent. He is the bearer of divine life because he stands in immediate relation with the " living Father" (vi. 57). He and the Father "are one" (x. 30) in the work of redemption. In this passage a unity of will and purpose, and not a unity of essence, is primarily referred to, as the context shows. The meaning is that his sheep are safe since the Father has given them to him, and the Father's power is therefore pledged to keep them. In this determination to guard them he and the Father are one. It is a "dynamic fellowship" (Meyer) which is here asserted. He and the Father perfectly co-operate in all that concerns the salvation of his people. Not even Calvin referred this passage to the unity of essence. This interpretation, however, in no way prejudices the question whether the metaphysical unity is presupposed and required by that ethical unity which is asserted. It accords with the whole purpose of the Gospel to present Christ as doing nothing of himself ($\dot{a}\phi'$ $\dot{\epsilon}a\nu\tau o\hat{\nu}$, v. 19), that is, in independence of the Father's will and purpose. Hence Jesus says: " He that hath seen me hath seen the Father" (xiv. 9), since he is conscious that he perfectly embodies and reveals the Father's will. This he does by virtue of that perfect fellowship which subsists between himself and the Father: "I am in the Father and the Father in me" (xiv. 11). His words and works are the proof of this mutual fellowship, this perfect moral

UNION OF THE SON WITH THE FATHER 115

unity. The same reciprocal fellowship in will and purpose is depicted in x. 38, where Jesus exhorts the Jews to acknowledge his works that they may "know and understand that the Father is in me, and I in the Father." That an ethical unity is referred to in xvii. 21 is evident from the fact that our Lord prays that his followers may be one even as he and the Father are one. Since an ethical union only can exist among believers, it must be the ethical aspect of his own union with the Father which he presents as the type of Christian fellowship. These passages do not, however, militate against the idea of a metaphysical unity, but leave the question open whether this perfect ethical or dynamic fellowship itself requires the supposition of a unity of essence. Much less can these passages justify a negative answer to the question whether, in other terms and for purposes different from those which are here in view, the Apostle John teaches that the Son exists in an eternal, essential unity with the Father.

The decision of this latter question — which must go a long way toward answering the former — hinges chiefly on the meaning of the passages which assert or imply the pre-existence of Christ. Wendt makes the ethical relations which we have noticed determining for the interpretation of these passages, which have been thought to assert more than ethical union.[1] He finds in the sayings of Jesus that his disciples were not of the world (xv. 19), and that the

[1] *Teaching of Jesus,* ii. 151 *sq.* (orig. p. 450 *sq.*).

unbelieving Jews were of the devil (viii. 44), the key to Jesus' meaning when he claims to come forth from God (xvi. 28). He concludes that Jesus comes from God and is sent by the Father into the world only in a "figurative" sense. But are these two classes of passages parallel, or even kindred in meaning and purpose? Can we reason from the significance of those passages which depict the moral kinships of men, to a figurative use of language on Jesus' part concerning his own person and the grounds of his authority and claims? Does Jesus ever apply to any other the "figurative" language which he applies to himself? Does he ever say of any other that he comes from God and that God has sent him into the world? Wendt reminds us that "believers are born of God and come from God,"[1] and appeals in illustration to passages like I. iv. 4: "Ye are of God" (ἐκ τοῦ θεοῦ). But it is self-evident that this expression is but the counterpart of the phrase "of the world" (verse 5), and is equivalent to the phrase "begotten of God." The whole passage shows that it is an ethical kinship to God, on the one hand, or to the wicked world, on the other, which is meant. Can any one seriously consider these passages as furnishing any parallel to those in which Jesus asserts that he was sent by the Father into the world, and that he abode at the Father's side, sharing his glory before the world was (xvii. 5, 22, 24)? This procedure treats the whole self-testimony

[1] *Teaching of Jesus*, ii. 161, note (orig. p. 458).

UNION OF THE SON WITH THE FATHER 117

of Jesus as "figurative" — where the language gives no sign of being such — on the ground that the figure of a new birth is common in John to express the idea of a moral renewal. The fact of chief significance remains that Jesus never applies to himself this language about being begotten from God which he applies to others, and that he never applies to any other the descriptions which he gives of his own coming from God. The two cases are so different that to make the former determining for the latter does not result so much in making the terms of the latter "figurative" as in making them meaningless and untrue. On this method of interpretation the statement "I came forth from God" (xvi. 28) means, I was chosen by God; and the assertion "I came down from heaven" (iii. 13, 31; vi. 38) means, I am in fellowship with God. It may well be doubted whether these texts can sustain to the meanings which they are thus made to yield the relation of *figure* to *reality*. But Wendt's interpretation may be further tested by his handling of the crucial texts, xvii. 5 and viii. 58.[1]

In his intercessory prayer (xvii. 5) Jesus uses these words: "And now, O Father, glorify thou me with.

[1] *Teaching of Jesus*, ii. 168 *sq.* (orig. p. 464 *sq.*). The passage vi. 62, "What then if ye should behold the Son of man ascending where he was before," Wendt rules out of court, because, in his view that our Fourth Gospel is a redaction by a later hand of memoranda preserved by John, he considers that this passage bears the marks of an interpolation by the editor. *Ib.* p. 168, note.

thine own self ($\pi\alpha\rho\grave{\alpha}$ $\sigma\epsilon\alpha\upsilon\tau\hat{\wp}$), with the glory which I had with thee before the world was." This passage seems plainly to refer to a mode of personal pre-existence on the part of Christ in heaven to which he expects to return; and Wendt admits that to modern ears the language naturally conveys this meaning. But he affirms that " according to the mode of speech and conception prevalent in the New Testament, a heavenly good, and so also a heavenly glory, can be conceived and spoken of as existing with God and belonging to a person, not because this person already exists and is invested with glory, but because the glory of God is in some way deposited and preserved for this person in heaven."[1] In illustration, reference is made to the treasure or reward which is said to be laid up for the disciples in heaven (Matt. vi. 20; v. 12 *et al.*). Wendt concludes that the glory which Christ had with the Father before the world was, could only have been the ideal glory for which the Father had destined him from eternity; and he thinks this view is confirmed by the way in which, in his teaching, he makes his prospective glorification to depend upon the accomplishment of his earthly ministry.

We must consider whether this alleged difference between New Testament and modern modes of thought in respect to the subject under discussion is established by adequate evidence. It is to be noticed, first of all, that our passage does not merely assert (as Wendt's argument seems to assume) the existence in

[1] *Teaching of Jesus*, ii. 169 (orig. p. 465).

UNION OF THE SON WITH THE FATHER 119

heaven of the glory with which Christ was to be endowed. The passage asserts the existence of *Christ himself*, not that of a glory destined for him, " before the world was." Wendt treats the passage as if its import were: Confer upon me now the glory which has been designed and kept for me from eternity; whereas it really says: Bestow upon me the glory which *I possessed* at thy side, in loving fellowship with thee, before the world existed. The difference between these two propositions is one that can be resolved by no known variation between New Testament and modern modes of thought. The passages cited by Wendt do not afford the slightest evidence that the New Testament ever speaks elsewhere of the pre-existence of persons, where it means only that some endowment or gift is prepared for them in God's purpose. The expressions respecting the laying up of the reward of well-doing (Matt. v. 12), and the preparation of the kingdom (Matt. xxv. 34), are designed to emphasize the *certainty* of the blessedness to which the terms refer. This result is already assured in God's fixed purpose. But who can imagine Jesus bringing out this truth by telling his disciples that *they themselves* had existed in eternity in the enjoyment of heavenly blessedness? If these representations were so changed as to be made really parallel in form and import to John xvii. 5, the meaning of Matt. xxv. 34 would be: Come, ye blessed of my Father, inherit the kingdom in which you have participated from the foundation of the world. But this is a very different statement from that which the passage actually contains; yet it is no more different from it than is the statement of John xvii. 5 from those of the passages which Wendt appeals to in explanation of its meaning.

It is very important in Biblical study to recognize all actual differences between ancient and modern modes of conception and thought. But I am not aware that the representation of a reward prepared and ready for those to whom it is to be given, is a mode of thought peculiar to antiquity; but, even if it were, I can see no ground in that fact for the opinion that the New Testament may even speak of the persons themselves who are to receive the destined rewards as already pre-existing in heaven in the enjoyment of them. If so, it is remarkable that Christ alone is so spoken of. It is, moreover, certain that the passages which Wendt cites from the Synoptists furnish no parallel to John xvii. 5. The truth is that these passages prove nothing in favor of his view of John xvii. 5, and that if they were of such a kind as to prove anything, they would prove too much, since they would justify the representation of Christ's disciples as also pre-existing.

The statement of Jesus in viii. 58, " Before Abraham was (*i. e.* was born, γενέσθαι), I am," Wendt explains as denoting the existence of Jesus "in the thoughts, purposes, and promises of God."[1] He admits that "the discourse is fashioned as if it treated of real

[1] *Teaching of Jesus,* ii. 176 (orig. p. 470).

UNION OF THE SON WITH THE FATHER

existence," but "we can still perceive from the connection that an ideal existence is intended."[1] Let us glance at the connection. The Jews reproach Jesus with claiming to be greater than Abraham (viii. 53). Jesus admits, and even maintains, the claim. Abraham longed to see the day of the Messiah, "and he saw it, and was glad" (viii. 56). Whether it was in prophetic hope on earth, or in paradise centuries afterwards, that he saw Messiah's work, the purport of the statement, in either case, is that Abraham's interest as a "man of religion" centred in the Messiah and presupposed the Messiah's superiority to himself. The Jews again object: If Abraham has seen you, you must have seen him; but you are not half a century old, and he lived centuries ago. The point of their objection is that centuries have intervened between Abraham's lifetime and that of Jesus. To this objection Jesus replies: "Before Abraham was born, I am." The purpose of this affirmation is to offset the charge that he could never have seen Abraham because he was never contemporary with him. Now, which assertion would best meet the point of his opposers, that of an *ideal* existence in God's purpose, before Abraham's birth, or that of a *real* existence? No doubt either statement, if admitted to be true, would serve to establish his general superiority to Abraham; only the latter, however, would meet the objection of the Jews which called it forth.

Wendt maintains that, since Abraham's seeing of

[1] *Teaching of Jesus*, ii. 177 (orig. p. 471).

Messiah's day must have been only prophetic and ideal, because Messiah's day was not a reality in Abraham's time, the existence of Christ before Abraham must, therefore, have been ideal also. I prefer the interpretation according to which Abraham is represented as seeing in paradise the day of the Messiah in its actual realization; but even if we adopt the view that this seeing was in prophetic vision, the conclusion which Wendt draws would not logically follow. The prophetic foresight of Messiah's *work* is as consistent with his real pre-existence as it is with his ideal pre-existence. The prevision of Messiah's earthly *mission* in no way prejudices the question as to the nature of his *person*. As in dealing with xvii. 5, Wendt overlooked the difference between the idea that Christ's glory was laid up in God's purpose for him and the actual assertion of the passage that Christ existed in eternity in the possession of heavenly glory, so here he lightly passes over the objection of the Jews which immediately called out Jesus' statement, and also leaves unnoticed the natural and very significant contrast between Abraham's *birth* and Christ's absolute *existence* ("I am").

Certain passages in the First Epistle also should be placed in connection with those already considered. In I. i. 1 we are told that the content of the gospel message was "from the beginning" (ὃ ἦν ἀπ' ἀρχῆς). Despite the involved construction of the opening verses of this epistle, the idea is plain. The substance of the message is eternal life. This life is in Christ, and was brought to the world by him. But before its manifestation it was with the Father (πρὸς τὸν πατέρα, verse 2) by virtue of the fellowship of the Son in whom it abides. Here the heavenly good which the apostle experienced in his fellowship with Christ is pictured as pre-existing "from the beginning;" then it was manifested in the life of Jesus, we saw and heard it, he says, and now declare it unto you. If these words fall short of a direct assertion that Christ himself was from the beginning, we cannot doubt that they imply it when later we read: "Ye know him which is from the beginning" (ἐγνώκατε τὸν ἀπ' ἀρχῆς, ii. 13, 14). The "word of life" to which the gospel message relates (περί, i. 1) is the record of the revelation of him (Christ) who is from the beginning.

We thus find that the ideas which are presented in the prologue are not without support in the writings of the apostle when taken as a whole. It is true that the pre-existence of the Son and his essential relation to the Father, are incidentally presented. It accords with the purpose of John's writings that these ideas should stand in the background, rather than in the foreground, of his picture of Christ. They are the presuppositions of his descriptions and arguments, rather than their immediate subject. But they are not on this account less fundamental in his whole view of the person and work of Christ. The prologue is seen to present, in its peculiar terms and for its peculiar purpose, a view of Christ's pre-incarnate nature and relation to God which the whole Gospel assumes. The prologue thus stands related to the Gospel as the vestibule to the house; it is a means of entrance, but it is also an integral part of the structure.

Respecting the term *Son of God*, our conclusion must be that it is used to denote a unique relation of fellowship and unity on the part of Jesus with God. It is more than a designation of his Messiahship. It denotes a permanent relation. Others *become* sons of God; he *is* the Son of God, and as such was sent into the world. While, therefore, the title is used chiefly to emphasize the authority of Christ as the agent of the divine will, it presupposes an essential relation of Jesus to God, since as Son he is sent into the world. The unique ethical or dynamic union of Jesus with God stands in the foreground, but this union requires and rests upon an essential union of nature. The phrase *Son of God* cannot, indeed, be said to carry in itself directly the significance which it bears in the Trinitarian creed, but it can be justly maintained that the term, in connection with the Logos-doctrine and with the assertions of Christ's pre-existence, inevitably gives rise to the problem with which theology has sought to deal in its doctrine of the hypostatic sonship of Christ. Although the title *Son* is not directly used by John in a metaphysical sense, it is so used as to imply a pretemporal relation of Jesus to God, and stands so related to explicit assertions of the pre-existence and divinity of Christ as to justify the conclusion that it is a fundamental assumption of John's theology that

UNION OF THE SON WITH THE FATHER 125

Jesus Christ, in his pre-incarnate form of being, existed eternally in an essential unity of nature with God.

This conclusion also determines our view of the import of μονογενής. It is not used in the sense of the Athanasian creed, to denote an eternal process of generation as contrasted with an act of creation. It is employed to add emphasis to the idea of Christ's unique relation to God as the perfect object of the divine love and the perfect representative of the divine will. The import of the term was determined for the apostle, not by metaphysical speculation, but by the analogy of human relations. The term can justly be appealed to as emphasizing that unique relation of Jesus to God which, as we have seen, presupposes a kinship of essence, but not as intended or adapted itself to describe or indicate the nature of that relation.

Criticism can only avoid the conclusion that Jesus possessed the consciousness of having personally existed previous to his life on earth in an essential life-fellowship with God, to which he knew that he should return after his work was finished, either by unnatural interpretations of the passages which speak of that relation, or by discrediting the historical trustworthiness of the Fourth Gospel. Those who consider the Gospel to be a product of second century speculation can consistently regard its Christology as a post-apostolic dogmatic development. Others who accept its direct apostolic authorship, as Beyschlag, or who accept it in a conditional form, as Wendt, can escape the conclusion that it teaches the pre-existence and deity of Christ only by resolving the Logos into an abstract principle, and by treating the statements of Christ's consciousness of a pretemporal life as examples of a Jewish mode of thought which is not current among moderns.

The total impression of John's conception of the person of his Master can be gained only by combining what he says of the Logos, of the Son, and of his pre-existence. When this is done and when the various passages are taken in their natural meaning and force, the conclusion — so far as the teaching of the Johannine writings is concerned — can be no other than that to which Cremer is led in view of the teaching of the New Testament as a whole: "It lies in the idea of the Messianic sonship to God, as this is embodied in the person and history of Jesus, that this sonship is something superterrestrial and eternal." "The Messianic Son of God is the pre-existent Son of God."[1]

[1] *Bibl.-theol. Wörterbuch der Neutest. Gräcität*, sub voce, ὁ υἱὸς τοῦ θεοῦ.

CHAPTER VI

THE DOCTRINE OF SIN

Literature. — REUSS: *Hist. Christ. Theol.*, Of the World, ii. 415-428 (orig. pp. 463-478); WESTCOTT: *Epistles of St. John*, The Idea of Sin in St. John, pp. 37-40; MESSNER: *Lehre der Apostel*, Die Sünde, pp. 328-334; FROMMANN: *Johann. Lehrb.*, Verhältniss der Menschheit zu Gott und dem Logos, pp. 242-345; PLUMMER: *The Epistles of St. John*, The Three Evil Tendencies in the World, and Antichrist, pp. 154-160; WENDT: *Teaching of Jesus*, Being from God or from the devil according to the Johannine discourses, ii. 114-121 (orig. pp. 420-426); BEYSCHLAG: *Neutest. Theol.*, Die Welt, Sünde und Teufel, ii. 428-432; WEISS: *Johann. Lehrb.*, Die beiden Menschenklassen, pp. 128-138; LECHLER: *Apostolic and Post-Apostolic Times*, The World and the Prince of this World, ii. 181-188 (orig. pp. 461-465); BAUR: *Neutest. Theol.*, Der Gegensatz des Lichts und der Finsterniss, u. s. w., pp. 359-362.

THE idea of sin is presented in the writings of John in a considerable variety of forms. The nearest approach to a definition of sin is found in the First Epistle (iii. 4): "sin is lawlessness" (ἡ ἁμαρτία ἐστὶν ἡ ἀνομία). The apostle is showing the inconsistency between sonship to God and the Christian's hope of attaining likeness to Christ, on the one hand, and the practice of sin (ποιεῖν τὴν ἁμαρτίαν), on the other. This contrariety is grounded in the fact that sin is a violation of the divine order. The precise nature and scope of the law to which sin is contrary is not defined. We are at liberty to regard it as an expression of the divine will in general, and to consider sin, as here described, as the selfish assertion of the human will against the divine. The passage yields us a generic idea only; for more concrete descriptions of sin we turn to other passages.

The apostle's tendency to employ ethical contrasts naturally leads him to define sin as "the darkness" ($\dot{\eta}$ σκοτία, τὸ σκότος). In these expressions the article is generally found, and designates the moral condition which is symbolized by "darkness" as characteristic of the sinful world. This contrast of light and darkness meets us in the prologue. The life which emanated from the Logos "was the light of men" (i. 4). This light "shineth in the darkness" (i. 5), a symbol for the sinful state of the world in its selfish isolation from God. Elsewhere in the Gospel the term is chiefly used in the expression, "to walk in darkness" (viii. 12; xii. 35; cf. I. i. 6), or "to abide in darkness" (xii. 46), and refers to the wicked moral blindness which disobedience to God induces. Similarly in the First Epistle "the darkness" — the sinful folly of the pre-Christian life — is described as "passing away" (ii. 8) from the true Christian man; where hatred is still indulged the darkness continues. We may say, then, that light is with John the symbol of goodness, love, and spiritual life, and that darkness is the synonym of evil, hate, and moral death.

THE DOCTRINE OF SIN

The question now arises, What is the nature of the dualism which the contrast implied in the use of the terms *light* and *darkness* involves? Is it physical, that is, grounded in the nature of man as consisting of matter and spirit; or metaphysical, that is, inherent in the essence of the universe; or ethical, that is, the result of free volition?

The contrast of flesh and spirit is most explicitly presented, in the writings of John, in the passage, "That which is born of the flesh is flesh; and that which is born of the Spirit is spirit" (iii. 6). This statement occurs in our Lord's conversation with Nicodemus respecting the new birth. It is intended to meet the difficulty of Nicodemus, who could only think of the "birth from above" after the analogy of man's natural birth. Jesus says to him in effect: "Man stands related to two orders, the natural and the spiritual. The first birth pertains to the lower sphere of being, the second to the higher." The point of importance for our present purpose is that these two spheres are not related to each other as evil and good, but only as lower or natural, and higher or spiritual. They are not here described as essentially and necessarily opposed to one another. In the contrast is implied a relative opposition, however, in so far as the lower elements of human nature which are comprised in the term *flesh* form the sphere in which animal appetites and passions operate, while the higher powers of our being, denoted by *spirit*, ally us to God and render us susceptible to moral and spiritual influences. The same contrast is presented in vi. 63 : "It is the spirit that quickeneth; the flesh profiteth nothing : the words that I have spoken unto you are spirit, and are life." The work of Jesus for man is in the realm of the spirit; it is concerned with his higher nature which connects him with God. No mere physical knowledge of Christ or contact with him (*cf.* the preceding verses) can avail to secure the new life which he would impart. Here, too, it is evident that flesh and spirit are not contrasted as specifically evil and good, but rather as outward or non-spiritual, and vital or essential.

One other passage should be cited in this connection: "For all that is in the world, the lust of the flesh (ἡ ἐπιθυμία τῆς σαρκός), and the lust of the eyes, and the vainglory of life, is not of the Father, but is of the world" (I. ii. 16). Here the flesh is conceived of as the seat, just as the eyes are regarded as the organs, of evil desires. An absolute identification of evil desire with the flesh is not, however, involved; much less an identification of sin in general with the flesh. The thought might be presented thus: Sensuous pleasures belong to the temporary, passing world, the κόσμος, and not to God's unchanging spiritual order. We conclude that these passages do not warrant the ascription to John of a natural dualism inherent in the human constitution.

Is, then, the "dualism" of John metaphysical? The question will recur in connection with various passages which are to be examined later, but should

THE DOCTRINE OF SIN

here be briefly considered with special reference to the meaning of the terms *light* and *darkness*. It is to be observed that in the prologue, where the light of the Logos is set in contrast with the world's darkness, the whole description has the practical aim of showing how the heavenly "light" came into the "darkness" and how "the darkness apprehended it not." The terms are obviously figurative, since they are freely interchanged with personal designations. The statement "The light shineth in the darkness; and the darkness apprehended it not" (i. 5) is only a figurative way of saying, "He came unto his own, and they that were his own received him not" (i. 11). The "light" is synonymous with the personal Logos; the "darkness" is synonymous with the sinful world, or, more specifically, with the people to whom Jesus came in his earthly manifestation. The references to the "light" and the "darkness" are set in unmistakable connection with free, personal action. The "dualism" which they imply must, therefore, be an ethical, not an essential or metaphysical dualism. This conclusion is confirmed by the way in which the contrast is employed throughout the Gospel. The conflict of light and darkness is the conflict of morally good actions and dispositions, on the one hand, with morally evil, on the other. One representative passage will make this clear: "And this is the judgment, that the light is come into the world, and men loved the darkness rather than the light; for their works were evil. For every one that doeth ill hateth the light, and cometh not to the light, lest his works should be reproved. But he that doeth the truth cometh to the light, that his works may be made manifest, that they have been wrought in God" (iii. 19-21). How obvious it is that the sphere of the conflict of light and darkness is here the sphere of free moral action (*cf.* viii. 12; xii. 35, 36, 46).

The passages from the First Epistle which bear upon the subject warrant no other view. The apostle's assertion that the substance of the gospel message is, "God is light, and in him is no darkness at all" (i. 5), has the practical purpose of showing that the moral conduct of men proves whether they really have fellowship with God or not (i. 6, 7). "Darkness" symbolizes the old sinful life, "light" the new spiritual life (ii. 8); "darkness" is practically synonymous with hate, "light" with love (ii. 9, 10).

The efforts which have been made, in connection with the modern denial of the apostolic authorship of the writings under consideration, to show the kinship between the ideas contained in them and those of Alexandrian speculation or of Gnostic dualism, are not supported by the natural force of the descriptions of evil and goodness which we have passed in review. Whether the terms employed be derived or original is of small consequence; their significance and use are distinctly ethical, and in this essential respect they illustrate a radical difference between the conceptions of sin and of the world which pervade these writings, and those which are characteristic either of Neo-

THE DOCTRINE OF SIN

Platonic Philosophy or of Gnosticism. Our author regards the world of human and divine action whose forces and agencies he describes, as a moral system, a sphere of free choice and of strict responsibility. From this standpoint we shall proceed to consider his doctrine of "the world" (ὁ κόσμος).

John uses the term *world* in three shades of meaning.[1] It designates, in the first instance, the created universe in general without regard to moral qualities, as in the expressions "before the world was" (xvii. 5), and "before the foundation of the world" (xvii. 24). More frequently it denotes, or at any rate prominently includes, the totality of rational and moral beings, — the world as the sphere of free and intelligent action. In this sense it is said that light came into the world when Christ came (iii. 19). So when the coming of the Son into the world (xi. 27; xvi. 28) is spoken of, it is his relation to mankind as the subjects of salvation which is primarily meant. It is now but a short step from this sense of the word to that which prevails in the writings of John, viz., the *sinful* world, mankind as alienated from God. Some passages seem to illustrate a use of the term which stands midway between these two shades of meaning last mentioned, as where Jesus speaks of coming into the world (of mankind) in order to "save the world" (xii. 46, 47), whose evil and lost condition is assumed. The three meanings are not perfectly dis-

[1] *Cf.* Reuss, *Hist. Christ. Theol.*, ii. 415 *sq.* (orig. ii. 463 *sq.*); Beyschlag, *Neutest. Theol.*, ii. 428 *sq.*

tinct but shade off into one another, as may be seen in i. 10: "He (the Logos) was in the world (of mankind), and the world (universe) was made by him, and the world (of sinful men) knew him not." From passages like this it appears that, even where no reference is made to moral qualities, it is assumed that the world is the sphere of evil, and that where mankind in general is referred to, the universality of sin is presupposed. We are here concerned chiefly with that prevailing usage in John in which "the world" means distinctly the sinful world in estrangement from God.

Only a few of the most emphatic passages which belong under this head need here be quoted. Speaking to the Pharisees who were plotting against him, Jesus said: "Ye are from beneath; I am from above: ye are of this world; I am not of this world" (viii. 23). He declares that his kingdom is not of this world (xviii. 36); that the world hates his disciples (xvii. 14); has not known God (xvii. 25); cannot, on account of its moral blindness and perverseness, receive the Spirit of truth (xiv. 17) and is subject to Satan as its prince (xii. 31; xiv. 30). To the same effect in the First Epistle the apostle exhorts his readers to "love not the world, neither the things that are in the world," on the ground that the love of the world and the love of God are essentially opposed (I. ii. 15, 16). Finally, the whole Johannine doctrine of the world may be summed up in the emphatic assertion, "The whole world lieth in the evil one" (ἐν τῷ πονηρῷ) (I. v. 19).

THE DOCTRINE OF SIN

That the dualism which is involved in the opposition between God and the world is not metaphysical but ethical, is made clear by the terms of the description. When Jesus says that "for judgment" he "came into this world, that they which see not may see; and that they which see may become blind" (ix. 39), he clearly means that his work must, by reason of its very nature, occasion a still greater obduracy in those who wickedly oppose him, through their continued rejection of his truth. The world, so far as his Pharisaic opponents represent it, is wicked by its own fault, and becomes more so through the inevitable recoil upon it in judgment of its own action in refusing the light. In iii. 19 the concrete synonym for the abstract "world" is "men," and the ground of the world's condemnation is affirmed to be that the men who compose it "loved the darkness rather than the light; for their works were evil." The world is opposed to God because it is wilfully wicked, is animated by hate to those who follow Christ (xv. 18, 19), and in relation to Christ personally is convicted "in respect of sin, because they [who compose it] believe not" on him (xvi. 8, 9).

In one striking passage (viii. 33–36) sin is described as a state of bondage. Jesus had said to certain Jewish believers that his truth should make them free (viii. 32). Not perceiving the profound spiritual significance of his words, they replied that as children of Abraham they had never yet been in bondage, — implying, apparently, that the captivities which the nation had experienced had not touched its essential life or annulled its inalienable prerogatives. Jesus does not drop his thought to the level of theirs, but proceeds: "Every one that committeth sin [ὁ ποιῶν τὴν ἁμαρτίαν— lives an habitual life of sin] is the bondservant (δοῦλος) of sin" (verse 34): If you continue the sinful life you will forfeit your place in God's house over which I have authority; you will lose your citizenship and rights in the spiritual order to which I belong; therefore I say again that the real freedom is that which the truth, as embodied and represented by me, bestows. True freedom is found only in obedience to God; sin is in its very nature slavery, because it involves the loss of God-given spiritual rights, the forfeiture of man's divinely intended destiny.

The words *sin* (ἁμαρτία) and *to sin* (ἁμαρτάνειν) occur frequently in our sources. *Sin* is commonly employed in an abstract sense to denote a power or principle, as in the phrases, "the sin of the world" (i. 29), "to commit sin" (viii. 34), "your sin" (viii. 21), etc. The word is also used to designate an act of sin as in the phrase, "a sin unto death" (I. v. 16, 17), but this meaning is chiefly found where the plural (ἁμαρτίαι) is used (*e. g.*, viii. 24; xx. 23; I. i. 9). The verb is also employed in a two-fold sense corresponding to that above noticed. It may have the force of the phrase ποιεῖν τὴν ἁμαρτίαν (viii. 34; I. iii. 4, 8, 9), to sin habitually, to live a sinful life, as in the following passages: " Whosoever abideth in him sinneth not: whosoever sinneth hath not seen him, neither knoweth him" (I. iii. 6); "Whosoever is begotten of God doeth no sin (ἁμαρτίαν οὐ ποιεῖ), because his seed abideth in him: and he cannot sin, because he is begotten of God" (I. iii. 9). In other connections ἁμαρτάνειν means to do an act of sin, as where the disciples ask Jesus concerning the man who was blind from his birth, "Who did sin, this man, or his parents, that he should be born blind?" (ix. 2, 3), and in I. i. 10 (cf. verse 8): "If we say that we have not sinned, we make him a liar and his word is not in us."

The importance of bearing in mind the distinction which we have just been tracing is especially seen in the apparent contradiction among certain passages in the First Epistle to which we have already had occasion, in other connections, to refer. It is affirmed, on the one hand, that no Christian can truly say that he has not sinned, and the apostle exhorts his readers to confess their sins (I. i. 9, 10); and yet we are told in the same Epistle that the Christian "sinneth not" and "cannot sin" (I. iii. 6, 9). The verbal contradiction is removed by attention to the two distinct meanings of the verb *to sin*. All Christians commit sinful acts, but they do not possess a sinful character. The Christian life and habitual sinfulness are absolute contraries; in this sense the Christian does not commit sin, and, indeed, cannot do so, since if he did he would not be a Christian at all. But just as little can he claim exemption from sinful impulses and acts. Just as the main direction of the river, notwithstanding its eddies and backcurrents, is ever toward the sea, so the central current of the Christian's life is set toward God, despite the hindering powers of evil which still check its progress and mar its perfection.

The way in which John speaks of sin as a power or principle clearly implies that he regards all men as naturally sinful and in need of redemption. It is "the sin of the world" (i. 29) which Christ comes to take away. One of the functions of the Spirit is to "convict the world in respect of sin" (xvi. 8, 9), that is, to make the world conscious of its sinfulness as evidenced by its unwillingness to receive Christ. Christians who have passed "into life" are conscious that they were naturally in a state of death (I. iii. 14). The love of God which was manifested toward the world in the sending of the Son aimed to secure the result that, through faith in him, men should not perish (iii. 16), as, apart from this work of love, they were in peril of doing. Hence the frequent emphasis upon the *saving* work of Christ (iv. 22, 42; v. 34; xii. 47; I. iv. 14). The world, apart from redemption, is a realm of moral darkness and death (i. 5; iii. 19; xii. 46; I. ii. 8; iii. 14), and is exposed, by reason of its sinfulness, to God's holy displeasure (iii. 16); in short, "the whole world lieth in the evil one" (I. v. 19).

Another set of expressions connects sin with demoniacal agencies. When the Jews charged Jesus with falsehood and blasphemous pretension they embodied their accusation in the statement: "Thou hast a demon" (δαιμόνιον) (vii. 20; viii. 48, 52; x. 20). In the Synoptic Gospels demoniacal "possession" is commonly associated with some physical and mental malady, especially with the more violent forms of mania. In the Fourth Gospel "possession" by evil spirits is referred to only in connection with the charges which the multitude made against Jesus, and seems to have been conceived of as a species of madness (vii. 20; x. 20); in viii. 48, the accusation "Thou hast a demon" is coupled with the charge, "Thou art a Samaritan," and appears to involve special bitterness of feeling against Jesus on the part of his accusers, and may imply the charge of wickedness as well as of madness. With this passage may be compared the Lord's reference to the character of his betrayer, Judas, in the words: "Did not I choose you the twelve, and one of you is a devil?" (διάβολος, vi. 70) — a strong expression to denote the source and base wickedness of his antagonism to his Master.

These passages lead us on to other representations in which human sinfulness is directly ascribed to the agency of the devil (ὁ διάβολος) or Satan. The devil is said to have put the suggestion or impulse to betray Jesus into the heart of Judas (xiii. 2). The Jews who opposed and accused Jesus claimed God as their father. Jesus denies that they are true children of God, and says to them: "Ye are of your father the devil, and the lusts of your father it is your will to do" (viii. 44). It is, of course, a moral kinship which is here under consideration. They are neither sons of Abraham nor sons of God, since they are not akin to either in the spirit of their action; on the contrary, they are, by reason of their falseness and murderous hate, akin to the devil. This idea of the sonship of wicked men to the devil — which is presented only in this one passage in the Gospel — appears also in the First Epistle: "He that doeth sin (ὁ ποιῶν τὴν ἁμαρτίαν) is of the devil (ἐκ τοῦ διαβόλου); ... In this the children of God are manifest, and the children of the devil" (τὰ τέκνα τοῦ διαβόλου) (I. iii. 8, 10). As those who are of faith are the sons of Abraham (*cf*. Gal. iii. 9, 29), and those who do God's will are sons of God, so those who habitually work iniquity are morally kindred to the devil in so far as they imitate his wickedness and embody his spirit.

Here arises the difficult inquiry, What conception of the origin and nature of Satan underlies the references to his agency in John's writings? Two passages, especially, give rise to this question: "He (the devil) was a murderer from the beginning (ἀπ' ἀρχῆς), and stood not in the truth (ἐν τῇ ἀληθείᾳ οὐκ ἔστηκεν),[1] because there is no truth in him. When

---

[1] Some editors punctuate this word ἔστηκεν (so Tischendorf, Meyer, Weiss). The former reading (imperfect of στήκειν) would mean *stood firm* or *steadfast*; the latter (perfect of ἵστημι with force of present) would express the permanent characteristic of the subject, and would mean that truth is an element foreign to his life.

THE DOCTRINE OF SIN

he speaketh a lie, he speaketh of his own: for he is a liar, and the father thereof" (ὁ πατὴρ αὐτοῦ) (viii. 44); "He that doeth sin is from the devil; for the devil sinneth from the beginning" (ἀπ' ἀρχῆς) (I. iii. 8). We must first consider the force of the phrase ἀπ' ἀρχῆς. In the first passage the interpretation of ἀπ' ἀρχῆς will be influenced by the view which is taken of the reference in the word "murderer." Many exegetes hold that when the devil is said to have been a murderer the allusion is to his agency in inciting Cain to slay his brother.[1] This explanation would determine the meaning of the passage to be: He was a murderer from the time when the race was in its infancy. Since, however, the act of Cain is not, in the Old Testament (Gen. iv. 3 *sq.*), referred to the instigation of Satan, it is more probable that the passage alludes to the temptation whereby Satan, represented under the figure of a serpent (Gen. iii. 1 *sq.*; *cf.* Rev. xx. 2), occasioned the fall of man. In this view the phrase ἀπ' ἀρχῆς would most naturally mean: from the beginning of the human race.[2] This interpretation seems to accord best with the natural force of our second passage (I. iii. 8), the purport of which is that there has never been a time in the history of the race when men have not been subject to the assaults of Satan. The connection shows that the sphere of human sin and salvation is that in which the sinning of Satan is

[1] So Nitzsch, Lücke, De Wette, Reuss.
[2] So Godet, Meyer, Müller, Weiss.

conceived of as taking place. Other interpretations seem less plausible. Especially objectionable is the view that ἀπ' ἀρχῆς is to be taken absolutely, which would imply either that God has created an evil being, or that Satan was eternal.[1] Many have taken the phrase as meaning: from the devil's own beginning *as such ;* that is, since by a fall from a previous state of holiness he became Satan.[2] This explanation, however, is unnatural in view of the reference in the word "murderer" and in view of the context of the passage from the Epistle. These considerations render it very improbable that in using the phrase ἀπ' ἀρχῆς the apostle's thoughts went back to any time or event anterior to the beginning of human history and experience.

It may be well to point out, in this connection, how slight is the support in the New Testament for the idea of a fall of Satan. There are but two passages (2 Pet. ii. 4; Jude 6) which can, with any degree of probability, be construed as alluding to it; and since between 2 Peter and Jude there is certainly some kind of literary dependence, these two really count as one. The passages read: "For if God spared not angels when they sinned, but cast them down to hell [Tartarus], and committed them to pits of darkness, to be reserved unto judgment," etc. (2 Pet. ii. 4); "And angels which kept not their own principality,

---

[1] So Hilgenfeld, Frommann, Reuss.
[2] So Augustine, Martensen, Delitzsch, and most Roman Catholic theologians.

THE DOCTRINE OF SIN 143

but left their proper habitation, he hath kept in everlasting bonds under darkness unto the judgment of the great day" (Jude 6). No mention is here made of Satan. The passage in Jude (which is probably the original) so closely resembles certain passages in the Book of Enoch [1] which is explicitly referred to and quoted a little further on (Jude 14 *sq.*) that little room is left for doubt that we have here an allusion to the popular Jewish doctrine of the fall of a heavenly host from their prior dominion ($ἀρχή$) to a state of bondage and punishment. If it is said that Satan must be regarded as included in this host, it is still to be remembered that the deutero-canonical character of the books in which these references occur, together with the certain dependence of these descriptions upon apocryphal sources such as the Book of Enoch, makes the derivation of a doctrine from the passages quite precarious. It is probable that the description in Gen. vi. 2 of the "sons of God" (angels) taking as wives the "daughters of men" lies at the root of the popular tradition which is found in the Book of Enoch. When the sources and affinities of the pas-

[1] "Announce to the watchers of the heaven, who have abandoned the high heaven and the holy, eternal place, and have defiled themselves with women," etc. (xii. 4); "Wherefore have ye left the high, holy, eternal heaven?" etc. (xv. 3); "I heard the voice of the angel saying: 'These are the angels who descended to the earth, and revealed what was hidden to the children of men, and seduced the children of men into committing sin'" (lxiv. 2). From the translation by R. H. Charles, Oxford, 1893.

sages in question are considered, it is quite evident that they can have no direct reference to the fall of Satan. Other passages which are often quoted in connection with the subject in question are quite inapplicable, as, for example, 1 Tim. iii. 6 : " Lest being puffed up he fall into the condemnation [κρίμα, judgment] of the devil." It is certainly difficult to determine the exact sense of this passage, but in any case no reference to the fall of Satan can be found in it. Still less can such a reference be found in Luke x. 18 : " I beheld Satan falling as lightning from heaven."

It is necessary for our purpose to distinguish between the rational grounds of the doctrine of the fall of Satan and the supposed Scriptural grounds. On no other supposition can the Biblical references to Satan be so naturally explained. It enables us to avoid the idea of an eternal dualism of good and evil, and the equally intolerable conception that God could create a being essentially evil. In no other way can these conclusions be escaped on the supposition of Satan's personal existence. If no one of the theories just alluded to be adopted, no course is left but to deny, as Frommann does, the personality of Satan, and to understand the Scriptural representations as popular descriptions of the operation of sinful principles or tendencies in the world. Frommann seeks to reduce the idea of Satan in John to that of an " evil worldprinciple," a " carnal tendency," the sum of the " temporal and perishable in contrast to God."[1] This view,

[1] *Der Johann. Lehrbegriff*, pp. 336, 367.

THE DOCTRINE OF SIN 145

taken in connection with the author's interpretation of ἀπ' ἀρχῆς in the absolute sense, approximates the Gnostic conception of the essential evil of matter and of an original dualism in the universe. One must go behind the text, and behind any results which legitimate exegesis can yield, if he will make the name Satan a symbol of the "sensuous principle" or an "evil tendency." In his whole discussion of this subject Frommann is really dealing with the thought of Paul more than with that of John, and proceeds, moreover, upon important misapprehensions of the teaching of the former.

So far as the Johannine writings bear upon the idea of the nature and origin of the devil we may sum the matter up by saying that all the passages assume the personality of Satan, but do not state or imply anything as to his origin. Speculation on this point, however, seems to be shut up to a single path. It can rest in no idea except that of a fall without giving place to conceptions which are inconsistent with the absoluteness, or subversive of the goodness of God.

Two ideas in John — scarcely less difficult than that which we have just been considering — remain to be examined, that of "antichrist" (I. ii. 18, 22 ; iv. 3 ; II. 7), and that of "sin unto death" (I. v. 16, 17). A clue, however, is afforded us for the understanding of the former term in the connection. In I. ii. 22, we are told that the antichrist is "he that denieth the Father and the Son;" in I. iv. 3 that "every spirit that confesseth not Jesus" is "the spirit of the antichrist," and in II. 7 that he who confesses not Jesus Christ as coming in the flesh [1] is "the deceiver and the antichrist." The distinguishing peculiarity of the sin which the term "antichrist" comprehends is the denial of the incarnation or messiahship of Jesus. This is a feature of the Gnostical tendency to which the Epistles so often refer. According to this doctrine the world is essentially evil, and nothing divine can abide in contact with it. The heavenly Christ could not really inhabit a material body, hence the denial of the incarnation; just as little could he submit to suffering, hence the denial that he came both "by water and blood" (I. v. 6). Against this denial John asserts that Christ was not only incarnate at his baptism ("came by water," $\delta\iota$' $\ddot{\upsilon}\delta\alpha\tau\sigma\varsigma$) but at his crucifixion ("came by blood," $\delta\iota$' $\alpha\ddot{\iota}\mu\alpha\tau\sigma\varsigma$). The antichristian spirit consists, then, in the denial of the Son's incarnation and passion which springs from a false notion of the divine transcendence, and from a corresponding error concerning the world and human nature in their relation to God.

The question remains, however, whether in speaking of antichrist John had in mind a person, or a tendency, or both. The prevailing view in the Church has been that "antichrist" designates a person. This view rests, however, upon the supposition of a close correspondence, or even identity, of the antichrist of

[1] The Greek is 'Ιησοῦν Χριστὸν ἐρχόμενον ἐν σαρκί. Neither of our English versions seems quite to reproduce the idea of the text.

THE DOCTRINE OF SIN 147

John's Epistles, the "man of sin" in the Pauline Apocalypse (2 Thess. ii. 3) and "the beast" in the Book of Revelation (Rev. xiii. 1 *sq.*). But this supposition is unwarranted. "The beast" of the Johannine Apocalypse is a symbol for the Roman Empire or for the Emperor Nero personally. The "man of sin" in 2 Thessalonians is a term for a false Messiah who was to arise with blasphemous pretensions, and who should represent forces of evil in the Jewish world which the Roman power ("that which restraineth," "the restrainer" ii. 6, 7) should hold in check for a time; then, when the pressure of restraint was taken away, the "mystery of iniquity" (Jewish hostility to the Messiah) which was working in secret should break forth into manifestation, and Christ should come and bring it to naught. The terms "beast," in Revelation, "man of sin" in Paul, and "antichrist" in John have widely different associations, and refer to manifestations of hostility to the gospel in widely different fields. "The beast" symbolizes Roman persecution; "the man of sin," fanatical Jewish opposition and pretence; "antichrist," a Gnostical subversion of the gospel. If the terms "beast" and "man of sin" are meant to indicate that the evil tendencies under consideration are embodied in a person, as is probably the case, it does not necessarily follow that the term "antichrist" is also a personal designation. The question can only be decided, if at all, by the passages in which the term appears.

The first of the four passages in which antichrist is

mentioned (I. ii. 18) seems to favor the view that the term designates a person. Prophecy concerning his appearing is alluded to, and the mention of "many antichrists," which appear to be distinguished from antichrist himself, seems to imply that many persons have arisen who embody the antichristian spirit, but that this spirit is to have its full and final incarnation in a person yet to appear. In the three other passages, however, the word is used in nearly the same sense as in the phrase "many antichrists" already noted, to mean persons who deny the true messiahship and incarnation of Jesus. The "whosoever" of ii. 23, shows that the name is applied to any person who makes the denial referred to. Still less in iv. 3 does "antichrist" appear to be a name for some one particular person. There prophecy concerning the coming of "the spirit of the antichrist" is alluded to, and this spirit is said to be in the world already. This verse seems to be the equivalent of ii. 18, and here it is quite certain that "the antichrist" is conceived of as a principle or spirit of denial, rather than as an individual. Finally, in II. 7, "the antichrist" is "the deceiver" who confesses not Jesus as coming in the flesh. We see, then, that in John's usage ὁ ἀντίχριστος is a title which he applies to many persons who have already appeared, — applies, in fact, to any one who denies the real coming of the Son of God into humanity. We further observe that the antichrist that is to come is synonymous with the spirit of the antichrist which is to come, but which is also already here. It appears to me, therefore, that the term is used to designate either a tendency, principle, or spirit, or to describe the men who embody that temper of denial which the apostle describes in the connection. If we reason from analogy it is certainly natural, in view of the references which are found in both canonical and non-canonical literature to persons who should embody special forms of wickedness, to think that John may have expected that some man was to appear who would be "the antichrist" by eminence. His references to the subject, however, do not warrant this conclusion, although they do not exclude it. It is better to abide by the actual indications of his language than to adopt the more uncertain course of reading him in the light of representations which, at most, are only analogous to his own. The discussion of the term "antichrist" in our sources has been too much complicated with the consideration of the terms of Paul and of the Apocalypse. The subject has been commonly treated as a general doctrinal topic, instead of a question of exegesis. Two of the most competent recent interpreters,[1] regarding solely the natural force of the passages where the term occurs in the First Epistle, pronounce in favor of the interpretation for which we have expressed a preference.

One further theme remains to be discussed, — sin unto death. The one passage which brings this topic before us is I. v. 16, 17 : " If any man see his brother

[1] Holtzmann, *Hand-Commentar*, *in loco*, and Westcott, *The Epistles of St. John*, *in loco*.

sinning a sin not unto death, he shall ask, and God will give him life for them that sin not unto death. There is a sin unto death (ἁμαρτία πρὸς θάνατον) : not concerning this do I say that he should make request. All unrighteousness is sin: and there is a sin not unto death." It is obvious that the writer means here to distinguish differing degrees of wickedness in sin. But this is almost the only assertion which can be made with certainty respecting the passage. Passing by minor points which do not essentially affect the meaning of the phrase ἁμαρτία πρὸς θάνατον, we need, if possible, to answer two questions : (1) Is a particular *act* of sin, or a certain *kind* of sin, here referred to? — that is, is ἁμαρτία best rendered as in our English versions, "a sin," or as in the margin of the R. V. "sin"? (2) In either case, what is the force of πρὸς θάνατον? What distinguishes this sin, or this kind of sin, from all others?

Respecting the first question I think, with Westcott and a majority of modern interpreters, that the translation "a sin" is too definite. If the apostle had in mind some particular act of sin, such as the denial of the Messiahship of Jesus (so Ebrard and Düsterdieck), or envy (so Augustine) it seems likely that he would have specified it, or that he would, at least, have written ἁμαρτία τις or μία. Nor may we, on the other hand, make the expression so vague and general as to interpret it to mean a state of extreme moral obduracy (so Bengel). We should rather understand by ἁμαρτία here a certain *type* of sin, a

THE DOCTRINE OF SIN

kind of sinning which might find expression in many different specific acts, all of which would, however, spring from one certain spirit or disposition. We think it probable that some particular attitude or habit of mind must have been in the apostle's thoughts in using this term. The question what this sinful disposition was is dependent upon the view which is taken of our second inquiry.

Several points connected with the passage as a whole require to be taken into account in estimating the force of ἁμαρτία πρὸς θάνατον. From the very terms of the passage it appears that the apostle, in the case which he supposes, is thinking of this sin as the act of a Christian, or at least of a professing Christian: "If any man see his *brother* sinning," etc. It would seem from this that the sin in question is something which is in a special manner the negation of the Christian profession. It seems also probable that other descriptions in the Epistle of specially heinous sins or sin would throw some light upon the meaning of this sin. Bearing in mind these two general considerations, let us briefly pass in review the leading theories respecting "sin unto death" in our passage.[1] It is well known that this passage is one of the supports of the distinctions made by Roman Catholic theologians between venial and mortal sins. The latter are such as destroy the friendship of God and cause the death of the soul. They are seven in number:

[1] For an account of the patristic comments on the passage, see Westcott, *Epistles of St. John*, pp. 210–214.

pride, covetousness, lust, anger, gluttony, envy, and sloth. But even if a valid distinction could be made between these particular sins and all others, no possible ground for it could be found in our passage, since in no case can ἁμαρτία be made to include a list of seven sins. Many earlier interpreters (as Calvin and Beza) identify "sin unto death" with the blasphemy against the Holy Ghost spoken of in the Synoptic Gospels (Matt. xii. 31 *sq.*; Mark. iii. 22 *sq.*; Luke xii. 10). There must unquestionably be a certain kinship between the thoughts expressed by the two phrases, but they cannot be strictly identical, because the "blasphemy" of which the Pharisees stood in danger consisted in ascribing the gracious works of Jesus to demoniacal sources, and involved an utter perversion of the moral nature, while the "sin" of our passage denotes some course of action in a professed Christian by which he cuts himself off from eternal life. To substantially the same opinion as that given above come the interpretations of Lücke, Huther, DeWette, and Haupt,[1] who agree in explaining the expression as denoting forfeiture of spiritual life through a wilful apostasy from Christ which involves a crisis of the soul, — a deliberate attitude of enmity to him taken from pure love of sinning. On this view "sin unto death" would simply be a name for consummate wickedness as shown by hostility to Christ. If John had in mind precisely this moral obduracy, by the very nature of which the subject is already excluded

[1] *Commentaries, in loco.*

from salvation, it seems strange that he should speak of it as the sin of a "brother" and should put his counsel regarding prayer for it in a negative and guarded form.

Bishop Westcott has advanced the view that "sin unto death" is sin "which in its very nature excludes from fellowship with Christians."[1] He thinks examples would be: hatred of the brethren, selfishness, and faithlessness. He defines ἁμαρτία πρὸς θάνατον as sin "tending to death, and not necessarily involving death. Death is, so to speak, its natural consequence if it continue, and not its inevitable issue as a matter of fact." It appears to me that this interpretation does not really distinguish "sin unto death" from any other sin. All sin tends to death if it continue, and even if some sins, such as those named, had a special effect to exclude the doer of them from Christian society, it would not thereby be proved that they were inherently worse than other sins. On Dr. Westcott's view it is difficult to find any reason for the apostle's hesitation in encouraging his readers to pray for the forgiveness of those who should sin unto death.

Those interpreters[2] seem to me to follow the indications of the Epistle who hold that sin unto death is the disposition or temper which expresses itself in the denial of Christ's incarnation, Messiahship, and saving work. This view sets our passage in close relation with the passages concerning antichrist, and

[1] *The Epistles of St. John*, p. 209.
[2] See, for example, Ebrard, *Commentary, in loco.*

proceeds, we believe, in the right direction. The underlying thought in respect to the antichristian spirit and in respect to sin unto death is probably the same. But the latter idea need not be made so definite as to mean a specific *act* of denial, but may most naturally be held to designate, as the term " antichrist " does, a temper of denial, a renunciation, on the part of one who has professed discipleship to Christ, of the saving significance of his person and work. We therefore hold that sin unto death is here equivalent in principle to the spirit of antichrist, and consists in apostasy or desertion of Christ.[1] With the authors just cited we hold that the New Testament passages outside our Epistle which are most closely analogous to that under review are Hebrews vi. 4–8 and x. 26–31, in which apostasy from Christ and its consequences are depicted. In these passages the thought probably is, If a man deserts Christ he will find no other Saviour ; there is no sacrifice for sins (Heb. x. 26) which can avail for him except that which Christ has made. Thus the impossibility of renewal which is asserted in case of any who have fallen away (Heb. vi. 6) is not absolute, but relative; it is an impossibility which lies within the limits of the supposition which is made in the immediate connection. In the case of one who turns away from Christ, and so long

---

[1] So Holtzmann, *Hand-Commentar, in loco*; Weiss, *Bibl. Theol.*, ii. § 151 *c*. note 10 (in the original of the 5th ed., note 8), and Dwight, in his notes appended to Huther's *Commentary on the Catholic Epistles* (in the Meyer-series), page 817.

as such apostasy lasts (note the *present* participles ἀνασταυροῦντας and παραδειγματίζοντας), there is no possibility of renewal.[1] This view alone accords with the drift and purpose of the Epistle as a whole, as the view which makes "antichrist" and "sin unto death" in 1 John refer to renunciation of Christ accords with the aim of that letter. The passages in Hebrews do not exclude the possibility of renewal in case the course of apostasy is repented of and forsaken; nor do the passages in 1 John pronounce this penalty of death upon any who turn away from the path of denial into which they have been beguiled. The idea which underlies both sets of passages is that the way of apostasy is the road to death; that renunciation of Christ is the renunciation of God's saving mercy, which will not be found elsewhere. This fearful goal, to which the repudiation of Christ will inevitably lead those who persist in it, is pointed out in the most solemn manner by both writers in order that their readers may be warned of the danger to which they are exposed in giving heed to the representatives of a fanatical and narrow Judaism, on the one hand, or to those of a proud and superficial Gnosticism, on the other.

[1] *Cf.* Dwight's notes on the passage in Lünemann's *Commentary* (Meyer-series), p. 551, and Farrar on Hebrews, *in loco*, in the *Cambridge Greek Testament*.

CHAPTER VII

THE WORK OF SALVATION

Literature. — WEISS: *Der Johann. Lehrb.*, Die Errettung der Welt, 157–164, and *Bibl. Theol.*, The Salvation in Christ, ii. 347–362 (orig. pp. 614–626); REUSS: *Hist. Christ. Theol.*, Of the Influence of the Word upon the World, ii. 429–445 (orig. pp. 479–498); BEYSCHLAG: *Neutest. Theol.*, Die Heilsstiftung, i. 261–277, Das Heilswerk, ii. 436–446; WENDT: *Teaching of Jesus*, Significance of the death of Jesus according to the Johannine discourses, ii. 251–262 (orig. pp. 530–539); SEARS, *The Heart of Christ*, The Johannean Atonement, 501–511; FROMMANN: *Johann. Lehrb.*, Jesus ist als der Christ der Heiland der Welt, 418–480; KÖSTLIN: *Der Lehrbegriff, u. s. w.*, Das Werk Jesu im Besondern, 160–209; BAUR: *Neutest. Theol.*, Die Lehre von der Erlösung, 368–389; DALE: *The Atonement*, The Testimony of St. John, 151–172.

A REVIEW of the references in the writings of John to the redemptive work of Christ may well begin with the claim which he makes for himself as the dispenser of life and as the bread of life in the fifth and sixth chapters of the Gospel. The way in which Jesus is led to assert his prerogative as the giver of life (v. 19 *sq.*) is significant. He had healed a man on the Sabbath. The Jews accused him of profaning the sacred day. He replied that in doing good on the Sabbath he was acting in accord with the unceasing beneficence of his Father. They then accused him of "making himself equal with God" (v. 18). This accusation called out an explanation of his mission. He does nothing, he says, independently of the Father's will and purpose (verse 19); he does the same things as the Father (verse 20), "For as the Father raiseth the dead and quickeneth ($\zeta\omega o\pi o\iota\epsilon\hat{\iota}$) them, even so the Son also quickeneth whom he will" (verse 21). These words should probably be understood in an ethical sense, since in the connection he says: "He that heareth my word, and believeth him that sent me, hath eternal life," etc. (verse 24), and again: "The hour cometh, and now is, when the dead shall hear the voice of the Son of God; and they that hear shall live" (verse 26). A present bestowment of spiritual life, on condition of faith, appears to be meant. In immediate connection with this right to bestow life stands its counterpart, the right to pronounce judgment (verses 22, 23). Those who do not honor the Son, and receive the message which the Father sends to them through him, are inevitably exposed to that process of judgment which, though not the immediate object of his coming into the world (viii. 15; xii. 47), is inseparable from his Messianic work. The Father has made him the bearer of life to the world, and through his incarnation and oneness with humanity, — which are the essential conditions of his achieving man's redemption, — has associated with this saving work, as its reverse side, the execution of judgment (verses 26, 27). At this point a transition seems to occur in the thought, which now passes over into the future and dwells for a moment upon the consummation of the life-giving process: "Marvel not at this: for the hour cometh, in which all that are in the tombs shall hear his voice, and shall come forth," etc. (verse 28). This resurrection, which is defined as a resurrection "of life" or "of judgment," according to its basis (so Weiss) or issue (so Meyer), can only be that which is conceived of as taking place at the end of the current age. While these expressions are very explicit in ascribing the work of salvation, both in its present realization and its future completion, to Christ, they are too general to indicate clearly by what means he effects this salvation.

After the miracle of the loaves (vi. 1–14) many followed Jesus in hope of securing further supply (vi. 26). He urges them to seek from him rather that spiritual food which he has come to provide for them (verse 27). To this they reply: What would you have us do? What do you hold that God requires of us? Jesus answers: He requires no deeds whereby you may win his favor; he requires only that you receive and obey me (verses 28, 29). To the Jewish mind the question at once presents itself: By what miracle do you sustain your claim to be a messenger of God and the bearer of life to the world? (verse 30.) Moses attested his mission by giving the people manna: "what workest thou?" (verses 30, 31.)

Such were the preliminary circumstances which occasioned the discourse on the bread of life. The

THE WORK OF SALVATION

reference to the manna which supplied only the temporary physical need of the passing hour affords Jesus an opportunity to set in contrast with it the spiritual nourishment which he gives for the permanent satisfaction of the soul. He tells them that the manna which Moses gave them was not the true, ideal bread of God (τὸν ἄρτον τὸν ἀληθινόν); this genuine bread from heaven God is now giving (δίδωσιν) them (verse 32); it is himself (verse 35). The saying gives great offence (verse 41), but Jesus reasserts, in other terms, his claim as the bearer of spiritual life. He is the way to the Father; he is the giver of the resurrection-life (verse 44); those who really hear God's voice recognize his message as divine; faith in him is the condition of eternal life (verses 45, 47). This stage of the discourse reaches its culmination in the repeated assertion that he is the living bread from heaven, and, especially, in the more specific statement that the life-giving bread is his flesh, which he will give for the life of the world (verse 51).

The final paragraph of the discourse presents the thought that spiritual life is secured by eating the flesh of the Son of man and drinking his blood (verse 53). What is its import? One answer is that reference is here made to the Lord's supper. This was the prevailing interpretation among the Latin and later Greek Church fathers, and is adopted by Roman Catholic writers and by several modern Protestant scholars.[1] But the exegetical difficulties connected

[1] *E. g.*, by Pfleiderer, Harnack, H. Holtzmann, and, in a modified form, by Plummer.

160 THE JOHANNINE THEOLOGY

with this view are very great. Jesus speaks of a present and continuous eating and drinking (verses 54, 56); moreover, it is difficult to conceive of Jesus as referring to the last supper in an argument with the Jews at a time so far in advance of its establishment, and especially in terms so mystical and so widely different from those actually used at the institution of that sacrament. If the words as they stand are referred to the eucharist, the conclusion can hardly be avoided that this application of them is due to the writer of the Gospel, — a conclusion of which those who deny its genuineness have naturally availed themselves. Westcott justly criticises this interpretation as follows: "To attempt to transfer the words of the discourse with their consequences to the sacrament is not only to involve the history in hopeless confusion, but to introduce overwhelming difficulties into their interpretation, which can only be removed by the arbitrary and untenable interpolation of qualifying sentences."[1]

The prevailing interpretation among Protestants refers the words to the propitiatory death of Christ. This was the opinion of Augustine and of the Reformers, and is presented in the commentaries of Lange, Godet and Meyer. It is favored by the following considerations: (a) The term *I will give* (δώσω, verse 51) points to a future saving act; (b) the ex-

---

[1] *Commentary, in loco.* For a detailed refutation of the interpretation just stated above in the text, see also Meyer, *in loco*

THE WORK OF SALVATION

pression, to drink his *blood*, necessarily refers to his *death;* (c) passages like i. 29, iii. 14, and I. iv. 10 confirm this explanation. All three of these points, however, are of doubtful validity. It is improbable that a reference to the death of Christ can be legitimately derived from the term *I will give* ($\delta\omega\sigma\omega$), either on account of the tense or on account of the significance of the word itself. The future may refer to a continuous giving of himself for the life of the world, as well as to one definite act, and the connection seems to show that the verb $\delta\iota\delta\acute{o}\nu\alpha\iota$ is used throughout, not in the sense of giving himself up to God in sacrifice, but in that of giving himself as food for man's nourishment (*cf.* verses 31–34).

The reference to the drinking of the blood of the Son of man (verse 53) may be regarded as parallel to that which is made to the eating of his flesh. If the latter does not necessarily refer to his expiatory death, it cannot be convincingly shown that the former does so. Certainly the fact that Christ is elsewhere spoken of as the Lamb of God (i. 29) and as a propitiation for our sins (I. iv. 10), does not of itself prove that he is presented in the same light in the discourse under consideration. It is almost as difficult to suppose that in this address to hostile Jews Jesus meant to dwell on the necessity of his sacrificial death as it is to suppose that his words had reference to the significance of the last supper. It would seem that his meaning must have been, in that case, altogether incomprehensible to his hearers.

The difficulties attending these interpretations have led many to adopt a third view which has, indeed, been held in varying forms. In this third theory the terms *flesh* and *blood* are understood in an ethical or mystical sense, and the eating and drinking spoken of are supposed to include the entire appropriation of Christ and his saving work. In this view the benefits of his death would be logically included, though not primarily or directly referred to in the terms *flesh* and *blood*. These words are regarded as symbols of his life or person. Westcott understands by the *flesh* "the virtue of Christ's humanity as living for us," and by the *blood* "the virtue of his humanity as subject to death."[1] For Weiss the *flesh* and *blood* together symbolize the weakness and finitude of human nature in contrast to the celestial glory of the spiritual nature. The eating and drinking therefore refer to the believing reception of Jesus' human appearance in his lowly form.[2] Taking a similar view of its terms, Wendt holds that the discourse is intended to confute the idea of the Jews that, because of his well-known human origin (verse 41 *sq.*), Jesus could not be the medium of eternal life to mankind. Thus the discussion " serves for the confirmation and explanation of the thought which he elsewhere briefly expresses by his self-designation as ' the Son of

---

[1] *Commentary, in loco.*

[2] *Life of Christ*, iii. 7. Weiss adds that the evangelist sees in these words intimations of Jesus' violent death, — an idea which is not involved in their original meaning.

man.'"[1] Others do not attempt to assign distinct senses to the words *flesh* and *blood* or to find in the statements concerning them any specific reference to Jesus' lowly human form, but understand that to eat his flesh and drink his blood is to make Christ wholly ours, to participate spiritually in his life.

Dr. John Lightfoot confirms this view by citations from Talmudic sources. In connection with them he says: "There is nothing more common in the schools of the Jews than the phrases of 'eating and drinking' in a metaphorical sense." "Bread is very frequently used in the Jewish writers for *doctrine*. So that when Christ talks of eating his flesh, he might perhaps hint to them that he would feed his followers not only with his *doctrines*, but with *himself* too." One Rabbi speaks of "eating the years of the Messiah;" another of "devouring" him. Lightfoot concludes: "To partake of the Messiah truly is to partake of himself, his pure nature, his righteousness, his spirit; and to live and grow and receive nourishment from that participation of him, — things which the Jewish schools heard little of, did not believe, did not think; but things which our blessed Saviour expresseth lively and comprehensively enough, by that of eating his flesh and drinking his blood."[2]

It appears to me probable that this third interpretation corresponds best with the primary import of the discourse. It is not impossible, however, that, as

[1] *Teaching of Jesus*, ii. 182 (orig. p. 475).
[2] *Horæ Hebraicæ, in loco*, Oxford trans., iii. 307-309.

164   THE JOHANNINE THEOLOGY

Weiss suggests, the writer, in reproducing the substance of the discourse in the light of subsequent events, thought of them as fulfilled in a special manner in Jesus' giving up his body to death, and even as directly referring to this event. But the discourse as a whole does not seem to warrant the supposition of a primary and direct reference to his atoning death, and in seeking an answer to the question, how, according to the Johannine writings, Jesus effects man's salvation, we are not carried by this discourse beyond the general truth that he does this by giving himself to men as spiritual food, or, dropping the figure, by offering himself as the object of faith and by entering into loving fellowship with men. More specific references to the work of salvation must be sought elsewhere.

In several places Christ is said to have come to *save* men. " God sent not the Son into the world to judge the world; but that the world should be saved (ἵνα σωθῇ ὁ κόσμος) through him " (iii. 17; *cf*. xii. 47). The connection shows that "the world " designates mankind in general, and that men are regarded as exposed — apart from his saving work — to condemnation or destruction (*cf*. verse 16), but the manner in which the salvation is effected is not intimated. Faith in himself and appropriation of the light which he has brought to men are spoken of (verses 18–21) as the *conditions* of the divine approval, but no *ground* of forgiveness in his death or sacrifice is alluded to. Elsewhere, in defending himself against the criticisms of

THE WORK OF SALVATION

the Jews, he affirms that although the testimony of the Baptist, which the Jews had sought, was favorable to him, he does not himself appeal to it for his own advantage, since his claims bear the direct authentication of God, and adds: "I say these things" (concerning John's testimony) "that ye may be saved" (ἵνα ὑμεῖς σωθῆτε, v. 34); it is for *your* sake, not for *mine*, that I refer to John's "witness," in the hope that you may heed it and believe on me. Here also we find only an implied reference to the believing acceptance of his Messiahship as the condition of salvation.

The passage in the allegory of the Door of the Sheepfold: "I am the door: by me if any man enter in, he shall be saved (σωθήσεται), and shall go in and go out, and shall find pasture" (x. 9), is figurative, and contains only the general idea of security through Christ from harm or danger. When we are told that "the salvation" (ἡ σωτηρία) — that is, the promised, long-expected Messianic salvation — "is from the Jews" (iv. 22), it is, no doubt, implied that Jesus is the Saviour who brings this salvation; but no suggestion of the way or means of accomplishing it is made. After the conversation with the Samaritan woman, in which the foregoing expression occurs, her countrymen declare that they are convinced by what they have heard from Jesus himself that he "is indeed the Saviour of the world" (iv. 42). In one other passage only is he designated as the Saviour (I. iv. 14) but the means by which he becomes such are not specified —

beyond the mention of confessing him and abiding in him as necessary (verses 13, 15). From this group of passages we may indeed infer the sinfulness of mankind; salvation is *from sin* and its consequences, but whether by an atonement for sin or not, we have as yet no indication. Thus far the whole soteriology of our sources may be summed up in the words: life-fellowship with Christ.

There are two passages, standing in close connection in the First Epistle, in which reference is made to the cleansing ($καθαρίζειν$) of men from sin (i. 7, 9). The apostle had declared that the substance of the gospel message is that God is light (verse 5); it follows that Christians must walk in the light (verse 6); in so doing they have fellowship with one another, and the blood of Jesus cleanses them from all sin (verse 7). The thought, then, is that the saving efficacy of Christ's blood is experienced only by those who walk in the light, that is, those who desire and strive to be pure and Godlike. The author now advances to the necessity of confession; if Christians confess their sins God's faithfulness to his promises and to his very nature is the guaranty of their forgiveness and cleansing (verses 8, 9). It will be noticed that in both these passages it is the cleansing of the Christian from the sin that still clings to him that is spoken of, and that in one case (verse 9) this cleansing is predicated of God, in the other (verse 7), of the blood of Jesus, his Son. From these passages we derive the same general conception as from those which speak of *saving* men; namely, that Jesus Christ wrought a deliverance for man from sin; and also the additional idea that this deliverance stands in some way connected with his death, since his blood is said to be the means of cleansing. It is further evident that the apostle speaks here, not of a juridical deliverance or acquittal, but of an actual moral purification.[1] It seems to be clearly implied in the first of these passages (verse 7) that the shedding of Christ's blood is the culminating act in his saving work. This is the only passage in John's writings where cleansing from sin is explicitly attributed to his blood or death. It remains to be seen whether this idea is clearly implied in other passages.

Closely resembling the passages just noticed are two others in which the taking away (αἴρειν) of sin is ascribed to Jesus. In I. iii. 5 it is stated that "he was manifested to take away sins" (ἵνα τὰς ἁμαρτίας ἄρῃ), or more exactly, "the sins," the sins of mankind. The other passage contains the exclamation of the Baptist when he saw Jesus approaching: "Behold, the Lamb of God, which taketh away (ὁ αἴρων) the sin of the world!" (i. 29.) Some interpreters have taken αἴρειν in the first passage in the sense of *to bear* as a sacrifice, in order to procure forgiveness,[2] and this meaning has been still more commonly given to the word in the second passage. But while αἴρειν in

[1] So Lücke, Huther, Haupt; *per contra*, Weiss, *Bibl. Theol.* § 148, *b.* 3.

[2] So, *e. g.*, Lücke and De Wette.

itself might in these passages mean *to bear*, the Johannine usage strongly favors another signification. The word is uniformly used by John in the sense of *to take away* (*cf.* xi. 48; xv. 2; xvii. 15; xix. 31, 38). Moreover, the Septuagint employs φέρειν to denote the *bearing* of sin, while it uses αἴρειν to express the idea of *taking away*. The context seems clearly to require the meaning *to take away* for ἄρῃ in I. iii. 5, since the point of the argument lies in the antagonism between the Christian life and sin, as shown by the purpose of Christ's manifestation, namely, to take away sins. If this view of I. iii. 5 be adopted, the presumption that ὁ αἴρων means "who takes away" is greatly strengthened.[1] In that case, the idea expressed in αἴρειν is substantially the same as that which we found in καθαρίζειν. Especially close would be the connection between I. i. 7 and i. 29, since the "blood" in the one passage corresponds with the "Lamb" in the other, and each term suggests the idea of a sacrificial victim.

On the interpretation of ὁ αἴρων in i. 29 which we think to be best supported, the question whether the sacrificial idea is found in the passage, will turn chiefly on the meaning of the phrase: "the Lamb of God." The sense in which we have taken αἴρειν is not prejudicial to this idea in the passage, since it may appear that the sin of the world is conceived of as taken away only through the expiation of it in the

[1] Among the interpreters who render ὁ αἴρων "who takes away," are Meyer, Westcott, Weiss, Godet, and Plummer.

sufferings and death of Christ. The grammatical force of the phrase, as determined by the article and the genitive, seems clearly to be : the expected Lamb which God has furnished or appointed, that is, the Lamb which God has set apart to a special function, and of which prophecy speaks. In the view of many the reference of the term is to the paschal lamb. This lamb was the symbol of Israel's deliverance from bondage, and Jesus may be regarded as the antitypical passover Lamb inasmuch as he accomplishes for men their deliverance from sin. It seems unnatural, however, to suppose that the Baptist should, at this time, have regarded Jesus in this special character ; and this impression is somewhat strengthened if the view be taken that in the quotation in xix. 36 : "A bone of him shall not be broken," the reference is not to the paschal lamb (Ex. xii. 46 ; Num. ix. 12), but to the description of Jehovah's protection of the righteous man in Ps. xxxiv. 20. But even if the apostle John does identify Jesus, after his death, with the paschal lamb (as Paul clearly does, 1 Cor. v. 7), a similar reference in our passage would not thereby be rendered especially probable, except on the view that this conception was imported into the Baptist's words by the evangelist *ex eventu*.

It seems, on all accounts, more natural to suppose that the phrase "the Lamb of God" is a reminiscence of Isaiah liii. 7, where the meekness of the suffering Servant of Jehovah is depicted by saying : "As a lamb that is led to the slaughter, and as a sheep that before her shearers is dumb; yea, he opened not his mouth." Some interpreters, connecting our passage with Isaiah liii. 7, and regarding the latter only as a figurative description of the innocence and patience of the Servant, conclude that the phrase "the Lamb of God" does not carry with it the sacrificial idea, but merely characterizes Jesus as the meek and gentle sufferer. But the sacrificial import of the passage Isaiah liii., taken as a whole, and especially of verses 10–12, renders this view improbable. Moreover, the recognition of a connection between our passage and Isaiah liii. 7 does not warrant the conclusion that the phrase under review is strictly limited in its meaning by the latter. The phrase "Lamb of God" is most naturally taken as an Old Testament symbol of a sacrificial victim, through the offering of which sin is done away. Similar allusions to Christ as the Lamb who dies in sacrifice for men are found in 1 Pet. i. 19, and in numerous passages in the Apocalypse (*e. g.*, v. 12; vii. 14). To me it appears highly probable that we have in our passage a symbolical expression, drawn from the Old Testament, for the sacrificial expiation of sin. If so, we must regard this idea as an element of the Johannine soteriology. But the justice of this conclusion will be found to be mainly dependent upon considerations connected with other passages yet to be examined.

In one passage (I. ii. 1) Christ is called a παράκλητος with or before the Father (πρὸς τὸν πατέρα):

"If any man sin, we have an Advocate with the Father, Jesus Christ the righteous." The word παράκλητος designates Christ as one who is summoned to our aid and who represents us in relation to (πρός) the Father. This passage does not, however, aid us in defining specifically the way in which Christ effects man's salvation. It bears mainly upon the mediation of Christ in securing forgiveness to the Christian man who falls into sin (ἁμάρτῃ, note the aorist). The thought is: If the Christian commits sin (in contrast to living in an habitual state of sin, I. iii. 6–9) he has as his Advocate before the "righteous Father" (xvii. 25) the sinless One who, having himself perfectly fulfilled his moral destiny in his human life, enters into perfect sympathy with those who are passing through the same process of trial. The passage bears, not upon the cause or ground of salvation, but upon its completion in the Christian man.

There are several passages in which some act of Christ, usually his death, is said to have been on behalf of (ὑπέρ) men. The first of these, "The bread which I will give is my flesh, for (ὑπέρ) the life of the world" (vi. 51), we have already noticed incidentally in our review of the discourse on the bread of life. On the interpretation of that discourse which I have adopted, a reference in these words to the death of Jesus for men cannot be confidently affirmed. For our present purpose this passage may be passed over, both because of the uncertainty of its meaning and because other passages are unambiguous upon the point in question. In the allegory of the Good Shepherd, Jesus, describing himself as "the good shepherd" says that he "lays down his life for (ὑπέρ) the sheep" (x. 11, 15). It is a question how far, in view of the figurative language of this whole description, we can draw doctrinal inferences respecting the significance of Christ's death from these words. If we consult the analogy made use of here we should say, the shepherd can only lay down his life in the protection of the sheep from danger; the parable does not carry us beyond the thought of the most self-denying sacrifice on the part of Christ for those whom he loves. Some interpreters, however (*e. g.*, Meyer, *in loco*), find the expiatory idea here in the verb (τίθησιν) which is used. It is claimed that the phrase τιθέναι τὴν ψυχήν means to pay down one's life as a ransom, in accordance with a frequent classical usage, and on the analogy of the expression to give one's life (διδόναι τὴν ψυχήν, Matt. xx. 28; *cf*. 1 Tim. ii. 6). In these passages the idea of a ransom is plainly expressed, and the force of the phrase τιθέναι τὴν ψυχήν cannot fairly be determined by simple comparison with them. The phrase in question is used in the New Testament only by John (x. 11, 15, 17, 18; xiii. 37, 38; xv. 13; I. iii. 16). This writer elsewhere employs the verb τιθέναι chiefly in the sense of to lay away (xi. 34; xix. 41; xx. 2, 13, 15), or to lay aside (xiii. 4). Westcott thinks that "the usage of St. John rather suggests the idea of putting off and laying aside as a robe," than the laying down of a ransom price. It is certain that the passages outside of this parable where our phrase is used do not support the idea of paying a ransom, e. g., xiii. 37 where Peter says: "I will lay down my life for thee" (τὴν ψυχήν μου ὑπὲρ σοῦ θήσω). When in xv. 13 Jesus alludes to his death he does so under terms of friendship which do not suggest the ransom-idea: "Greater love hath no man than this, that a man lay down his life for his friends" (ἵνα τις τὴν ψυχὴν αὐτοῦ θῇ ὑπὲρ τῶν φίλων αὐτοῦ). In the remaining passage (I. iii. 16) the apostle makes the laying down of Christ's life for men parallel to that laying down of life for one another which is the duty of Christians, and expresses both acts in the same terms: "He laid down his life for us (ἐκεῖνος ὑπὲρ ἡμῶν τὴν ψυχὴν αὐτοῦ ἔθηκεν), and we ought to lay down our lives for the brethren" (ὑπὲρ τῶν ἀδελφῶν τὰς ψυχὰς θεῖναι). Surely no payment of life as a ransom-price can be thought of in the mutual laying down of life for one another among Christians; if not, it is unwarranted to derive this idea from the parallel phrase.

The opinion of Meyer does not seem to be warranted by the facts of the case. The substitutionary idea can be derived from the references to the giving of his life by the good shepherd only in case the preposition ὑπέρ can be shown to involve this idea. This preposition strictly means *on behalf of, for the benefit of*, and not *instead of* (ἀντί). It is more generic than ἀντί, and might comprehend its idea if the connection required. One might die for the benefit of another by dying in that other's stead, but he might do so in other ways also. In the present instance the figure of the good shepherd in his relation to his sheep, warrants us in saying that Jesus, according to the parable, held his life at the service of men, and when the occasion arose laid down his life that they might live. As the faithful shepherd dies in protecting his sheep from wild beasts or robbers, so Jesus dies to save men from sin and death. The analogy would suggest that this death is experienced in the course of an effort to save men by other means; that it represents the culmination of effort to secure that end, but it would be unwarranted thus to limit the thought by the terms of the allegorical form. We think that the passages under review, fairly interpreted, teach that the death of Jesus is a means to man's rescue from sin and its consequences. This conclusion, however, we should regard as somewhat doubtful did these passages stand alone. It may be escaped by separating these clauses in which ὑπέρ occurs from others found elsewhere, and by adhering strictly to the limits of the parabolic analogy. In any case our passages do not, on our interpretation, indicate in what way or on what ground the death of Christ avails for man's salvation. Respecting the two passages just passed in review (vi. 51; x. 11), we must agree with Weiss in saying: "In both images there is nothing said of any bearing of punishment, but of a service of love, which Jesus discharges to the world by

THE WORK OF SALVATION. 175

giving his life, in that he thereby delivers it from death and keeps it in life."[1]

The next passage in which the relation of the death of Christ to men is denoted by ὑπέρ is that where the high priest Caiaphas is said to have uttered an unconscious prophecy of the necessity and purport of Christ's death (xi. 47–53). The passage presents considerable critical difficulties, but the meaning which appears on the face of the narrative is as follows: In a meeting of the Sanhedrin the Pharisees express their concern because so many of their fellow-countrymen have believed on Jesus. They argue: If he is permitted to go on winning adherents thus without interruption, the attention of our Roman rulers will surely become directed to the matter. They will regard the excitement attending adherence to this pretended Messiah and King as a sign of possible sedition, and they will promptly destroy forever the remnant of independence which is now ours; they will annihilate our holy city and completely extinguish our national life (xi. 47, 48). To this argument Caiaphas, who was high priest during that fateful year, answered: You Pharisees are altogether lacking in shrewdness. We can turn this whole situation to our advantage. By sacrificing Jesus we can show our loyalty to Rome, and thus avert all possible suspicion from ourselves. Thus he, not the Jewish people, will perish. Let the penal stroke, which you so much fear, descend upon him, instead of us.

[1] *Bibl. Theol.* § 148, *c.*

It is clear that the suggestion of Caiaphas was dictated by selfish policy. It is through wicked enmity to Jesus, and cruel betrayal of him, that the advantage of his death is to be secured to the people. They are to shield themselves by turning base injustice to Jesus into a semblance of devotion to Rome (verses 49, 50; *cf.* xviii. 14). On this counsel of Caiaphas the evangelist now makes a comment based upon the Old Testament idea of the high priest as the recipient of oracular communications from Jehovah (Ex. xxviii. 30; Num. xxvii. 21). He says that the very words which Caiaphas uttered in a worldly and wicked spirit contained, despite his purpose, a great divine truth; he, in virtue of his sacred office, was made the organ of a word of God of which he was all unconscious. His words — little as he meant them so — express the great truth that Jesus was to die for ($\hupér$) the Jewish nation, and not only that, but that by his death he was to gather together into a spiritual unity all those in every nation who are true, obedient sons of God (verses 51, 52). Whatever view we may take of John's assertion of a divine determination controlling the words of Caiaphas and directing them to the expression of truth wholly foreign to the mind of the speaker, it is evident that the whole narrative assumes it to be a great central truth of Christianity that Jesus died to save the Jewish nation, and to constitute all the children of God into one family. Moreover, as in I. i. 7 fellowship among Christians and their cleansing from all sin by the blood of

THE WORK OF SALVATION

Christ were placed side by side, so here we have a correlation of the idea of salvation and of Christian unity as together representing the object of Christ's death. For our purpose the main point to be noted is the way in which the whole narrative assumes the centrality of the truth that Christ's death was the means of effecting the Messianic salvation for the Jewish nation, and of constituting the one communion of true believers. But in what sense, in the light of our passage, does Christ die for ($\dot{v}\pi\acute{e}\rho$) men? We certainly cannot carry the idea of a divine overruling of Caiaphas' words so far as to find in them the true conception of Jesus' vicarious death. To the high priest's mind his death would be the result of crafty policy, whereby suspicion of political treachery should be averted from the Jewish people. He did not connect the death of Christ with God's order, or contemplate it as subserving moral and spiritual ends. Our passage, then, does not involve more than the assertion which the evangelist held to be fundamental and axiomatic, that Christ secured the salvation of men by his death; but to the questions, why, or in what way, our author gives us, as yet, no answer.

In xv. 13 Jesus refers to his laying down his life as a proof of his great love: "Greater love hath no man than this, that a man lay down life for ($\dot{v}\pi\acute{e}\rho$) his friends." It accords with the purpose of the discourse in which this passage occurs that Jesus should speak of his death here as being experienced for the benefit of his immediate disciples, without thereby justifying any limitation of its intended benefits. But the passage does not carry us beyond those previously cited in respect to the way in which his death secures the benefits to which the preposition points. The same may be said of the kindred passage I. iii. 16: " Hereby know we love, because he laid down his life for (ὑπέρ) us: and we ought to lay down our lives for (ὑπέρ) the brethren." In this case, however, if we are to press the parallelism, we should have to conclude that the death of Jesus is for the benefit of men only in the sense in which self-sacrificing suffering on the part of men is for the benefit of its objects. The context shows that in this passage the death of Jesus stands as a symbol of self-sacrificing love which men are to share and illustrate. That this is, in general, its entire significance in John, would be, however, an unwarranted conclusion.

The words " For their sakes (ὑπὲρ αὐτῶν) I sanctify (ἁγιάζω) myself, that they themselves also may be sanctified in truth " (xvii. 19) are understood by most interpreters [1] in a sacrificial sense, and ἁγιάζειν is taken as equivalent to προσφέρειν θυσίαν (Chrysostom, cf. Eph. v. 2). On this view the meaning would be: For the salvation of my disciples I consecrate myself, through death, as a sacrifice unto God. This explanation is sustained by Septuagint examples of the use of ἁγιάζειν in the sense of consecration to death in sacrifice (Ex. xiii. 2; Deut. xv. 19, etc.). Considerations drawn from the connection in which our pas-

[1] So, e. g., Lücke, DeWette, Meyer, Weiss, H. Holtzmann.

THE WORK OF SALVATION

sage stands, however, render this view, to say the least, very doubtful. Jesus prays for the consecration of his disciples (xvii. 17), and adds that he consecrates himself for them that they themselves also (καὶ αὐτοί) may be consecrated in truth (xvii. 19). It seems incredible that ἁγιάζειν as applied to the disciples should refer to their consecration to death as martyrs (so Chrysostom), and, if it did, the usage would not be parallel to that in which it applies to Jesus, who, according to the supposition, dies, not as a martyr, but as a sacrifice. The language of verse 19 most naturally "implies two consecrations of a homogeneous character" (Godet). It seems unnatural to attribute, as Weiss does, a double sense to ἁγιάζειν in the passage. It appears to me preferable to understand the words comprehensively of Christ's whole devotion of himself to his appointed work, which would include his life as well as his death. The thought is unduly narrowed by Neander, who defines Christ's self-consecration as "the realization of the ideal of holiness."[1] The phrase more naturally denotes that whole self-giving of Jesus to men by which he becomes the author and finisher of their salvation.[2]

Jesus implies the necessity of his death for the realization of his saving work in the statement, "Verily, verily, I say unto you, except a grain of wheat fall into the earth and die, it abideth by itself alone; but if it die, it beareth much fruit" (xii. 24). But neither

[1] *Planting and Training*, ii. 39 (Bohn ed.).
[2] So, substantially, Godet and Westcott.

the figure in which the principle of sacrifice is presented, nor the context of the passage, suggests the idea of vicarious or sacrificial death. The principle is directly applied to the life of the disciples, who are not to " love " their lives, but to " hate " them (xii. 25), that is, not to withhold from others their interest, sympathy, and efforts, but freely to give them. To follow Christ in a life of service and self-giving is the practical thought of the passage, "If any man serve me, let him follow me " (xii. 26).

The necessity of Jesus' death is, however, presented in other terms: " As Moses lifted up the serpent in the wilderness, even so must the Son of man be lifted up ($\dot{v}\psi\omega\theta\hat{\eta}\nu\alpha\iota$ $\delta\epsilon\hat{\iota}$): that whosoever believeth may in him have eternal life" (iii. 14, 15; *cf.* xii. 34). The comparison here made involves (*a*) that as the brazen serpent was lifted up on a pole (Num. xxi. 8 *sq.*), so Jesus must be lifted up on the cross (*cf.*, especially, viii. 28); and (*b*) that, as looking upon the serpent secured healing, so belief on the crucified One secures eternal life. This passage and those in which Jesus is described as the Lamb of God (i. 29, 36) it is particularly important to bear in mind in seeking to determine the idea which underlies the assertions of his voluntary devotion of his life for the good of men.

Again, Jesus says: " And I, if I be lifted up from the earth, will draw all men unto myself " (xii. 32), which the evangelist explains by saying: " This he said, signifying by what manner of death he should die " (xii. 33). Here the cross seems to be thought of,

THE WORK OF SALVATION 181

not only as the symbol of death, but of exaltation above and beyond the earth (ἐκ τῆς γῆς). The combination of ideas is similar to that which is presented by Paul in Phil. ii. 8, 9, where the humiliation to the death of the cross is presented as the ground of the exaltation. Since the heavenly reign and kingly authority of Jesus were attained on the path of suffering, the cross may fitly stand, not only as the symbol of the suffering, but of its result also. In asserting that in consequence of being lifted up on the cross he would exert his great attractive power upon mankind, Jesus seems not only to have signified, as John affirms, the manner of his death, but also to have proclaimed the ground of his exaltation and the impelling motive of his matchless influence in the world.

The two most important passages, in their bearing on the Johannine idea of atonement, are found in the First Epistle: "He is the propitiation (ἱλασμός) for (περί) our sins," etc. (ii. 2), and, "Herein is love, not that we loved God, but that he loved us, and sent his Son to be the propitiation (ἱλασμός) for (περί) our sins" (iv. 10). These are the only passages in which any of the technical terms which express the ideas of atonement, reconciliation, or propitiation (καταλλάσσειν, καταλλαγή, ἱλάσκεσθαι, ἱλαστήριον, κ. τ. λ.) occur in the Johannine writings; they are also the only passages in which the word ἱλασμός, on which their meaning chiefly turns, is found in the New Testament.

In order rightly to estimate the force of these passages it is necessary to give a brief account of the Biblical use of ἱλάσκεσθαι and its kindred forms.[1] In the Septuagint the two principal uses of ἱλασμός (and of its strengthened form ἐξιλασμός) are, (a) as the equivalent of כִּפֻּרִים, " coverings " [of sin by sacrifice], meaning atonement or expiation (e. g., Lev. xxv. 9; Num. v. 8) ; (b) as a translation of הַטָּאת, sin offering (Ezek. xliv. 27 ; xlv. 19) ; and (c) in the sense of סְלִיחָה, forgiveness (Ps. cxxx. 4 ; Dan. ix. 9). The verb ἱλάσκεσθαι and its compound ἐξιλάσκεσθαι are chiefly used to translate כִּפֶּר, to cover, that is, to atone for, sin. The subject of the action, expressed or implied, is, in this usage, God or some human agent; the object is the sins expiated, expressed in the accusative (Ps. lxv. 4), dative (Ps. lxxviii. 38), or after περί (Lev. v. 18) or ὑπέρ (Ezek. xlv. 17) ; the verb is also used to translate סָלַח, to forgive, and in the passive signifies to be merciful (as in Luke xviii. 13). This verb is found but twice in the New Testament, in both instances in accord with Septuagint usage. In Luke xviii. 13, ἱλάσθητί μοι τῷ ἁμαρτωλῷ means, be propitious, etc., as in 2 Kings v. 18, ἱλάσεται τῷ δούλῳ ; cf. Ps. xxv. 11 ; lxxix. 9. In Hebrews ii. 17 the phrase εἰς τὸ ἱλάσκεσθαι τὰς ἁμαρτίας τοῦ λαοῦ corresponds to the prevailing Septuagint usage, and means, " in

[1] For a full exhibition of the Septuagint usage I would refer to Westcott's note on the subject in his *Epistles of St. John*, pp. 85–87. The Biblical use of this and other terms bearing upon the doctrine of atonement is fully discussed in Cremer's *Bibl.-Theol. Lexicon*, sub voce, and in Trench's *New Testament Synonyms*.

THE WORK OF SALVATION

order (as high priest) to expiate by sacrifice the sins of the people."

Attention has often been called — and justly — to the difference between the classical and the Biblical use of this class of words. In Homer and most ancient authors ἱλάσκεσθαι means to render the gods favorable by sacrifices or prayers, — the assumption being that they are not, apart from these appeasing acts, disposed to be favorable to men. In Biblical Greek the conception is quite different; only in Zech. vii. 2, do we find any expression which seems to answer to the idea of ἱλάσκεσθαι τὸν θεόν. There the phrase is, ἐξιλάσασθαι τὸν κύριον, which, as the context and the Hebrew show,[1] is not used in a sacrificial sense, but means to implore or "intreat the favor of the Lord" (R. V.). We have therefore no example of a phrase meaning "to propitiate God." Biblical language avoids the expression of the idea that God is, in his disposition or feeling, averse to forgiveness. He does not have to be made willing by expiations to forgive sin. He is, and always has been, willing. The Biblical idea is that the obstacle to forgiveness lies in his essential righteousness which so conditions his grace that without its satisfaction God cannot, in self-consistency, forgive. In the heathen view expiation renders the gods willing to forgive; in the Biblical view expiation enables God,

[1] The Hebrew is, לְחַלּוֹת אֶת־פְּנֵי יְהוָה, literally, to smooth or stroke the face of Jehovah. The verb is frequently used of imploring the favor of men (Job. xi. 19; Prov. xix. 6).

consistently with his holiness, actually to do what he was never unwilling to do. In the former view sacrifice changes the sentiment of the gods toward men; in the latter it affects the consistency of his procedure in relation to sin. The divine character is in no way changed. In the expiation (which God himself provides) is fulfilled a condition of the operation of that grace in which the whole work of salvation has its origin and ground. In heathenism men win the favor of the gods; in Biblical religion God's favor is sovereign and free, but it manifests itself in accord with the whole nature of God; its operation in the forgiveness of sin is conditioned upon the manifestation, at the same time, of the divine displeasure at sin and the assertion of its desert of punishment. God cannot forgive as if he were mere goodnature. He can forgive only in accordance with his changeless, essential righteousness, which must be vindicated and satisfied. To effect this vindication and satisfaction is the function of sacrifice or expiation in the Bible.

In the light of the foregoing considerations there can hardly be a doubt that when Christ is said to be an ἱλασμὸς περὶ τῶν ἁμαρτιῶν ἡμῶν (I. ii. 2; iv. 10) the meaning is that he accomplishes for us a reconciliation with God on account of our sins by himself atoning for them. He is the means of rendering God favorable in so far as by his sacrificial death he has accomplished, on our behalf, the ends of punishment, and is thus in respect to our sins a means of reconciliation with God.

THE WORK OF SALVATION 185

It is frequently asserted that in John's writings we have no trace of an objective atonement for sin, or of those legal conceptions of God's character or government which are the presuppositions of the sacrificial idea.[1] It is true that John has not developed the idea of expiation for sin by the suffering and death of Christ, but it is none the less true that he several times alludes to it in such a way as to show that it was an underlying assumption of his teaching. After making the fullest allowances for the doubtful passages, there remain several references to the sacrificial idea of Christ's work which no unprejudiced exegesis can set aside. Such are the description of Jesus as " the Lamb of God " (i. 29, 36); the designation of him as our Advocate, in respect to sin, before the Father (I. ii. 1); the statement that he died for ($ὑπέρ$) men (xi. 51; xv. 13; I. iii. 16); the allusion to the necessity of his death (iii. 14), and the presentation of it as the condition of founding his kingdom (xii. 32); and the assertion that he is the propitiation or reconciliation in respect to the sins of the world (I. ii. 2; iv. 10). To these may be

[1] "We have not been able to discover anywhere in the writings of the apostle John any trace whatever of a vicarious satisfaction," etc. — REUSS: *Hist. Christ. Theol.* ii. 443 (orig. ii. 496).

"The atonement (according to John) . . . is the believer himself brought into harmony with the divine mind, purpose, and will, through the Mediator; and it involves a knowledge of the love of Christ, and its exceeding and abounding peace." — SEARS: *The Heart of Christ*, p. 501.

added the reference in I. ii. 12 to the forgiveness of sins "for his name's sake" (διὰ τὸ ὄνομα αὐτοῦ).

We have seen that several expressions which have been thought to illustrate the sacrificial conception of Christ's saving work are, at least, of doubtful application to it. We may summarize a part of the foregoing discussion by quoting the following as the principal examples: cleansing from sin (I. i. 7, 9), probably refers, not to satisfaction for the guilt of sin by atonement, but to actual deliverance from the power and defilement of the sin itself; ὁ αἴρων (i. 29) probably refers to the taking away of sin, that is, the abolition of it, and not to the penal endurance of its guilt; the giving of his flesh, etc. (vi. 51), is probably a symbolic expression for Christ's self-communication to the believer, rather than an assertion respecting his sacrificial death; I incline to a similar explanation of xvii. 19: "For their sakes I sanctify myself;" and when in xii. 32 the drawing of all men to Christ is conditioned upon his being lifted up from the earth, this last expression seems to include not only his death, but his resurrection and ascension. In that case the passage bears, indeed, upon the saving significance of Christ's death, but less directly and exclusively than it would do if the lifting up referred only to the cross, as in iii. 14 and viii. 28.

There is no doubt that John dwells less than most of the New Testament writers upon the legal aspects of the divine nature, but there are not wanting evidences that the conception of the divine love which

THE WORK OF SALVATION 187

underlies all his religious ideas includes the notion of righteousness, that self-respecting attribute of God which occasions his holy displeasure at sin and requires to be expressed and vindicated while sin is forgiven. It accords with John's mystical type of mind to dwell more upon the union of the believer with Christ than upon the ground of forgiveness which is laid by Christ's redemptive work. The apostle is fond of leaving behind " the first principles of Christ" and of pressing on unto "perfection" (Heb. vi. 1) or maturity. He is less concerned with the method in which salvation has been provided than with the actual realization of that salvation in its fulness of blessedness and peace. He thinks and speaks less of the provision for forgiveness than he does of the life of fellowship with Christ and of likeness to God; in a word, he is less concerned for theology than for religion.

John wrote after the great conflicts with Judaism in the Church, which were at their height about the middle of the first century, had ceased to stimulate and shape the thought of Christian teachers. Except in certain allusions in the First Epistle, his writings (leaving aside for our purpose the Apocalypse) are not controversial. He undertook to interpret to his readers, in a constructive spirit, the gospel of Christ. He wrote after many years of Christian experience and reflection. He had little or no occasion to use the weapons of a distinctively Jewish logic, or to run his thoughts into Jewish legal forms. He did not, it would seem, feel called upon to argue the case for the various doctrines of Christianity at all. He simply set forth characteristic facts of Christ's manifestation as they had taken shape in his memory, emphasized the essential principles of his teaching, and pointed out the bearing of these principles upon life. Hence we do not find subjects analyzed and reasoned out by John. His mode of thought is synthetic, and the particulars of a subject are generally touched only by suggestion. It need not surprise us, therefore, that we find no developed doctrine of redemption in John. The circumstances of the case explain why few Jewish sacrificial forms of thought appear. All that we should expect is to find certain suggestions and allusions, quite incidentally introduced, which enable us to judge whether or not John assumed that the death of Christ was sacrificial in its significance and saving in its effect. We have already indicated the answer which we think must be given to this question.

CHAPTER VIII

THE DOCTRINE OF THE HOLY SPIRIT

Literature. — WEISS : *Bibl. Theol.*, The Paraclete, ii. 405–410; *Johann. Lehrb.*, Der Paraklet, 280–285; REUSS : *Hist. Christ. Theol.*, Of the Spirit, ii. 469–481 (orig. 524–538) ; KÖSTLIN: *Johann. Lehrb.*, Geschäft des Geistes, u. s. w., 196–209; MESSNER : *Lehre d. Apostel*, Der Geist, pp. 343–345; BEYSCHLAG: *Neutest. Theol.*, Die Heilswirksamkeit des erhöhten Christus, ii. 444–446; BERNARD: *The Central Teaching of Jesus Christ* (John xiii.–xvii.), *passim ;* DODS : *The Gospel of St. John*, The Spirit Christ's Witness, ii. 205–225; EWALD : *Old and New Test. Theol.*, The Power of the Holy Spirit, pp. 324–340; BAUR: *Neutest. Theol.*, Die Mittheilung des Geistes, pp. 384–386; MAURICE : *The Gospel of St. John*, The Comforter and his Testimony, pp. 396–410; HARE : *The Mission of the Comforter*.

THE teaching concerning the nature and office of the Holy Spirit is found chiefly in chapters xiv.–xvi. of the Gospel. This teaching is the leading theme of those farewell discourses which appear to have been spoken in connection with the last supper. It was called out by the wonder and grief of the disciples at the Lord's approaching departure. Its primary object seems to have been to assure the disciples that, although he was soon to be no more with them in visible form, a substitute for his bodily presence would be given them in the indwelling Spirit. The work of the Spirit, therefore, is the final subject of his instruction, and stands connected with the completion of his own mission.

Let us first pass in review the principal designations of the Spirit, from which we shall naturally be led to consider the questions concerning his personality and work. Besides the term τὸ πνεῦμα, or τὸ πνεῦμα τὸ ἅγιον, the Spirit is designated as ὁ παράκλητος, the Paraclete, in four passages: "And I will pray the Father, and he shall give you another Comforter (ἄλλον παράκλητον), that he may abide with you forever" (xiv. 16); "But the Comforter (ὁ παράκλητος), even the Holy Spirit, whom the Father will send in my name," etc (xiv. 26); "But when the Comforter (ὁ παράκλητος) is come, whom I will send unto you from the Father," etc. (xv. 26); "If I go not away, the Comforter (ὁ παράκλητος) will not come unto you," etc. (xvi. 7).

The rendering "the Comforter," for ὁ παράκλητος, dates from Wicklif's translation, and has been perpetuated in almost all later English Bibles, including our Revised Version. It is formed from the Latin *con* and *fortis, confortare*, and means *one who strengthens*. While in these various English translations, from Wicklif's onward, παράκλητος is rendered *Comforter* in the Gospel, it is translated *Advocate* in the First Epistle (ii. 1), — a fact which is probably due to a similar variation in the rendering in several ancient versions. Although the word "Comforter" conveys very well the practical import of the Spirit's work, it cannot be

THE DOCTRINE OF THE HOLY SPIRIT

defended as an accurate translation of παράκλητος. It will not serve as a rendering in I. ii. 1, where Christ is called our παράκλητος πρὸς τὸν πατέρα; nor does it bring out the passive force of the word παράκλητος. In the passage just referred to it is evident that παράκλητος means *advocate* or *intercessor*. Now since in xiv. 16 the Holy Spirit is designated as ἄλλος παράκλητος, — that is, since the Holy Spirit is a Paraclete as really as Christ is, — it is evident that some uniform translation of παράκλητος should be adopted. The passage applies by clear implication the same designation to Christ and to the Holy Spirit, and applies it in the same sense. The word should, therefore, be rendered, in both applications of it, in the same way. Furthermore, the word παράκλητος is passive in termination; it means one who is called in to the side of another, and, in usage, one who is called to counsel or help. In its classic use it is applied to an advocate in a case at law, especially to the advocate for the defence.[1] From these considerations it is evident that the term is best translated *Advocate* or *Helper* (margin, R. V.). This translation, no less than the other, implies the positive, active work of the Spirit, since it portrays him as One who pleads the Christian's cause, instructs him in the truth of Christ, and accuses and convicts the world of sin.

Another kindred designation for the Spirit is "the Spirit of truth" (τὸ πνεῦμα τῆς ἀληθείας) (xiv. 17 ; xv.

[1] *Cf.* the Commentaries of Westcott and Lange, on John xiv. 16.

26; xvi. 13; *cf.* I. iv. 6; v. 7). The phrase denotes the Spirit who belongs to the truth in such a sense that he is its possessor, bearer, and mediator. The passages just cited set its meaning in clear light. As "the Spirit of truth" the evil world does not receive or know him (xiv. 17), because it has no spiritual affinity for "the truth" which Jesus has revealed, and which the Spirit seeks to make effective in human life. Again, he is "the Spirit of truth" because he bears witness of Christ to the disciples, that is, interprets and enforces the teaching of Jesus, and fosters in them the life which corresponds to it (xv. 26). Even more explicitly is the function of the Spirit of truth defined in xvi. 13 *sq.*, where it is said that he shall guide the disciples "into all the truth" ($\epsilon\dot{\iota}\varsigma$ $\tau\dot{\eta}\nu$ $\dot{a}\lambda\acute{\eta}\theta\epsilon\iota a\nu$ $\pi\hat{a}\sigma a\nu$), that is, into the knowledge and experience of that specific truth which Jesus reveals and embodies in his own person (*cf.* xiv. 6). The truth as Jesus proclaimed and illustrated it, the truth as matter not of knowledge only, but of conduct and life (iii. 21; II. 4), is the sphere of the Spirit's work. His work is, therefore, set in the closest connection with the work of Christ in the world, since in unseen but effective ways he continues to interpret and apply his truth, and to make men feel the need and the blessing of its possession.

Of the two terms descriptive of the Spirit which we have reviewed, the former is more general, designating him as our Helper, but not describing the nature or method of his help; the latter is more specific, and indicates the means by which his work for men is accomplished. "Paraclete" is a legal term, and the relations which it implies need to be understood in the light of what is said of the Spirit of truth and of the relation in which his ministry stands to the work of Christ. But before entering further upon this topic, it is necessary to discuss the question whether *the Spirit* in John designates an impersonal principle or a distinct personality.

Many scholars have called in question the current view that by the Holy Spirit in our sources is meant a self distinct from Christ, and have asserted that under this term we must understand Christ himself glorified into a spirit, or the spiritual presence and manifestation of Christ to his disciples after his departure from earth.[1] The principal exegetical considerations which are urged in support of this view are the following: In close connection with the promise of the Spirit's coming, and as apparently identical with it, Jesus mentions his own coming to his disciples, "I will not leave you desolate (ὀρφανούς): I come to you" (xiv. 18). This promise, it is said, must refer to his own spiritual presence with his followers to the end of time; "it follows that these are not two distinct and different manifestations, but that what is said of the Paraclete is a theological formula by which the idea of the relation between Christ and the believer is analyzed and changed into a hypos-

[1] So Tholuck, *Commentary on John, ad loc.* xiv. 16; Reuss, *Hist. Christ. Theol.*, ii. 469 *sq.* (orig. ii. 524 *sq.*).

tasis" (Reuss). To the same purport is the assurance that they shall soon see him again (xiv. 19; xvi. 16). Moreover, after his resurrection, Jesus, on one occasion, breathed on his disciples and said: Receive ye the Holy Spirit (xx. 22). This, it is said, was a symbolic act in which Jesus conferred on them a power from himself, a principle of spiritual life which was derived from his own invisible presence with them. The Spirit is identical with himself. Appeal is also made to I. ii. 27, 28, where "the anointing" (τὸ χρῖσμα), that is, the bestowment of the Spirit, is closely associated with Christ's own promised manifestation. Before discussing the bearing of these passages upon our subject, let us review the exegetical arguments which are presented in support of the view that the Spirit is conceived of in the discourses of chapters xiv.-xvi. as a personality distinct from Christ.

We direct attention, first, to those passages in which the Holy Spirit is expressly distinguished from Christ. He is described as ἄλλος παράκλητος, "another Advocate" (xiv. 16). Christ was an Advocate; the Holy Spirit will be another, distinct from Christ and supplying his place, as the term ἄλλος, which designates a distinction of persons, necessarily implies. Again, it is said that the Father will send the Holy Spirit in Christ's name, and that he will bring to the remembrance of the disciples what Christ has taught (xiv. 26). Here the Spirit is clearly distinguished from Christ. Similarly in xv. 26 Jesus says that he will send the Paraclete from the Father, and adds: "He shall bear witness of me" (περὶ ἐμοῦ). To the same effect is the repeated assertion that the Spirit shall take of that which is Christ's — that is, his truth — and shall declare it unto the disciples (xvi. 14, 15). How could the distinction of personalities be more clearly marked than by the juxtaposition of the two emphatic pronouns which we observe in this passage: ἐκεῖνος ἐμὲ δοξάσει, "Me shall he (the Spirit) glorify" (xvi. 14). Even more explicitly, if possible, does Jesus distinguish the Spirit from himself in the words, "It is expedient for you that I go away: for if I go not away, the Paraclete will not come unto you; but if I go, I will send him unto you" (xvi. 7).

Let us next observe the use of pronouns in connection with the passages just noticed. Since the word πνεῦμα is grammatically neuter, all pronominal designations of the Spirit which have πνεῦμα for their immediate antecedent must, of course, be neuter. These words obviously have no bearing upon the question of the personality of the Spirit.[1] That which is of especial importance in this connection is that as soon as πνεῦμα ceases to be the *immediate* antecedent of pronouns designating the Spirit, masculine forms

[1] The neuter relative ὅ, which occurs three times with πνεῦμα for its antecedent (xiv. 17, 26; xv. 26), is rendered "whom" in both our versions except in the last instance (xv. 26), where it is rendered "which," no doubt to distinguish it from the immediately preceding ὅν, which has ὁ παράκλητος for its antecedent. Similarly is αὐτό rendered "him" in xiv. 17 where it occurs twice, referring to πνεῦμα.

are employed. In xiv. 26, for example, we read: τὸ πνεῦμα τὸ ἅγιον ὃ πέμψει ὁ πατὴρ ἐν τῷ ὀνόματί μου, ἐκεῖνος ὑμᾶς διδάξει πάντα, κ. τ. λ. The force of the change of pronouns may be exhibited in English thus: "the Holy Spirit *which* (ὅ) the Father will send in my name, *he* (ἐκεῖνος) shall teach you all things," etc. The same usage is observed in xv. 26: τὸ πνεῦμα τῆς ἀληθείας ὃ παρὰ τοῦ πατρὸς ἐκπορεύεται, ἐκεῖνος μαρτυρήσει περὶ ἐμοῦ, which we may render thus: "the Spirit of truth, *which* (ὅ) proceedeth from the Father, *he* (ἐκεῖνος) shall bear witness of me." It is obvious that, in John's usage, as soon as the necessity of referring to the Spirit by neuter pronouns which arises from the immediate antecedence of τὸ πνεῦμα, is removed, he instinctively adopts masculine designations. Accordingly in all the passages where the neuter word πνεῦμα is not used, we find the masculine pronouns αὐτός and ἐκεῖνος employed (xvi. 7, 8, 13, 14). In the first of these passages (xvi. 7, 8) the pronouns αὐτόν and ἐκεῖνος (πέμψω αὐτὸν πρὸς ὑμᾶς. καὶ ἐλθὼν ἐκεῖνος ἐλέγξει, κ. τ. λ.) have, indeed, the noun παράκλητος for their antecedent, but in neither of the other passages is the form of the pronoun influenced by a masculine antecedent, and in one of them (xvi. 13) ἐκεῖνος is used notwithstanding the apposition to it of τὸ πνεῦμα (ὅταν δὲ ἔλθῃ ἐκεῖνος, τὸ πνεῦμα τῆς ἀληθείας). It thus appears that John, when not prevented from so doing by the grammatical gender of πνεῦμα, uniformly designates the Spirit by masculine pronouns implying personality.

THE DOCTRINE OF THE HOLY SPIRIT 197

What, now, does John predicate of the Spirit to whom he thus refers in personal terms? To the Spirit is ascribed speaking (λαλήσει, xvi. 13), teaching (διδάξει, xiv. 26), the announcing of future events and the proclamation of the truth of Christ (ἀναγγελεῖ, xvi. 13, 14), the guiding of the disciples into all the truth (of Christ) (ὁδηγήσει ὑμᾶς εἰς τὴν ἀλήθειαν πᾶσαν, xvi. 13), the bringing of the teachings of Jesus to the recollection of the disciples (ὑπομνήσει, κ. τ. λ., xiv. 26), the glorification of Christ (ἐκεῖνος ἐμὲ δοξάσει, xvi. 14), the bearing of testimony concerning Christ (μαρτυρήσει περὶ ἐμοῦ, xv. 26) which is likened, by implication, to the testimony which his disciples bear concerning him (xv. 27), and the conviction of the world concerning sin, righteousness, and judgment (ἐλέγξει, κ. τ. λ., xvi. 8). To this series of personal actions which are ascribed to the Spirit may be added the references to his always being in fellowship with the disciples (ἵνα ᾖ μεθ᾽ ὑμῶν εἰς τὸν αἰῶνα, xiv. 16), and to his abiding at their side for succor (παρ᾽ ὑμῖν μένει), and within them (καὶ ἐν ὑμῖν ἐστίν xiv. 17) as a power and inspiration. We summarize, then, the considerations which have been adduced in proof of the personality of the Spirit: (1) the Spirit is expressly distinguished from Christ; (2) he is described by personal designations; and (3) to him is ascribed a series of personal activities. We regard these considerations as decisive upon the point now at issue. Even Reuss admits that exegesis alone sustains this conclusion. He thinks it inconsistent with "practical logic," and therefore deems it necessary to seek some explanation of the way in which John was led into this inconsistency. He declares that "the solution of the problem (as to the personality of the Spirit) does not belong to exegesis."[1] As we are here concerned primarily with the exegesis of the text, while Reuss is chiefly concerned with an effort to explain the alleged misconceptions which the text presents, we may decline to follow this author on his *a priori* road. He finds, however, in the text itself, as we indicated on an earlier page (p. 193), traces of the true, rational idea that the Spirit is "a power, a manifestation, a quality." There are thus, in his view, two inconsistent representations respecting the nature of the Spirit. One of these accords with practical logic; the other is a speculative idea whose motive is to be accounted for. Let us turn again to the principal passages which present, in the judgment of Reuss, the tenable view that the Spirit is an impersonal force, and test their alleged inconsistency with those which so clearly describe the Spirit as personal.

We think there can be no doubt that the passages which presuppose the distinct personality of the Spirit are much more explicit than those which have been supposed to imply the opposite idea. We might therefore justly appeal to these clearer and more numerous passages as furnishing the norm for the interpretation of those which are more vague and

[1] *Hist. Christ. Theol.*, ii. 472 (orig. ii. 527).

indefinite. Let us, however, review the latter set of passages, and see what is the nature of the alleged inconsistency between them and those which we have just examined. One of the most important of these is xiv. 18, 19: "I will not leave you desolate: I come unto you. Yet a little while, and the world beholdeth me no more; but ye behold me," etc. Interpreters are divided on the question, To what event do the *coming* and *beholding* here spoken of refer? Some (as Augustine and Hofmann) suppose that the parousia is meant; others (as Weiss and Holtzmann) find here a reference to the appearance of Jesus after the resurrection. On neither of these views can the passage come into any possible conflict with those which describe the personality of the Spirit, since no reference to the Spirit is made. The more common and, I think, the preferable view, however, is that the *coming* spoken of is the coming of Christ to his disciples through the Spirit, and that the *beholding* is the spiritual vision of Christ which is involved in their communion with him through the operation of the Spirit (so Lücke, Tholuck, Meyer, Godet, Plummer). Many interpreters have attempted a combination of these last two views (as DeWette, Lange, Ebrard, Westcott), — an effort which leads, I think, to no clear and satisfactory result.

Assuming, then, the correctness of the third interpretation, does it involve any inconsistency between this passage and the idea of the personality of the Spirit? Since the Spirit comes, as we have seen, as the continuator of Christ's work in the world, and has it for his mission to interpret and apply Christ's truth and to quicken and foster in men the life which corresponds to that truth, Christ himself may fitly be said to come to his disciples, only in another form of manifestation, in the coming of the Spirit. His promise to come to them (in the Spirit) is made in contrast to the idea entertained by them that, in withdrawing his bodily presence, he might abandon them altogether. In saying: "I come unto you" the emphasis does not lie upon the strict identity in respect to the form of manifestation of the "I" who is coming and the "I" who is speaking, but, as the parallelism shows, upon the certainty that they will not be deserted by him when he withdraws from their sight. "I come to you" is the positive equivalent of the negative: "I will not leave you desolate." The emphasis lies, therefore, upon the certainty that he will be with them still, and not upon any assertion that he will be with them in the same manner or form as he has been. It is only by a misplaced emphasis that the passage can be made inconsistent with the idea of a distinction between Christ and the Spirit. The same remarks, substantially, apply to xvi. 16: "A little while, and ye behold me no more; and again a little while and ye shall see me," and to xvi. 22: "But I will see you again, and your heart shall rejoice," etc., provided they be interpreted as referring to the mission of the Paraclete. The interpre-

THE DOCTRINE OF THE HOLY SPIRIT 201

tation of xiv. 18 is, of course, determining for these verses.[1]

Whatever view be taken of the meaning in detail of the passage which describes Jesus as breathing on his disciples and saying, "Receive ye the Holy Spirit" (xx. 22), and of its relation to the scene at Pentecost, it furnishes no just objection to the view that between Christ and the Holy Spirit a distinction is implied. Even if, as Reuss supposes,[2] the scene presents a parallel to the narrative in Genesis (ii. 7) which describes Jehovah as breathing into the nostrils of man the breath of life, it would by no means necessarily follow that the Holy Spirit designates here Christ's own spirit, subjectively considered, and is undistinguishable from his own person. If the distinction is well founded upon other clear passages, it is applicable here without violence to the passage.

[1] There is almost as much variation of opinion respecting the *coming* referred to in xiv. 3, "I come again, and will receive you unto myself," as in respect to the *coming* spoken of in the later verses which we have just reviewed. Some refer it to his spiritual personal presence (De Wette, Scholten, Keim); some to the coming of the Paraclete (Lücke, Olshausen, Neander, Godet); others to the coming of Christ at the death of his disciples (Reuss, Tholuck, Lange, Holtzmann); and still others to the personal second advent of Christ (Frommann, Hofmann, Lechler, Meyer, Weiss). This last interpretation harmonizes best with the immediate context, which speaks of Christ's going away to prepare a place for his disciples, and of his taking them unto himself at his coming; only upon the second of the views above mentioned could the passage have any direct bearing upon our subject.

[2] *Hist. Christ. Theol.*, ii. 480 (orig. ii. 537).

Concerning the last of the passages which we shall examine in this connection (I. ii. 27, 28) Reuss says: "See, again, the passage which says distinctly: 'The anointing which ye received' (that is to say, the Spirit, or the Paraclete) 'teacheth you concerning all things. And now abide in him, that if he shall be be manifested, we may have boldness, and not be ashamed before him at his coming.' Evidently here, he whose coming was expected and the Paraclete are one and the same person. If this be so, it is natural that the action of the Paraclete should be represented sometimes as personal, sometimes as impersonal; and in the former case, sometimes as distinct from that of Christ, sometimes as one with it."[1] This does not seem to me to be an accurate statement. In the first place, the abbreviation of the passage by Reuss brings the idea of the anointing and that of Christ's appearing into closer proximity than that in which they actually stand in the passage. Again, in the context of our passage the "anointing" is clearly distinguished from Christ from whom it comes: "And ye have an anointing ($\chi\rho\hat{\iota}\sigma\mu\alpha$) from the Holy One" ($\dot{\alpha}\pi\grave{o}\ \tau o\hat{v}\ \dot{\alpha}\gamma\acute{\iota}ov$), (I. ii. 20), provided, as seems almost certain, "the Holy One" be understood to refer to Christ. (So Rothe, Haupt, Huther, Westcott, Plummer and Holtzmann, vs. Neander and Weiss, who refer the words to God.) The language of the verses in question is in no respect unfavorable to the same distinction. It is true that the anointing, the gift or

[1] *Op. cit.* ii. 479, 480 (orig. ii. 536, 537).

THE DOCTRINE OF THE HOLY SPIRIT 203

grace of the Spirit, is closely associated in idea with abiding in Christ, and with preparedness for his parousia, but it is also to be noticed that the chrism is said to have been *received* from Christ, and is not identified with him. There is throughout the passage, as so commonly in the Epistle (*cf.*, *e. g.*, iii. 2, 3), a use of pronouns which is grammatically ambiguous, and an abrupt transition from one subject to another, but there is no confusion of the Spirit with Christ. Even if τὸ χρῖσμα (personified) be regarded as the subject of ἐδίδαξεν, there can be no doubt that the following ἐν αὐτῷ refers to Christ, and that he is the subject of all that is said in the following verse (28). We conclude that the close association of the gift and work of the Spirit with the ideas of abiding in Christ and of readiness for Christ's coming, can give no ground whatever for denying or doubting the distinction between Christ and the Spirit which is elsewhere so explicitly affirmed. Reuss, indeed, candidly admits that "literal exegesis pleads for the distinction of persons," and that "speculative reason admits and sanctions it; but (he adds) practical logic demurs."[1] We are here concerned with exegesis, and it is no presumption to maintain that the results of exegesis must be abandoned, and an *a priori* method of dealing with the subject must be adopted by him who would call in question the personality of the Spirit.

Let us now turn from the question of the nature to that of the mission and work of the Holy Spirit. For

[1] *Op. cit.* ii. 478 (orig. ii. 534).

this purpose we must review several of the passages already examined, but from a different point of view. Three points require to be considered: (1) the relation of the Spirit to the historical work of Christ; (2) the work of the Spirit in believers; and (3) his work in the unbelieving world.

Under the first head we notice that God sends the Spirit in Christ's name (ἐν τῷ ὀνόματί μου, xiv. 26). The force of the expression will be appreciated by recalling the significance of the " name " in the Hebrew mode of thought. The name is the symbol of the nature, essence, and import of the thing or person which it represents. The name of Christ, therefore, stands for that which Christ *is*; it is the symbol of his saving life and power. When, then, the Spirit is said to be sent in Christ's name, the meaning is that the sphere of the Spirit's working is the same as that of Christ; that the mission of the Spirit is a part of the redemptive economy in which lie the whole purpose and meaning of Christ's work. The work of the Spirit is therefore inseparably linked to God's historic action in the redemption of mankind through Christ. "Christ's 'name'—all, that is, which can be defined as to his nature and his work—is the sphere in which the Spirit acts; and so little by little through the long life of the Church the meaning of the primitive confession 'Jesus is Lord' (Rom. x. 9; 1 Cor. xii. 3) is made more fully known."[1] " God sends the Spirit in the name of Jesus, that is, so that what the name

[1] Westcott, *Commentary, in loco.*

of Christ comprises in itself forms the sphere in which the divine thought, counsel, and will lives." It is "this name the complete saving knowledge of which, its confession, influence, glorification, etc., is to be brought about and advanced through the mission of the Spirit, as, in general, all that God has done in the carrying out of his redemptive counsel he has done ἐν Χριστῷ (Eph. i. 3 sq.)."[1]

Of kindred significance are the assertions that the Spirit shall bring to the remembrance of believers all that Jesus had said to them (xiv. 26), that he shall bear witness of the Saviour (xv. 26), guide the disciples into all the truth (xvi. 13) and glorify Christ by taking of his and declaring it unto them (xvi. 14, 15). The operation of the Spirit is wholly in the line of Christ's work on earth; it belongs to the same sphere, and contemplates the same ends. It represents a stage of the redemptive process which lies beyond the historic work of Christ; it is the continued operation of God's saving, redeeming love, interpreting, applying, and perfecting the work of the Saviour. The Spirit's work is the invisible operation of those forces and influences of divine grace which were revealed in visible manifestation in the earthly life of Jesus. This work, therefore, represents a carrying forward and completion of God's redemptive purpose. Hence the historic action of God in the work of Christ on earth must come to its close and find its fulfilment in this final stage of the great saving process. Such seems

[1] Meyer, *Commentary, in loco.*

206   THE JOHANNINE THEOLOGY

to be the import of the Saviour's words: "It is expedient for you that I go away: for if I go not away, the Paraclete will not come unto you; but if I go, I will send him unto you" (xvi. 7).

The same general conception of the Spirit's relation to the work of Jesus which meets us in these discourses, is found in the First Epistle. In contrast to the "antichrists" (ii. 18) who deny the Messiahship and incarnation of Jesus, and who have gone forth out of the Church, the true and faithful Christians are said to "have an anointing from the Holy One" and to "know all things" (ii. 20). The "all things" of this verse is synonymous with "the truth" which they are said in the next verse (21) to know, and with "all the truth" (xvi. 13), into which Jesus had said that the Spirit should guide the disciples. "The truth" is the specific truth which he came to proclaim and to embody in his own person. He not only declares the truth, but he *is* the truth (xiv. 6). The truth is the true life of fellowship with God and of likeness to him. Of this life Jesus presents the perfect type. The work of the Spirit is to teach men all things that pertain to that life, and to lead them on in a more and more perfect experience and realization of it. Since the Spirit thus continues and completes the work of Christ, it is natural that the operation of the Spirit should be in the closest manner associated with abiding in Christ: "The anointing which ye received of him abideth in you, and ye need not that any one teach you; but as his anointing teacheth you con-

THE DOCTRINE OF THE HOLY SPIRIT 207

cerning all things, and is true, and is no lie, and even as it taught you, ye abide in him " (I. ii. 27).

These passages which connect the Spirit's work with that of Christ involve to some extent the second topic to be considered, — the work of the Spirit in believers. This work is to foster the Christian life in those who receive Christ. The principal terms in which it is defined are *teaching* (xiv. 26 ; I. ii. 27), *guiding into all the truth* (xvi. 13), and *bearing witness of Christ* (xv. 26; I. v. 7). The faith of the first believers was largely due to the visible presence of Jesus with them. Because they saw and heard him and witnessed his miracles, they were led to trust in him. It was the purpose of Jesus that men should be brought more and more to ground their faith, not upon signs or miracles or the impression made by his visible presence, but upon that which he *taught* and *was*. Those who believed on him because they beheld the signs which he did, Jesus himself did not confidently trust (ii. 23–25). It was necessary that the faith of men be founded upon deeper and more enduring reasons. Only the experience of the joy and richness of the new spiritual life, only the certainty which the living fellowship with God imparts, can supply an immovable foundation for faith. Hence Jesus said to Thomas : " Because thou hast seen me thou hast believed : blessed are they that have not seen, and yet have believed " (xx. 29).

We are to read the statements concerning the work of the Spirit in the light of these ideas. Certain defects in the faith of the disciples were connected with their inborn prejudices and misunderstandings, and even with their attachment to his own person. Faith must become larger, deeper, more spiritual. It must rest upon more adequate grounds. It must be fortified by richer experience. It must penetrate beneath the surface of Christ's person, to his very heart, and must draw its life from his own inmost, divine life. This could only happen by his departing from them. For this reason, he said, his departure was expedient, for if he went not away the Paraclete would not come to them (xvi. 7). He seems to mean that while he is present with them, a veil of sense hangs before their eyes and prevents them from seeing the deepest things of his gospel.[1] Only under the guidance of the Spirit can they live their way into an appreciation of these. Under this guidance his truth shall open to them its hidden depths; it shall disclose its inner meanings; it shall assert in their lives its inherent power. Their traditional prejudices shall gradually give way; their failures to comprehend his mission and to learn the nature of his kingdom shall be overcome; they shall cease to know Christ after the flesh. The narrow limitations which their Jewish training led them to set to his work shall be broken

[1] "So long as he continued with them, they lived by sight, rather than by faith; and sight disturbs faith, and shakes it, and weakens it. Sight, as belonging to the world of sense, partakes its frailties and imperfections. To put forth all its power, faith must be purely and wholly faith." — HARE: *The Mission of the Comforter*, p. 140.

THE DOCTRINE OF THE HOLY SPIRIT

down and the world-wide significance of his mission and kingdom shall appear.

The whole history of the apostolic age is an illustration and fulfilment of the promise of Jesus concerning the work of the Spirit. The slow but certain process by which his truth and kingdom burst the bonds of Jewish particularism and asserted their universal significance and destination; the gradual enlightenment of the minds of the apostles whereby they were led to see that God is no respecter of persons; the providential opening of the door of faith to the Gentiles; and the matchless missionary career of that champion of a universal gospel, the apostle Paul, — are proofs of the Spirit's presence and power in guiding the disciples into all Christ's truth and in revealing to them its true import for themselves and for the world.

No less marked was the work of the Spirit in deepening the personal lives of those men. How many illustrations do the gospels give us of the utter failure and inability of the first disciples to understand their Master's words. "Are ye so without understanding also?" (Mark vii. 18) was his sorrowful rejoinder to them when they asked the meaning of one of his plainest lessons. When he portrayed the nature of his kingship John tells us that his disciples did not understand his meaning (xii. 16), and he himself asserted that he had many things to tell them which as yet they could not bear (xvi. 12). The author of the writings which we are studying is a striking illustration of the Spirit's influence in deepening the first disciples' understanding of the person and truth of Jesus. Like the others he at first looked for an earthly kingdom, to be founded and extended by force (Luke ix. 54); his views of the aim of the gospel were as inadequate as those of his associates; his appreciation of his Master's spiritual truth was as defective. Yet it was he who gave us that interpretation of the gospel which has been aptly called "the heart of Christ." No other mind has risen to conceptions so broad, so lofty, and so purely spiritual concerning the great themes of religion. His conception of God's nature is the sublimest which the New Testament anywhere presents; his insight into the depths of Jesus' person and teaching is the profoundest; and to his thought the gospel is as wide and all-embracing as the needs of man and as the love of God which gave it birth. It is utter folly to attempt to explain the matchless splendor of these conceptions apart from the working of that promised Spirit which unsealed the heavenly secrets of Christ to the mind of his beloved disciple.[1]

Our third and final topic is the relation of the Holy Spirit to the unbelieving world. This relation is most fully set forth in xvi. 8–11 : " And he (the Paraclete), when he is come, will convict the world in respect of

[1] Fitly, therefore, did the mediæval church, in its effort to express this heavenward flight of the apostle's spirit, adopt as his symbol the eagle soaring against the sun. This conception finds expression in the noble hymn, commonly attributed to

sin, and of righteousness, and of judgment: of sin, because they believe not on me; of righteousness, because I go to the Father, and ye behold me no more; of judgment, because the prince of this world hath been judged." Several particular points connected with the passage require brief mention before its import as a whole is considered. The word ἐλέγξει should be rendered *will convince* or *convict* (R. V.), instead of *will reprove* (A. V.), which is too weak a translation. The term is a legal one. The Spirit is represented as having a controversy, so to speak, with the world respecting sin, righteousness, and judgment; and the Spirit asserts and maintains his true view as against the world's false view. The Spirit sets the world clearly in the wrong, that is, *convinces* it in respect to the matters of difference, and pronounces the world's guilt in consequence, that is, *convicts* it. Both the ideas of *convincing* and *convicting* are, no doubt, involved in ἐλέγξει, but I am of opinion that the condemnatory idea expressed by *convict* is rather secondary than primary, and that *will convince* is the best available English translation.

The rendering of the preposition περί by "of"

Adam of St. Victor, a stanza of which we here quote in the original and in Dr. Washburn's translation: —

Volat avis sina meta	Bird of God! with boundless flight
Quo nec vates nec propheta	Soaring far beyond the height
Evolavit altius;	Of the bard or prophet old;
Tam implenda, tam impleta,	Truth fulfilled, and truth to be, —
Nunquam vidit tot secreta	Never purer mystery
Purus homo purius.	Did a purer tongue unfold.

in the A. V. did much to obscure the sense of the passage. The meaning is not merely that the Spirit will, in general, convince the world of its sin, of the true righteousness, etc., but that in respect to the matter of sin, etc., the Spirit will work a certain special conviction by certain special means. The ὅτι clauses of verses 9–11 explain the special manner or means of the convincing in respect to sin, righteousness, and judgment. Some interpreters assign to ὅτι in these clauses a simple causal meaning, and connect them with the verb ἐλέγξει, and thus the sense would be (to take one example): He will convince the world concerning sin *because* of its unbelief. Others make ὅτι mean *so far as*, and treat the ὅτι clauses as more exact definitions of the preceding nouns (ἁμαρτίας, κ. τ. λ.); for example: He will convince the world concerning sin in so far as they do not believe on me. The former is simpler and more natural, and I shall proceed upon that view of their force.

While there are scarcely any generic differences among critical interpreters in regard to the meaning of this passage, there are considerable variations in respect to emphasis and to the scope of its terms. Speaking very generally we may say that there is a narrower, and a broader view of its meaning. The narrower view holds the terms of the passage in close relation to the person of Jesus. It is the specific sin of rejecting him of which the Spirit convinces the world; it is his personal righteousness which the Spirit vindicates; it is as the enemy of his work and kingdom that the Spirit proves Satan to have been judged. This mode of treating the passage, which limits the terms more closely, is illustrated in the comments of Meyer and Weiss. This view of the passage is certainly just as against those loose and vague interpretations which explain "sin," "righteousness" and "judgment" almost without reference to the special explanatory statements of verses 9-11. The older theologians, for example, explained "sin" as sin in general as a condition of condemnation, and " righteousness," as justification by faith, or even as imputed righteousness. But without falling into these inaccuracies, many interpreters, like Godet and Westcott, assign a larger sense to the terms than that which we have just described. My judgment is that strict exegesis requires us to adhere to the more specific reference of the words, but we do not thereby limit the wider ranges of truth which they suggest and involve.[1] The meaning of the passage, taking its three subjects in order, seems to be: The sinful world rejects Christ; in this it is contrary to truth and right. The Spirit in his work will take up the cause of truth and right, and set the world clearly in the wrong in this matter of refusing to believe on Christ. The Spirit will prove the world to be in the wrong in this matter, *just because* it is in the wrong; that is, the Spirit will take the world in its wrong attitude

[1] The larger bearings of the passage, without carelessness of exegesis, are admirably set forth in Hare's *Mission of the Comforter*.

toward Christ and show it that it *is* wrong; the Spirit will disclose to the world the real nature of its opposition to Christ *as sin*. The passage treats, in this part of it, primarily and directly of the sin of rejecting Christ and his mission, and of the fact that the Spirit will convince the world that in so rejecting him it was in the wrong, and will convict it of its guilt in consequence. By analogy, however, the passage may be applied to the relation of unbelief to sin in general, as by Westcott: " The want of belief in Christ, when he is made known, lies at the root of all sin, and reveals its nature. . . . The Spirit therefore starts from the fact of unbelief in the Son of Man, and through that lays open what sin is." [1]

The second proposition of the passage is more difficult: The Spirit will convince the world concerning righteousness, because Jesus is going to the Father, and the disciples will see him no more. If the sin which the previous indictment contemplates is primarily the sin of rejecting Christ, the righteousness in question here is probably the righteousness of Christ. The world has deemed him unrighteous, and has put him to death as such. The Spirit will prove that he was righteous, and will put the world in the wrong. This the Spirit will do by appeal to Christ's ascension and glorification. The withdrawal of his visible presence from them is the condition of the Spirit's coming and work (xvi. 7), and the ascension to heaven is the perfect vindication of his mission. These

[1] *Commentary, in loco.*

facts the Spirit can, as we may say, urge against the world's view of Christ's character. When the Father takes him to his side, and when the hindrances — such as prejudice, disappointment, and personal antipathy — to a just appreciation of him which have been incidental to his visible presence among them are withdrawn, then it will appear that the world misjudged him. If the strict demands of exegesis yield this more limited sense of the words, it is not thereby denied that they suggest, and are legitimately applied to, the true *idea* of righteousness as represented in the life of Jesus. This application of them is made by President Dwight: "The Spirit, while laying hold upon and pressing the fact that Christ goes away to the Father, so that he is seen no more, — that is, the great consummation of his work in the ascension to heaven, — will convince the world of his idea of righteousness: that righteousness consists in the union of the heart with God, the entrance to which is through faith." [1]

The third element in the conviction of the world by the Spirit is in respect to judgment. The Spirit will prove to the world that its prince stands condemned ($\kappa\acute{\epsilon}\kappa\rho\iota\tau\alpha\iota$). This result is viewed as already accomplished when Jesus spoke. The work of Jesus is the victory over Satan. "Now," he says as he contemplates its completion, "now is the judgment of this world: now shall the prince of this world be

[1] Notes added to the American edition of Godet's *Commentary*, ii. 514.

cast out" (xii. 31). The finished work of Jesus involves the final sentence of him in whom the spirit of opposition to himself is concentrated; the Spirit will affirm and justify that sentence and so in the matter of judgment convince the world.

In what manner is this work of the Spirit effected? Is it by his direct operation upon the hearts of unbelieving men, or indirectly, through the testimony and teaching of believers? The indications point to the latter as the method which the passage contemplates. The work of the Spirit in question is described in immediate connection with the statement that he will be sent to the disciples ($\pi\rho\grave{o}s$ $\dot{v}\mu\hat{a}s$, verse 7). The phrase: "When he is come" ($\ddot{\epsilon}\lambda\theta\omega\nu$) in verse 8 clearly refers back to the *coming* to the disciples ($\dot{\epsilon}\lambda\epsilon\dot{v}\sigma\epsilon\tau\alpha\iota$) spoken of in verse 7. The specific conviction of the world which our passage describes is wrought through the instrumentality of the disciples in whom the Spirit dwells. The illustration or proof of it which lies nearest at hand is found in the successful preaching of the apostles. Nothing is here said as to how far the world will acknowledge itself to be in the wrong respecting sin, righteousness, and judgment. According as it does or does not acknowledge the truth of the Spirit's indictment against it, is the way open to faith and conversion, or to increased unbelief and moral hardening. In understanding, with most interpreters, that the conviction of the world in question is conceived of as wrought mediately through believers, we in no way call in question the universal operation of the Holy Spirit upon mankind; especially is this the case if the more specific interpretation of the Spirit's ἔλεγξις be adopted. The considerations which favor the view of the Spirit's work here described, as mediated through believers, are favorable to the more specific reference of the passage as a whole.

CHAPTER IX

THE APPROPRIATION OF SALVATION

Literature. — REUSS: *Hist. Christ. Theol.*, Of Faith, ii. 455–468 (orig. ii. 508–524); WEISS: *Johann. Lehrb.*, Der Begriff des Glaubens, pp. 18–28, and *Bibl. Theol.*, Faith and Fellowship with Christ, ii. 363–370 (orig. 626–632); WENDT: *Teaching of Jesus*, Faith in Jesus according to the Johannine Discourses, ii. 329–339 (orig. 595–602); FROMMANN: *Johann. Lehrb.*, Aneignung des Heils, u. s. w., p. 548 *sq.*, especially pp. 551–563; BEYSCHLAG: *Neutest. Theol.*, Der Glaube, u. s. w., ii. 447–452; NEANDER: *Planting and Training*, Faith as the Principle of a New Life, ii. 41–47 (Bohn ed.).

SALVATION is appropriated by faith. We accordingly turn to a study of its nature and contents. The word *faith* (πίστις) does not occur in the Fourth Gospel, and is found only once in the Epistles (I. v. 4). The verb *to believe* (πιστεύειν) is, however, one of the commonest words in our sources, occurring more than one hundred times. There is no lack of emphasis, therefore, upon the idea of faith in John's writings. We shall soon see that the conception of faith is not so uniform and definite in John as in Paul and the Epistle to the Hebrews. I do not think that any definition of faith could be framed which would adequately cover all the shades of meaning and variety

THE APPROPRIATION OF SALVATION 219

of emphasis in which John employs the word. It naturally results from this variation in usage that interpreters differ considerably in their judgment as to the central and characteristic idea in John's doctrine of faith. It will be our first task to illustrate this variety by studying the uses of the terms in question.

There are numerous passages in which πιστεύειν is used in the sense of believing that a thing is true. It is assent to a proposition, a *Fürwahrhalten*. Thus the apostle states that his aim in writing the Gospel was that his readers might "believe that Jesus was the Christ, the Son of God," although he immediately carries us beyond the idea of mere theoretic assent by adding: "and that believing ye may have life in his name" (xx. 31). In the First Epistle, where the writer is refuting and condemning that false gnosis which denied the true incarnation and saving work of the Son of God, he represents faith as the opposite of this denial: "Whosoever believeth that Jesus is the Christ is begotten of God" (I. v. 1). This belief is the "confession" (ii. 22; iv. 15) of Jesus as the Son of God in contrast to the antichristian spirit of denial. In this connection, therefore, faith is an affirmation. Similarly in xi. 27 Martha asserts her faith in the words: "I have believed that thou art the Christ, the Son of God, even he that cometh into the world;" and in his highpriestly prayer Jesus asks that his disciples may be one, in order that the world may believe that the

Father sent him (xvii. 21). We can only justly estimate the full religious significance and contents of this assent to Jesus' sonship to God and mission to the world after we have passed in review other classes of passages.

In several places *to believe* means to credit some word or assertion or to accept the testimony of some person. After the resurrection, the disciples are said to have remembered the saying of Jesus, "Destroy this temple, and in three days I will raise it up," "and they believed the scripture, and the word which Jesus had said" (ii. 22). Jesus declares to the Jews: "If ye believed Moses, ye would believe me; for he wrote of me. But if ye believe not his writings, how shall ye believe my words?" (v. 46, 47). Again, he accuses the Jews of not believing him just because he speaks to them the truth (viii. 45, 46); and elsewhere he tells them that even if they give no credence to him they should "believe the works," that is, should admit the truth of the testimony which is contained in his miracles (x. 37, 38). It is obvious that in all the passages thus far cited, the intellectual aspect of faith is placed in the foreground. Whatever more may be fairly implied in consequence of the nature of the truths believed in, these passages speak of an assent of the mind to certain statements or testimony. To believe — in the sense of these passages — is to hold for true the statement that Jesus is the Son of God, or to cherish the conviction that his teaching is true.

THE APPROPRIATION OF SALVATION   221

In close connection with this set of passages should be placed another, in which Jesus distinctly recognizes a gradation in faith as respects its religious significance and value. Some reason will be found for the view that faith is conceived of in the Fourth Gospel as a development having its incipient and defective stages, when it reposes upon inadequate grounds, and advancing toward perfection as it comes to rest more completely upon the best and deepest reasons. An illustration is found in the conversation between Jesus and Nathanael (i. 47–51). The latter is astonished at Jesus' supernatural knowledge of himself, and at once confesses him as the Son of God and King of Israel. "Jesus answered and said unto him, Because I said unto thee, I saw thee underneath the fig tree, believest thou ? thou shalt see greater things than these." The meaning is, that his penetration into Nathanael's thoughts is a slender basis for faith in himself, and that a faith so supported must be correspondingly deficient. More adequate grounds for his faith will be disclosed as time goes on, when he shall see how Jesus lives in constant intercourse with God his Father,— symbolically described under the figure of angels ascending from him into the open heavens, and descending thence upon him in ministries of comfort. Another illustration is found in the fact that many Jews in Jerusalem at the passover "believed on his name (ἐπίστευσαν εἰς τὸ ὄνομα αὐτοῦ), beholding his signs which he did." "But," adds the apostle, "Jesus did not trust himself unto them," —

did not yield his confidence to them (αὐτὸς δὲ ᾽Ιησοῦς οὐκ ἐπίστευεν αὐτὸν αὐτοῖς, ii. 23, 24). Why ? Because the greatest element of their belief was mere wonder at his miracles. Their faith was based upon no proper appreciation of his person and work. It was wanting, therefore, in real spiritual power; it rested upon deficient grounds, and was itself correspondingly defective. The point which the apostle emphasizes by the play on the word πιστεύειν may be partially brought out by rendering : They believed on him, but he did not believe in them, for he knew the real super · ficiality of their professed faith.

A gradation in the quality of faith corresponding to the character of its grounds, is recognized in the narrative concerning the belief of the Samaritan woman and her neighbors (iv. 39–42). Many of her acquaintances " believed on him" on the basis of her statement respecting the supernatural knowledge of her life which he had shown. But when they afterwards, during two days, heard Jesus himself, they said to the woman, " No longer (οὐκέτι) do we believe because of thy speaking (λαλιά): for we have ourselves heard, and know that this is indeed the Saviour of the world" (iv. 42). The difference between a confidence which rested upon the testimony of another and a faith which was won from personal contact with Jesus, is here sharply emphasized. Nor would it be merely prophetic or supernatural knowledge which those with whom he abode two days would find in him. This association would inevitably give them some larger idea of his work and mission, some fuller appreciation of his personality and spirit.

A striking illustration of the fact that John presupposes a development of faith which proceeds in proportion as faith finds its truest and deepest grounds, is seen where Jesus explains to the Jews his mission and work, and chides them for their hostility to himself (viii. 12–30). "As he spake these things," says the apostle, "many believed on him" (viii. 30). But what was the nature of this faith? The following verses make the answer clear: "Jesus therefore said to those Jews which had believed him, If ye abide in my word, then are ye truly my disciples; and ye shall know the truth, and the truth shall make you free" (viii. 31, 32). Theirs certainly was a faith which was but superficial and rudimentary; it was the result of a passing impression and interest. It was scarcely more than a germ of real, enduring, saving faith. Jesus did not therefore regard it as *truly* making them his disciples, nor as yet involving the knowledge of the truth and securing the freedom which the truth bestows; this it could do only if it was completed by a continuance in his word, that is, by a thoroughgoing reception of his truth, and by a life which answered to its demands.

From those in whom the capacity for this higher and completer faith is wanting, Jesus seeks to call forth the lower kind of faith, for the lower contains the germ of the higher, and is capable of ripening into it. The expectation of the Jewish people that a very prominent part of the Messiah's work should be to do "signs and wonders" made them more susceptible to the evidence of miracles than to any other proof which Jesus gave of his divine commission. Jesus welcomed a confidence in himself which was based only upon his works, not so much for its own immediate religious value as because it might conduct in those whom it attached to himself to a true personal trust, which should be based upon adequate reasons. But he distinctly asserted the inferiority of such belief. He distinguished between believing *him* and believing his *works* (x. 38). He says, in effect, to his disciples, in allusion to their partial and defective faith: Believe on me for such reasons as you can appreciate; believe on me for what I *am*, if you can, but if miracles alone seem to you to be plain proof of divinity, believe me on account of them (xiv. 11). A faith which is based upon external evidences of his divine power is better than none, because it may ripen and deepen into a faith which grasps the divinity which speaks in his whole life and spirit, and which meets and satisfies the spiritual longings and wants of the soul; but such a faith is wanting in vitality and spiritual power, because it does not spring from what is deepest in man, or lay hold upon what is deepest in Christ.

A concrete example which illustrates a similar distinction is found in the narrative concerning the transition of Thomas from doubt to belief in regard to the reality of the Lord's appearance after the resur-

THE APPROPRIATION OF SALVATION 225

rection (xx. 24-29). Thomas demanded tangible evidence before he would believe. Jesus made this demand the occasion of laying down the great general truth, "Because thou hast seen me thou hast believed: blessed are they that have not seen and yet have believed" (verse 29). This is the beatitude of those who have never seen Christ in the flesh. A special blessing is pronounced for those who believe, though not having seen, because their faith must rest upon deeper reasons than any which can offer themselves to the senses. Such faith springs from a sense of spiritual need and from the recognition of the adaptation of Christ to satisfy it. It rests, therefore, upon grounds which lie deep in human nature, and has its motive in the clear recognition of Christ as the bread of life to the soul. A true faith thus finds itself embracing more and more that which is central in the life and person of Jesus, and depending less and less upon whatever is incidental or extraneous. Such faith rises into the heavens and finds its home in the very heart of Christ. Its true sphere is the sphere of the spirit. Though it may once have known Christ after the flesh, yet as it grows and deepens, it at last knows him so no more (2 Cor. v. 16).[1]

---

[1] The distinction which we are tracing in the Fourth Gospel between outer and inner, or sensuous and spiritual, aids to faith, Mr. Whittier has beautifully illustrated in his poem *Palestine*, the closing stanzas of which I quote: —

"And what if my feet may not tread where He stood,
Nor my ears hear the dashing of Galilee's flood,

To these illustrations of the gradual enlarging and deepening of faith may be added, in conclusion, an example which is presented quite incidentally. At the miracle in Cana of Galilee in which Jesus "manifested his glory," it is said that "his disciples believed on him" (ii. 11), — that is, entered upon a new stage of faith as they gained new assurance of his divine power and glory.

A common construction with πιστεύειν is the preposition εἰς followed by the object of faith, God, Christ, or the name of Christ. Thus in xiv. 1: "Ye believe in God (εἰς τὸν θεόν), believe also in me" (εἰς ἐμέ). The preposition designates the act and disposition denoted by πιστεύειν as terminating upon its object (i. 12; iii. 16, 18, 36; vi. 40; xii. 44). We shall have occasion later to discuss the question, what is the nature of the relation expressed by the phrase πιστεύειν εἰς. Meantime let us note in passing the connections in which several of these passages stand. In i. 12 those who "received (ἔλαβον) him" (the Word) or "believe on his name" are they to whom the

> Nor my eyes see the cross which He bowed him to bear,
> Nor my knees press Gethsemane's garden of prayer ?
>
> "Yet, Loved of the Father, thy Spirit is near
> To the meek, and the lowly, and penitent here ;
> And the voice of thy love is the same even now
> As at Bethany's tomb or on Olivet's brow.
>
> "O, the outward hath gone ! — but in glory and power,
> The *Spirit* surviveth the things of an hour;
> Unchanged, undecaying, its Pentecost flame
> On the heart's secret altar is burning the same !"

right (ἐξουσία) has been given "to become children of God." Here, evidently, faith in Christ, or the reception of him, and sonship to God are involved in each other. In iii. 36 the result of believing on the Son is declared to be eternal life, and it is implied that faith involves obedience, since the contrast to "He that believeth" is "He that obeyeth not."

In the discourse on the Bread of Life faith is several times referred to, as in vi. 35: "Jesus said unto them, I am the bread of life: he that cometh to me shall not hunger, and he that believeth on me shall never thirst." Here, believing on him and coming to him are identical, and both phrases are equivalent to the eating of the bread of life, as both the context (*cf.* verses 33, 50, 51) and the use of the figurative terms "hunger" and "thirst" in the verse itself show. In verse 40 believing on the Son is associated with beholding him, and its result is declared to be eternal life; while in verse 47 believing is clearly equivalent to coming to him (*cf.* verse 45), and is said to be the result of having heard and learned from the Father. In xii. 44–46 belief on Christ is affirmed to involve belief on God. This faith in him who is "come a light into the world" secures for its possessor the result that he does not walk in darkness. It will be necessary to recur to these ideas with which faith is associated, in a closer consideration of the nature of faith, to which our review of passages will conduct us.

In several passages πιστεύειν stands without an object and without any expressed or implied explanation (*e. g.* i. 7; iii. 12). In these cases it is obvious that it denotes the right religious attitude or disposition of the soul toward Christ. Eternal life is said to be its consequence: "He that believeth hath eternal life" (vi. 47, *cf.* iii. 15). This believing is conceived of as identical with that possession of Christ which is mentioned in the First Epistle, whose result is also "the life" (ἡ ζωή), that is, the true, eternal life: "He that hath the Son hath the life; he that hath not the Son of God hath not the life" (I. v. 12). The fact, too, that the consequence of faith is the *present* possession of eternal life — "*hath* (ἔχει) eternal life" — is not to be overlooked in considering the nature of faith. In John's view faith is certainly used in a sense sufficiently comprehensive to include all that man can do, or is required to do, in appropriating the salvation which is offered in Christ. When, therefore, the disciples asked Jesus what they must do that they might work the works of God, his answer was: "This is the work of God," — the sum of God's requirement, — "that ye believe" (note the present, ἵνα πιστεύητε, "continue to believe;" *cf.* the aorist, ἵνα πιστεύσητε, xiii. 19) "on him whom he hath sent" (vi. 28, 29).

Our review of the principal passages which bear upon the subject gives rise to the general inquiry as to the nature and contents of Christian faith as presented in our sources. The opinion of Weiss on this question is that faith in John's writings is the persuasion that Jesus is what he claims to be, the confession that he is the Christ or the Son of God. This author rejects the view that the notion of mystical union with Christ is any part of the Johannine idea of faith. " The confident persuasion that Jesus is the Son of God" is faith.[1] The result is that faith is regarded as a stage of knowledge, and we have already seen (pp. 66, 67) that Weiss seeks to exclude from the knowledge of God and of Christ every touch of mysticism. Our author, therefore, makes a sharp distinction between faith in Christ and being in Christ. " Abiding in Christ is not faith, but it presupposes faith. This abiding is the personal surrender to him in which the new relation to Christ which faith has brought about is continually completed anew with conscious self-determination."[2] It is obvious that faith is thus conceived as the subjective condition of abiding in Christ, or the condition precedent of the religious life, rather than as the actual entrance into that spiritual relation to the Redeemer. Union with Christ is a result of faith, quite distinct from it and following upon it both logically and chronologically. Faith is an intellectual assent to the claims of Jesus, a mental affirmation of the proposition: He is the Messiah or the Son of God.

It is a matter of some interest that on this point Weiss coincides with the school of Ritschl, to whose opinions in general he is so strenuously opposed.

[1] *Bibl. Theol.*, § 149 a, note 2. *Cf. Johann. Lehrbegriff*, p. 19 sq.
[2] *Bibl. Theol.*, § 149 c.

Both are at one in eliminating from faith the mystical element. This disposition may be illustrated, on the side of the school of Ritschl, by the following citations from Wendt: " In these Johannine discourses the disposition designated as that which should be shown toward the *person* of Jesus is, according to its peculiar nature, regarded as the right disposition toward his *teaching* (Verkündigung), and the faith which is required in him consists in nothing else than in the trustful and obedient recognition, reception, and following of that teaching, which revealed God, showed the right, and effected salvation, and which constitutes his Messianic calling."[1] This author, however, carries his exclusion of mysticism much farther than Weiss, and goes so far as to deny that the allegory of the Vine and the Branches (xv. 1 *sq.*), the discourse on the Bread of Life (vi. 32 *sq.*), and other passages which describe the *abiding* of his disciples in Christ, imply anything of the nature of " a mystical union of the disciples with his glorified heavenly nature. They are rather the energetic declaration of the fact that Jesus based his saving significance entirely upon the word of teaching which he, as man, exercised upon earth, and that he regarded the necessary disposition of other men towards him as consisting in the inward reception of his teaching exercised by him on earth as man." [2] In this view the idea of union with Christ is

---

[1] *Teaching of Jesus*, ii. 331 (orig. p. 597).
[2] *Ibid.*, ii. 335 (orig. pp. 599, 600).

THE APPROPRIATION OF SALVATION 231

not only excluded from faith, but it is banished altogether from Christianity; it does not even remain as a result of faith, distinct and generically different from it, as in the opinion of Weiss.

For purposes of comparison let us now set beside these anti-mystical expositions of faith in John, some examples of another mode of view. For Neander, faith is, with John as with Paul, self-surrender to Christ and entrance into communion with him. " By this faith entrance is made into fellowship with the Redeemer, and at the same time a participation obtained in his divine life. . . . According to John's conception, it is impossible to separate either faith or knowledge from the life." [1] The definition of Frommann is of similar import: "Faith presupposes the knowledge of Christ, and is a necessary consequence of it. But according to its inner nature faith is an inward, humble trust in the saving love of God which is revealed in Christ, and must accordingly express itself in a trustful obedience to the Redeemer, and in the life and conduct of men." [2]

Beyschlag has taken up this question with special reference to the opinions of Weiss.[3] He maintains that in the Johannine applications of the idea of faith the two sides, conviction and confidence or trust, are separably bound together, and that the recent opinion as held by Weiss ("If I rightly understand him,"

[1] *Planting and Training*, ii. 42, 43 (Bohn ed.).
[2] *Johann. Lehrbegriff*, p. 557.
[3] *Neutest. Theol.*, ii. 447–449.

adds Beyschlag in a note) that in distinction from Paul and the Epistle to the Hebrews, John means by faith only the conviction of the truth of the fact that Jesus is the Christ, but not trust (das Vertrauen) in God's love in Christ, is as incorrect as possible (möglichst verfehlt). "The full Johannine idea of faith is, the laying hold and appropriation of eternal life, which God offers in Jesus."[1]

Our review of the leading passages which speak of faith in the writings of John has already shown to which of these expositions we must give our adherence. The opinion of Weiss may be maintained in its application to some passages, but it cannot be made to square with others. When in the First Epistle John is contrasting faith with the spirit of antichristian denial, it is no doubt assent to the Messiahship and divine sonship of Jesus which he means by faith, although it can be shown that, in the nature of the case, faith, in that connection, also involves much besides. But to make the passages which speak of faith in ($\pi\iota\sigma\tau\epsilon\acute{\upsilon}\epsilon\iota\nu$ $\epsilon\acute{\iota}\varsigma$) Christ or in his name, and especially when they are associated with the idea of receiving him, appropriating him as the heavenly bread, or as involving the present possession of eternal life, — to make these passages, I say, refer only to a conviction of Jesus' sonship to God, is little less than preposterous. Who can believe that when Jesus said, "Ye believe in God, believe also in me" (xiv. 1) he meant, "You believe that God exists, believe also

[1] *Neutest. Theol.*, ii. 449.

that I am the Christ"? To believe is to have the Son (I. v. 12); it is to receive Jesus Christ (i. 12, 13); it is to come to the Son (vi. 35); it is to enter into the possession of eternal life (vi. 47). It is impossible that such functions and effects should be ascribed to any faith which is not in its very nature a trustful surrender of the soul to Christ, a self-renouncing acceptance of his person, and an entrance into life-fellowship with him.

It is true, as our examination of the passages has shown, that there is recognized in John an incipient or rudimentary faith which, in certain specified cases, amounted to little more than an intellectual conviction. Such was the "faith" of those who were won by miracles only, to whom Jesus would not trust himself (ii. 23, 24); such was the "faith" of the Samaritans, who believed from hearsay that Jesus had supernatural knowledge (iv. 39). But it is easy to see that this sort of "faith" is represented in the gospel as inadequate. Eternal life is never said to be the effect or reward of such faith. True faith, the believing reception of Christ as Saviour, is clearly distinguished from this mere belief or opinion. Where the *true* nature of faith is set forth, it is seen to involve the constitution of a new spiritual relation to Christ.

If the question be considered abstractly rather than exegetically, the view of Weiss does not commend itself. There lies in the very nature of the objects of faith a reason for maintaining that faith is no mere conviction, opinion, or holding for true, but also, and much more, a personal relation of sympathy and fellowship. Take, for example, the faith which is represented in the First Epistle as the confession that Jesus is the Son of God, or that he is come in the flesh (iv. 2, 15; v. 5). This confession is not a mere theoretic assent. It is also described as a confession of the Son involving the possession of the Father (ii. 22), as a receiving of the witness of God (v. 9), as a possession of the Son and an obtaining of life in consequence (v. 12), and as believing on the name of the Son of God. The apostle is clearly speaking of a faith which is the condition of the new spiritual birth, and which is the secret of the Christian's victory over the world (v. 4). As well might one maintain that to Paul's mind the earliest Christian confession of faith, "Jesus is Lord" (1 Cor. xii. 3), excludes the idea that faith in the Pauline epistles means a personal trust in Jesus Christ and an entrance into fellowship with him, as to hold that John's Christian confession, which he is upholding against those who deny it, is in any way inconsistent with the so-called mystical element in faith. Less clearly and explicitly, but not less really, than Paul, does John represent faith as the subjective principle of the new life. It stands organically related to the abiding fellowship with Christ, which constitutes the Christian life. It is the initial act, on man's part, by which he enters into that relation with Christ in which eternal life has its cause and ground.

THE APPROPRIATION OF SALVATION 235

Faith in Christ, as commonly represented in our sources, is related to abiding in Christ as the beginning is related to the continuance of any process or relation. They may be distinguished, but they cannot be separated. Faith is not a mere condition of indwelling in Christ, distinct in nature from it. It is the act of entering upon that relation whose continuance is designated in John as abiding in Christ. There is a *life* of faith as well as an *act* of faith; in other words, faith designates a permanent characteristic of the Christian life, that is, self-renouncing trust, although its significance as the initiatory act of the Christian life is that which is brought more prominently forward. Faith is commonly presented in John as the appropriation of salvation, while abiding in Christ is the realization of salvation in its development and effects. We, accordingly, distinguish these for convenience, and devote a chapter to each; but we cannot distinguish them in such a way as to imply that the believer ever passes beyond faith and leaves it behind. As truly as the Christian life is with Paul a matter of faith all the way through (Rom. i. 17), so truly is it with John a life of love and obedience, divinely implanted in man, and a constant moral victory over the world through faith (I. v. 1–4).

It remains to define more particularly the various grounds of testimony or evidence upon which Christian faith is represented in the Johannine writings as resting. Three sources of testimony are recognized which are adapted to awaken faith. The first is the word of human witnesses. John the Baptist is said to have come "for witness, that he might bear witness of the light, that all might believe through him" (i. 7), — that is, through John's testimony. Here the believing reception of the light of the Logos is regarded as mediated through the witness-bearing of John. This testimony consisted in John's asserting the pre-eminence and pre-existence of Jesus (i. 15), and the fact of the Spirit's descent upon him at his baptism (i. 32), which he witnessed, and on the basis of which he declares that Jesus is the Son of God (i. 34).

The second source of evidence is Jesus' own testimony concerning himself. His teaching springs from his direct, intimate knowledge of the things of God, and bears in itself the marks of a divine origin for those who can perceive its true meaning and character (iii. 11, *cf.* verses 20, 21). The Son penetrates the depths of the Father's will and working, and his whole mission of teaching and labor is a revelation of the Father's nature (v. 19–21). Only the Son who is in the bosom of the Father can adequately reveal him (i. 18; vi. 46), and this revelation carries its own attestation; those who have an affinity of mind for divine things believingly accept it and come to Christ (vi. 45).

But chief emphasis is laid on the testimony of God to the truth of the claims made by Jesus. Of himself, that is, apart from God, Jesus does nothing. His witness of himself is not an isolated self-witness.

THE APPROPRIATION OF SALVATION 237

The evidence which attests his claims is primarily divine. John, indeed, testified to his Messiahship, but he does not rest his case upon human testimony. His miracles also attest his divine mission, but only because they are the works which the Father gave him to accomplish. All testimony is secondary to that which God himself gives. Human attestation, his own self-witness, and the evidence of miracles are all grounded in the fact that God has set his seal upon him as the true Messiah and Saviour. Other testimony is valuable only as it accords with and reflects the direct testimony given by the Father. This testimony God has already given in the Old Testament, and the force of it appears to all who can discern the true import of Sacred Scripture in the correspondence between the person and work of Jesus and the prophetic Messianic ideal. The Jews fail to appreciate and receive this testimony because they search the Scriptures to so little purpose. Their spiritual blindness, their selfish wilfulness, their lack of love to God, their vainglorious spirit, — these are the reasons why they do not receive God's testimony concerning the Messiah and accept him (v. 30–47; *cf*. xii. 41–43).

Jesus makes his appeal to the minds and hearts of men on the ground that the Father dwells in him and speaks through him (xiv. 9, 10). He offers himself to men on the assumption that those who have the capacity and disposition to perceive God revealing himself in him will do so, and will take a practical

238 THE JOHANNINE THEOLOGY

attitude towards him which corresponds to this perception. He is, indeed, attested by works which none who came not from God could do. This species of testimony John sums up in the First Epistle in stating the three-fold witness which God has borne to Jesus: " There are three who bear witness, the Spirit, and the water, and the blood: and the three agree in one" (I. v. 8). The bestowment of the Spirit, his Messianic consecration at his baptism, and his redemptive sufferings and death, sum up into themselves the testimony by which his mission is attested. They stand out as prominent and significant features of the incarnation. The work of the Saviour is authenticated not only by the significance and attending circumstances of his baptism, which proved him to be the true Messiah and the incarnate Son of God (as the Docetic errorists whom the apostle is confuting would themselves admit), but also by his sacrificial death, and by the pouring out of the Spirit upon the early Church, both of which bear the evidence in themselves of divine saving deeds.[1] In close connection with this

---

[1] I have given what seems to me to be the probable meaning of this passage. There are, however, many differing interpretations. By some "the Spirit" is understood to mean the Spirit which descended upon him at his baptism, and by others is interpreted subjectively of Christ's own spirit. "Water and blood" are sometimes referred to the water and blood which issued from Christ's side at the crucifixion (xix. 34), but are more commonly supposed to designate the sacraments. A majority of interpreters could probably be cited for the view which I have embodied in the text.

objective testimony on which faith is founded, is the inner experience which corresponds to it. The external becomes internal, so that "he that believeth on the Son of God hath the witness in him," "and the witness is this, that God gave unto us eternal life, and this life is in his Son" (I. v. 10, 11).

Faith rests upon objective grounds; it appeals to historic facts for its justification. But it is not mere opinion respecting these facts. John never conceives of faith as consisting in a mere intellectual possession of the truths of the gospel. The whole nature embraces them, or, more exactly, faith embraces him in whom all these truths centre. Faith is neither a subjective play of feeling nor a speculative conviction or assent; it is a personal relation. It carries man out of himself, and commits him to another. It is self-renouncing trust, repose of soul in Jesus Christ. It involves, therefore, an experience which tests and proves the external grounds on which it reposes, and which gives to the soul an assured certainty of their validity. Thus faith and knowledge are seen to be, to John's mind, essentially one. Either may be called the condition of salvation (I. iv. 16 ; vi. 47 ; xvii. 3). The true knowledge of divine things is an ethical and spiritual knowledge; it is the certitude which faith begets. The mysticism of John, then, for which we contend, is not a subjective mysticism which absorbs the soul in self-contemplations and revery, but an objective and rational mysticism which lives in a world of realities, apprehends divinely revealed truth, and bases its experience upon it. It is a mysticism which feeds not upon its own feelings and fancies, but upon Christ. It involves an acceptance of him and a life of obedience to him. Its motto is: abiding in Christ.

CHAPTER X

THE ORIGIN AND NATURE OF THE SPIRITUAL LIFE

Literature. — WEISS: *Johann. Lehrb.*, Christus das Leben, und das Leben in Christo, pp. 29–41, Das Sein in Christo, u. s. w., pp. 68–85, and Die Geburt aus Gott, u. s. w., pp. 86–100; *Bibl. Theol.*, Fellowship with God and Sonship with God, ii. 371–376 (orig. 633–637); WESTCOTT: *The Epistles of St. John*, Divine Fellowship, pp. 174, 175; BAUR: *Neutest. Theol.*, Die Lehre und die Reden Jesu, u. s. w. (chs. v., vi.), pp. 372–378; WENDT: *Teaching of Jesus*, The Life-bringing Message, etc., ii. 203–211 (orig. pp. 492–498); BEYSCHLAG: *Neutest. Theol.*, Das Leben in Gott; die Gotteskindschaft, ii. 452–455; LECHLER: *Apostolic and Post-Apostolic Times*, Fellowship with the Father and with the Son, ii. 201–207 (orig. pp. 473–479); VAN OOSTERZEE, *Theol. of the New Test.*, The Son of God in relation to the World, pp. 93–100 (Pt. ii. ch. ii. § 20); SCHMID; *Bibl. Theol. of the New Test.*, Fellowship with Christ, etc., pp. 540–548.

IN the present chapter I wish to collate the principal materials for the study of John's conception of the nature and sources of the religious life and character. We have considered faith as the act by which a new relation to God is constituted. It is the subjective condition of the realization of salvation. Corresponding to faith as initiating the work of salvation from the human side, is the impartation of life from God, or the birth from above, which expresses the objective or divine side of the sinner's change of relation. Following the spiritual birth comes the spiritual life, which is described under various terms, such as fellowship with God, abiding in Christ, partaking of his body and blood, and so forth. The subject of this chapter, then, is, John's conception of this life of religion which is begotten of God in the soul. The theme stands in close connection with the idea of faith which we have already examined, and certain special sides or aspects of it will come into view in the subsequent study of the doctrines of love, prayer, and eternal life. Our present inquiry is particularly directed to ascertaining the import of such terms as, begotten from God, sonship to God, abiding in Christ, and feeding upon him.

We begin with an examination of the phrase "born" or "begotten from God," or "from above" (γεννηθῆναι ἐκ θεοῦ, ἐκ τοῦ θεοῦ, ἄνωθεν), which occurs eight times in our sources (counting the whole passage iii. 3–8, and verses in which the word is repeated, as furnishing single instances of its use). The first example of the employment of the phrase meets us in the prologue (i. 13) where a contrast is drawn between the natural and the spiritual birth. The thought is: The Word came to the Jewish people, who of right belonged to him by reason of their privileges and training, but they rejected him (verse 11). He then offered himself to any and all who would accept him, and opened to them the privilege of sonship to God (verse 12). This he did on conditions which were purely spiritual, and irrespective of natural birthright or inheritance. Not descent from the theocratic people, but acceptance of a new life from God, was his requirement. The nature of this divine impartation of life is not defined, except so far as a definition of it is implied in its contrast to natural birth or descent, and in its co-ordination with receiving Christ and believing on his name (verse 12).

Attention may here be called to the fact that the phrase in question is best rendered " begotten " rather than " born of God " except in the passage iii. 3–8, where the thought is slightly different. The A. V. rendered " born " in all cases except in I. v. 1, and 18. In the first of these passages the active participle (γεννήσαντα) occurs, which can only be translated " begat; " but notwithstanding this, the passive forms (γεγέννηται, γεγεννημένον) were rendered in one case " born," and in the other " begotten." In verse 18 two passive participles occur (γεγεννημένος and γεννηθείς), and the same inconsistency is observed in the rendering of the A. V., where no apparent reason diverted the translators from their favorite rendering ("born"), as was the case in verse 1. The R. V. has correctly translated the terms by " begotten " in all cases in the First Epistle, but in i. 13 has rendered " born " (" begotten " in the margin), probably in view of the passage iii. 3–8. The correct translation here (i. 13) is " begotten," since the thought relates primarily to the first origin of life, and not to a change in the sphere or mode of life. The phrase γεννηθῆναι ἐκ θεοῦ in this passage, and uniformly in the First Epistle, refers to the initiation of spiritual life from God, to a divine begetting or impartation of life. The force of the phrase is amply illustrated in the First Epistle.

In I. ii. 29, the habitual doing of righteousness is said to be the test which determines whether or not one is begotten of God: "If ye know that he [God] is righteous, ye know that every one also that doeth righteousness (ὁ ποιῶν τὴν δικαιοσύνην) hath been begotten of him" (ἐξ αὐτοῦ γεγέννηται). Likeness of character to God is the mark of those to whom God has imparted his own life, so that they become and remain his sons (note the force of the perfect tense).[1] The thought is similar in I. iii. 9: "Every one that has been begotten of God [and that remains his child — γεγεννημένος] does not do sin (ἁμαρτίαν οὐ ποιεῖ), because his seed abideth in him," — the new germ of life which God has imparted to him remains as a transforming power in his life, — "and he cannot sin," that is, cannot live the sinful life, cannot habitually sin (ἁμαρτάνειν is here equivalent to ποιεῖν ἁμαρτίαν), "because he has been begotten of God" (ἐκ τοῦ θεοῦ γεγέννηται). As in the two passages just noticed, the doing of righteousness and the not doing of sin are given as the tests of having been begotten from God, so in iv. 7 love is pre-

---

[1] I have rendered the Greek perfect tense in all cases by our English perfect, instead of by the present, "*is* begotten" (R. V.). This tense expresses a permanent relation begun in the past and continued in the present. The present tense in English reproduces only the second element in this two-fold force, which our perfect, no doubt, fails in part to represent.

sented in the same relation: "Beloved, let us love one another: for love is of God; and every one that loveth hath been begotten (γεγέννηται) of God, and knoweth God." It is obvious that righteousness and love are regarded as tests of the divine impartation of life because they are its consequences. The divine begetting is the logical *prius* of the spiritual life and of all its fruits. This relation of the thoughts is made clear in I. iii. 9, and is particularly emphasized in the conversation of Jesus with Nicodemus (iii. 3–8).

Still another test of the divine begetting is faith: "Whosoever believeth that Jesus is the Christ hath been begotten of God: and whosoever loveth him that begat (τὸν γεννήσαντα, that is, God) loveth him also that hath been begotten of him (God)" (I. v. 1): He that loves God who bestows spiritual life, loves also the child of God upon whom he has bestowed it; love to God involves love of the brethren. Nothing is here intimated as to the logical or chronological relation of faith to the divine begetting; it is only said that every one who believes in Jesus as the Christ has been begotten from God and is a child of his. Such faith is the unfailing mark of sonship to God. An effect of the possession of divine life is stated, in an abstract form, in I. v. 4: "Whatsoever hath been begotten of God overcometh the world." This reminds one of the statement in I. iii. 9 that the divine life-principle brings about a moral impossibility of sinning. How closely the begetting from God and faith — the divine and human factors in salvation — are co-ordinated by John is apparent from the parallelism of this verse (I. v. 4), where to the statement that what is born of God overcomes the world, he adds that faith is the power that overcomes the world.

The final passage in the Epistle (v. 18) resembles in general iii. 9. It reads: "We know that whosoever hath been begotten of God (ὁ γεγεννημένος ἐκ τοῦ θεοῦ) sinneth not; but he that was begotten of God (ὁ γεννηθεὶς ἐκ τοῦ θεοῦ) keepeth him (τηρεῖ αὐτόν) and the evil one toucheth him not." Considerable difficulty besets the phrase ὁ γεννηθεὶς ἐκ τοῦ θεοῦ τηρεῖ αὐτόν (or ἑαυτόν). Most modern editors (Treg., Tisch., Alf., W. & H., R. V.) adopt the reading αὐτόν (so A[1] B Vulg.). Some, however, support the reading of the Textus Receptus, ἑαυτόν (so ℵ A[2] K L). If ἑαυτόν be read, the meaning is plain: He that was born of God keeps himself, that is, maintains his proper character, as a Christian (*cf.* iii. 3; 1 Tim. v. 22; Jas. i. 27). The great majority of interpreters favor this view of the text and meaning, notwithstanding the contrary verdict of the textual critics.[1] Other exegetes, however, adopt the reading αὐτόν.[2] In that case, ὁ γεννηθείς is most naturally referred, so far as grammatical considerations are concerned, to Christ. Westcott and Plummer adopt this supposition, and regard it as explaining the change from the perfect

---

[1] See, for example, the Commentaries of Lücke, Huther, Haupt, Weiss, and Holtzmann. The same view of the meaning is presented in our King James's version.

[2] So Alford, Westcott, Plummer.

THE NATURE OF THE SPIRITUAL LIFE 247

participle (uniformly used by John in application to the believer) to the aorist. The theory is that γεννηθείς refers to a past fact, or a "timeless relation" (Plummer). But the fact that John never elsewhere applies the verb γεννηθῆναι to Christ presents a great difficulty for this interpretation. Alford, therefore, though adopting the reading αὐτόν, holds that ὁ γεννηθείς refers to the same person as ὁ γεγεννημένος, and supposes that the construction is broken after the word γεννηθείς, and that the immediate subject of τηρεῖ is the idea or fact of the divine begetting which is implied in ὁ γεννηθείς. To bring out this interpretation the sentence may be rendered: "But he that was born of God, — the divine begetting keeps him." Weiss says that if αὐτόν is read, this is the correct interpretation of the sentence.[1] On this view the change to the aorist participle is explained as marking his divine birth as a past fact which severed his connection with the prince of the world and with evil (Alford). This explanation avoids the difficulties which beset that of Westcott, but, in point of grammar, is very harsh and arbitrary. All things considered, the interpretation seems preferable which rests upon the reading ἑαυτόν, and which translates: "He that was begotten from God [the Christian] keeps himself," — with which should be compared the words of this same Epistle: "Every one that hath this hope [of seeing Christ as he is] set on

[1] The Vulgate embodies this explanation: *sed generatio Dei conservat eum.*

him [Christ] purifieth (ἁγνίζει ἑαυτόν), even as he [Christ] is pure" (I. iii. 3). But whichever reading and interpretation be adopted, the main thought is that it is against the nature of the new life to continue in sin, and that the Christian is to be kept free from Satan's power.

The final example of the form of thought under consideration is found in the conversation of Jesus with Nicodemus (iii. 3–8). Here, as we have before intimated, the form of thought seems to be that of birth rather than of begetting. Jesus speaks rather of a transformation than of an origination of life. "Except a man be born anew (ἄνωθεν), he cannot see the kingdom of God" (iii. 3). For our purpose it makes no essential difference whether ἄνωθεν be rendered "again" (A. V.), "anew" (R. V.), or "from above" (so most commentators). In any case the meaning is that a spiritual renewal, wrought by God, is necessary for participation in the divine kingdom. After the incredulous question of Nicodemus as to the possibility of a birth in addition to that by which we enter the world, Jesus repeats the thought in somewhat different terms: "Except a man be born of water and the Spirit, he cannot enter into the kingdom of God. That which is born of the flesh is flesh; and that which is born of the Spirit is spirit. Marvel not that I said unto thee, Ye must be born anew" (verses 5–7). Nicodemus had spoken of natural birth as the only one that was conceivable. Jesus replies that man is related to two spheres, the natural and the spiritual; that as physical birth marks the beginning of his personal natural life, so a spiritual birth marks the beginning of the higher life of the spirit. He implies that as great a change in man's disposition and character is involved in his entering the divine kingdom as took place in his natural life at his birth. The new birth is a spiritual transformation; it is an entrance into a new world of motives, interests, and hopes. This spiritual process is, he adds, an inscrutable mystery, like the movement of the wind, whose sound is heard, but whose nature and sources none can trace.

Such is the general import of the conversation. The principal exegetical difficulty appears in connection with the phrase (verse 5), " born of water and the Spirit " (ἐξ ὕδατος καὶ πνεύματος). Most commentators, ancient and modern, hold that there is in the word " water " some kind of a reference to baptism. This supposition is considerably strengthened by the passage, " There are three who bear witness, — the Spirit, and the water, and the blood: and the three agree in one " (1. v. 8), where " the water " is most naturally taken as referring to Christ's baptism. Weiss is the only modern interpreter among those whom I have consulted, who supposes that " water " is here contemplated only symbolically as the purifying element which takes away sin. He does not make " water " and " spirit " mean the same thing (as Calvin and Grotius had done, on the supposition of a hendiadys), but regards the effective, life-giving power of the

Spirit as the positive counterpart and completion of the cleansing symbolized by "water." But if a reference to baptism be assumed, is it primarily and directly to Christian baptism (so De Wette, Meyer, Holtzmann), or to the baptism of John? Many scholars adopt the latter view (Tholuck, Alford, Westcott, Plummer, Godet), but generally hold that an indirect or prophetic reference to Christian baptism is also veiled in the word. Lücke finds the force of the thought in the phrase ἐξ ὕδατος, not in the outward rite of baptism, but in its idea and significance. This seems to me to be a helpful suggestion, but it should not be pushed so far as to exclude the objective import of the rite. Baptism expresses not only the repentance of the recipient, but also God's promise and pledge of forgiveness. Bearing this in mind, I think it most natural to suppose that in speaking of "water" and "Spirit," Jesus is thinking primarily of the repentance-baptism (βάπτισμα μετανοίας, Mk. i. 4) of John, and of the spiritual cleansing which he himself effects. The two aspects of thought expressed in "water" and "Spirit" correspond to the distinction made by John the Baptist between his preparatory work and the positive renewal of men which Christ should accomplish: " I baptized you with water (ὕδατι); but he shall baptize you with the Holy Spirit" (πνεύματι ἁγίῳ, Mk. i. 8). " Water " expresses rather the preparatory or negative aspect of the renewal, corresponding to baptism, which is a sign of repentance of sin and of divine forgiveness; " Spirit " expresses the positive bestowment of a new life. There is thus a natural progress of thought in passing from the idea of birth by water to that of birth by Spirit. Although in speaking to Nicodemus Jesus would hardly think directly of Christian baptism, the distinct and yet complementary significance of ὕδωρ and πνεῦμα is in principle equally applicable to it. We think, then, that the sense is, substantially, this: Repentance and forgiveness (expressed in baptism) and the bestowment of a new life from God are essential to participation in his kingdom.

Those who have been begotten from God, or born anew, are children of God. That to believe, to be begotten of God, and to be a child of God, are kindred and inseparable ideas is clearly shown by the passage, "As many as received him, to them gave he the right (ἐξουσίαν) to become children of God, even to them that believe on his name; which were born (or begotten), not of blood, nor of the will of the flesh, nor of the will of man, but of God" (i. 12, 13). The complete co-ordination of receiving Christ, believing on Christ, and being begotten of God shows that faith is not here contemplated merely as a condition precedent of becoming a son of God (as Weiss insists). To believe, and to be begotten of God are two inseparable aspects of the same event or process (I. v. 1), and in being begotten of God one becomes a child of God; equally, therefore, does he become such in the very act of believing. Faith, therefore, does not merely make sonship to God possible; it is the actual entrance into the relation of sonship so far as man has to do with constituting that relation. Weiss stands alone, so far as I know, among critical interpreters in sharply separating off from one another the various phases and stages of the work of salvation which John designates by the different words or phrases which we have quoted. His version of the passage just cited is: "To those who accept him by faith, Christ has given not sonship itself, but the power to *become* the sons of God; the last and highest realization of this ideal, a realization for the present fathomless, lies only in the future consummation."[1] But the word ἐξουσία here is best taken, not as referring to a mere future *possibility* which faith opens, but as emphasizing the loftiness of the privilege of becoming sons of God which is accorded to believers.[2] The arbitrary analysis of Weiss involves his whole discussion of this and allied subjects in a maze of refinements, which illustrate, not the apostle's method of religious thought, but an over-subtle quality of some modern minds which the Germans themselves aptly designate as " Spitzfindigkeit."

It may be well to notice here again what we have observed in another connection, that John always speaks of τέκνα τοῦ θεοῦ, not of υἱοὶ τοῦ θεοῦ. Weiss suggests that John may have chosen the word τέκνα " so as not to seem to approach too near " (in the language which he applies to Christians) " the peerless

[1] *Bibl. Theol.* § 150, *d.*
[2] So Beyschlag, *Neutest. Theol.*, ii. 453.

THE NATURE OF THE SPIRITUAL LIFE 253

position of the only begotten Son of God." [1] A more satisfactory motive for the choice of this word may be found in John's mode of religious thought. The term τέκνον suggests the personal and intimate relations which are involved in sonship rather than the legal standing and privileges which Paul's favorite word υἱός expresses. The force of τέκνον, as used by the apostle, and the distinction between it and υἱός, are thus stated by Bishop Westcott: "The idea of τέκνον, as it is thus presented by St. John, includes the two notions of the presence of the divine principle and the action of human growth. The child is made to share in his Father's nature, and he uses in progressive advance the powers which he has received. It is therefore easily intelligible why St. John never uses the title υἱός, the name of definite dignity and privilege, to describe the relation of Christians to God. He regards their position not as the result of an 'adoption' (υἱοθεσία), but as the result of a new life which advances from the vital germ to full maturity." [2]

The way in which John associates the idea of childship with relations of loving fellowship between man and God may be easily seen from the First Epistle. "Behold what manner of love the Father hath bestowed upon us, that we should be called children of God" (ἵνα τέκνα θεοῦ κληθῶμεν — should bear a title

[1] *Bibl. Theol.* § 150, d.
[2] *The Epistles of St. John*, additional note on I. iii. 1, pp. 123, 124.

of such honor and dignity): "and such we are" (καὶ ἐσμέν): We not only bear the name of children of God, but we are in reality that which the name imports. "Beloved, now are we children of God," etc. (I. iii. 1, 2). It is the purpose (ἵνα) of God's love to secure to us the high privilege of sonship, and this privilege is not a mere possibility or prospect, but a present possession: καὶ ἐσμέν· νῦν τέκνα θεοῦ ἐσμέν.

Not only is a loving relation to God involved in childship to him; loving fellowship among men is equally involved in it. The test of childship to God is the doing of righteousness and the loving of one's brother, that is, fellow-Christian (I. iii. 10). Both the relations of love which we have just mentioned — that to God and that to man — are emphasized together in I. v. 1, 2: "Whosoever believeth that Jesus is the Christ is begotten of God: and whosoever loveth him that begat [God] loveth him also that is begotten of him [the Christian brother]. Hereby we know that we love the children of God, when we love God, and do his commandments." These examples show that with John sonship to God is a personal relation of obedience and love, involving mutual devotion among all who share this relation. They illustrate his spiritual mode of viewing the nature and obligations of religion. These relations are viewed quite simply, and are described under natural analogies which widely remove them from all suggestions of legal processes or of an extended *ordo sa-*

THE NATURE OF THE SPIRITUAL LIFE 255

lutis. It may be observed in passing that they also confirm the view taken in an earlier chapter in regard to the question whether or not in John all men are regarded as sons of God (pp. 70–73).

A passage of great interest in its bearing upon our theme is found in the speech of Caiaphas before the Sanhedrin (xi. 49–52). He declared that it was expedient that Jesus should die, not for the (Jewish) nation only, but "that he might also gather together into one the children of God that are scattered abroad" (verse 52). The contrast between τὰ τέκνα τοῦ θεοῦ and "the [Jewish] nation" shows that by the former certain Gentiles are meant. It must not be forgotten that it is here the high priest, and not the evangelist, who is speaking and giving his philosophy of vicarious sacrifice,—in certain respects a false and perverse one. Still, the apostle gives the opinion of Caiaphas as expressing certain truths which lay beneath the speaker's immediate, conscious meaning. We may then regard the idea that there were "children of God" outside Judaism as true to John's mind, especially if it be involved in other passages. The question arises, How are we to conceive and define this idea? Hilgenfeld understands the words to refer, in a dualistic sense, to a natural sonship of some men to God, in contrast to others who are children of the devil.[1] This opinion is connected with the theory of the Tübingen school respecting the origin and character of the Fourth

[1] *Das Evangelium und die Briefe Johannes,* p. 297 *sq.*

Gospel as a specimen of Gnostic speculation applied to Christianity. Most interpreters hold either that some Gentiles are spoken of as "children of God" by anticipation, as being such in the purpose of God (Calvin, Luther, Meyer, Holtzmann), or that they are so described because they have an incipient faith, a susceptibility or predisposition, which would lead them to accept the truth and work of Christ when the knowledge of it should be brought to them (so, substantially, Lücke, Weiss, Godet, Westcott). This is the preferable view. These scattered believers among the heathen are already children of God, not, indeed, naturally, but by the grace of God which manifests itself wherever there is a receptivity for it. Jesus recognizes in men different degrees of receptiveness for his truth. He says to a certain company of Jews: "He that is of God" — he that has the disposition and desire of obedience — "heareth the words of God: for this cause ye hear them not, because ye are not of God" (viii. 47). We hold, therefore, that these Gentile "children of God" are the "other sheep (ἄλλα πρόβατα) which are not derived from (ἐκ) this [Jewish] fold" which he would bring [1] (ἀγαγεῖν), that all his sheep may together constitute one flock under the one Shepherd (x. 16). It does not

[1] Many interpreters (as Meyer, Weiss, Westcott, Plummer) render ἀγαγεῖν *to lead*, and do not find the idea of *bringing together* the scattered sheep, either to himself or into one flock, contained in our passage (*per contra*, Tholuck, Luthardt, Godet). This question does not essentially concern our present use of the passage.

THE NATURE OF THE SPIRITUAL LIFE

seem natural (with Meyer and others) to take the words "Other sheep I have" as prophetic, especially in view of the statements of the prologue that the life of the Logos "was the light of men" (i. 4), "the true light which lighteth every man, coming into the world" (ὃ φωτίζει πάντα ἄνθρωπον ἐρχόμενον εἰς τὸν κόσμον, i. 9). Whichever of three possible constructions [1] be adopted for the participle ἐρχόμενον here, the passage asserts the universality of revelation through the Logos; nor does it merely assert that the Logos enlightens all men in general (πάντας ἀνθρώπους), but that he lighteth every individual man (πάντα ἄνθρωπον). If God reveals himself to each man in some way and measure and touches men universally with the influences of his grace, it is certainly conceivable that there should be at all times and in all nations those who — notwithstanding the limitations of their light and knowledge — may, by reason of their disposition and susceptibility, be truly called "children of God" and members of Christ's true flock. In this view sonship to God does not rest

[1] Ἐρχόμενον may be construed (1) with ἦν at the beginning of the sentence, making a periphrastic form: The true light which lighteth every man *was coming* (or came) into the world (so Lücke, DeWette, Weiss, Godet, Westcott, Rev. Vers.); or (2) with the relative ὅ: There was the true light which, by (or on) coming into the world, lighteth every man (so Luther's first ed., "*durch seine Zukunft,*" u. s. w.); or (3) with ἄνθρωπον: which lighteth every man that cometh (or as he cometh) into the world (so most of the Fathers and Reformers, Vulg., A. V., Meyer, Plummer, Dwight). A majority of modern exegetes adopt the first construction.

upon a basis of nature or of desert: it rests upon divine grace alone, but upon a grace which is not restricted, but world-wide in its operation.

The nature of the Christian life is further exhibited by the use of a considerable variety of descriptive phrases, the most important of which are, abiding or being in Christ (or in God), the dwelling of Christ (or of God) in the believer, — both forms of expression are sometimes combined, — fellowship with Christ (or with God), and eating the flesh of the Son of Man and drinking his blood.[1] What the significance and consequences of this "abiding" are may best be determined by a careful observation of the connections of thought in which the expression occurs. The test of abiding in Christ is said to be obedience to his commandments and the following of his example: "Hereby know we that we are in him: he that saith he abideth in him ought himself also to walk even as he (Christ) walked" (I. ii. 5, 6). Again, the holding fast of the truths which were first taught his Christian readers is urged by the apostle as the condition of abiding in the Son and in the Father (I. ii. 24). This verse has been paraphrased thus: "Let the truths which were first taught you have a home in your hearts: if these have a home in you, ye also shall have a home in the Son and in the Father" (Plummer). In verses 27 and 28 the abiding of the believer in Christ is closely associated (not strictly

[1] The passages are tabulated in Westcott's *Epistles of St. John*, pp. 174, 175.

identified) with the "anointing" ($\chi\rho\hat{\iota}\sigma\mu a$) which the Christian has received, that is, with the gift of the Holy Spirit. This chrism is personified and represented as abiding in the Christian and teaching him, — a work which seems to be thought of as a condition or preparation for his abiding in Christ. These verses appear to be explained by I. iv. 13: "Hereby know we that we abide in him, and he in us, because he hath given us of his Spirit." Another clear note respecting the meaning of abiding in Christ is struck in I. iii. 6: "Whosoever abideth in him sinneth not ($o\dot{v}\chi$ $\dot{a}\mu a\rho\tau\dot{a}\nu\epsilon\iota$ — does not live the sinful life): whosoever sinneth ($\pi\hat{a}\varsigma$ $\dot{o}$ $\dot{a}\mu a\rho\tau\dot{a}\nu\omega\nu$ — every one who lives the life of habitual sin) hath not seen him, neither knoweth him."

From these passages it appears that to abide in Christ (or in God) is to forsake the sinful life, to keep his words and to exemplify his spirit. In short, it is to live the life of love: "God is love; and he that abideth in love abideth in God, and God abideth in him" (I. iv. 16). But the further question arises, whether a personal, mystical relation is also involved in this and kindred expressions. It seems difficult to doubt that this is the case when one reads the allegory of the Vine and the Branches (xv. 1–6). Even Weiss, who seeks to exclude all mysticism from the Johannine idea of faith, admits that "abiding" in Christ implies a "mystical union, a oneness of person with him."[1] The allegory depicts the necessity of

[1] *Bibl. Theol.* § 149, *d*, note 12.

an organic and vital union between the believer and Christ. To abide in him (verse 4) is equivalent to bearing a relation to him analogous to that of the branch to the vine (verse 2) from which it draws its life. Such a union is the condition of all fruitfulness (verses 4, 5). Apart from him the disciple can do nothing, that is, can bear no fruit of Christlike love and service. It is noticeable that the thought passes directly from the figure of the vine to that of loving fellowship between him and his disciples: " Even as the Father hath loved me, I also have loved you: abide ye in my love" (verse 9). The fundamental idea of the allegory is that of the close, constant, loving fellowship of life between the believer and his Lord.

This fellowship of the believer with Christ involves fellowship with the Father and the indwelling of Christ and of God in the Christian man. " Our fellowship is with the Father, and with his Son Jesus Christ" (I. i. 3). He who keeps God's commandments abides in God, and God in him (I. iii. 24). God abides in those who love one another (I. iv. 12). A reciprocal abiding of the believer in Christ, and of Christ in him, is more than once mentioned (xiv. 20 ; xv. 5); and the possible closeness of this union is emphasized by its being compared to that which subsists between the Son and the Father: " And the glory which thou hast given me I have given unto them; that they may be one, even as we are one ; I in them, and thou in me, that they may be perfected into one; that the

THE NATURE OF THE SPIRITUAL LIFE 261

world may know that thou didst send me, and lovedst them, even as thou lovedst me" (xvii. 22, 23).

We have already had occasion, in treating of the Johannine doctrine of salvation, to consider the three principal interpretations of the expressions eating the flesh, and drinking the blood of the Son of man (vi. 52–59; see pp. 159–164). In the view which we adopted these phrases are descriptive of the living appropriation of Christ to the heart. "Flesh" and "blood" stand as symbols of his very self. To partake of these is spiritually to appropriate Christ by an intimate life-union with him. This conception of his meaning is the most comprehensive one. It does not wholly exclude the ideas which are derived from them by other explanations, but, in a measure, includes them. The appropriation of Christ, in the fullest sense of the word, includes the believing acceptance of the benefits of his sacrificial work which are perpetually symbolized and attested in the Lord's supper. Christ is himself, in his whole person, work, and spirit, the bread of life; and to eat his flesh and drink his blood is the same as to feed upon that living bread of God which came down out of heaven (verses 57, 58); it is to live "because of him;" it is to strike the roots of one's life into Christ.

This review of the passages which illustrate the nature of the relation which the Christian sustains to the source of his spiritual life, may fitly close with a notice of a passage which is a complex of the religious ideas found in the writings of John: "Yet a little while, and the world beholdeth me no more; but ye behold me: because I live, ye shall live also.[1] In that day ye shall know that I am in my Father, and ye in me, and I in you" (xiv. 19, 20). Jesus had just been speaking of his coming to them through the presence of the Spirit (verse 18), and now adds that soon his bodily form — which is all that the world can see of him — will be withdrawn from human sight; the literal, physical beholding of him will be no longer possible, but his disciples will continue to behold him with the eye of the spirit; he will still seem real and present to them through the spiritual perception which they have of him. When the senses can no longer discern him he will still disclose himself to the mystic vision of the soul. To this conception is added that of living through his life. Removed though he will be from the world's natural sight, his life will not be quenched. He will live on and work on in unseen, unknown ways in the world of the Spirit. Because his life and power are changeless and eternal he will continue to be the source of spiritual life to all who look to him. Such words carry the mind beyond the realm of time and sense

[1] Many scholars (so Meyer and Weiss; *per contra*, Godet and Westcott) would translate the latter part of this verse thus: "but ye behold me because I live and (because) ye shall live," making the two assertions "I live" and "ye shall live" assign the reason for the statement "ye behold me," instead of treating them as together constituting an independent proposition. The rendering of our English versions appears to me to give the more forcible sense.

into the world of eternal reality. To this world Christ belongs, — in it he lives and works; into that world the eye of faith pierces, and up to its heavenly heights of holy peace and calm he lifts those who join their lives to him.

But even in this region of transcendent mystery the mind is not "in wandering mazes lost." Thought is still held captive by the sense of those personal relations which lie at the basis of all religious life and experience. "In that day ye shall know that I am in my Father, and ye in me, and I in you" (xiv. 20). The spiritual vision of Christ, and spiritual life through his life, shall but make more clear and certain his own perfect union with the Father, and the mutual fellowship of his disciples and himself. And what is the bond of this union? Love (verses 21, 22). These high, mystic terms — beholding, living, indwelling — are at once translated into that practical but all-embracing principle of love. He who loves and obeys me, he it is to whom the vision of God comes. Our passage, therefore, forms a fitting transition to the special study of the idea of love in our sources. But before passing on to the consideration of that subject, let us cast a glance backward over the religious conceptions which we have just reviewed, and seek to make some practical estimate of their import.

In the first place, the ideas which we have been considering illustrate what I may call an intensely *religious* view of Christianity. I mean that they all rest upon the supposition that God is very near us, and that the forces of the spiritual and eternal order constantly penetrate our world. Religion is a very personal affair. It is not depicted as consisting in the performance of sacred rites, or even in the doing of specific duties. It is rather a relation of fellowship with God as revealed in Christ, and therefore a relation of likeness to him. The religious life is not a play of feeling within ourselves; it is not a mere collection of good deeds and virtues which we have achieved; it is a divine impartation from God; it is the response of the human spirit to the life-giving touch of the Father of our spirits. The descriptions of Christian life and experience which we have studied assume that religion is the divine life in man; that the world of religious thought and feeling is a world of realities, and not of phantoms.

Again, the Johannine conception of religion is especially favorable to *devotion*. It appeals powerfully to the imagination and the heart; it keeps alive the sense of a real and present Saviour; it fills life, not merely with hopes of a future blessedness, but with a present fulness of joy and richness of experience. No New Testament writer has so vividly conceived the powers of the heavenly world as operative here and now, as the apostle John. If, as his legend describes, he has soared into the sun, he has brought down into our sinful world and common life something of the warmth and glory of the everlasting Light. Eternal life is already here; the world of time and sense is swallowed up in the world of the spirit; and life is transfigured by the presence and the love of God.

Our author's religious ideas are also very *practical*. Religion is character. " He that doeth righteousness is righteous, even as he [Christ] is righteous " (I. iii. 7). Christ has interpreted the nature of God to man; his life is therefore the true norm of character. Likeness to him is the all-comprehending requirement of religion. To be like God in love, in sympathy, in helpfulness, is the sum of every Christian obligation. All duties repose upon this deep foundation. This is the reason for living the Christian life upon which all other reasons rest. Any conception of religion must involve a high standard of character which presents, as John's does, a pure and spiritual idea of God, and then defines the religious life to be a fellowship and affinity of spirit with him. We may sum the matter up by saying that, while there is little in the Gospel and First Epistle of John which is adapted to promote the strifes of sect and the disputes of theological parties, these writings remain what they have ever been since their composition and will probably be to the end of time, — the two incomparable manuals of religion, matchless portrayals of the richness, beauty, and blessedness of the spiritual life.

CHAPTER XI

THE DOCTRINE OF LOVE

Literature. — REUSS: *Hist. Christ. Theol.*, Of Love, ii. 482–491 (orig. ii. 538–549); WESTCOTT: *Epistles of St. John*, The Idea of Love, pp. 130–133; BEYSCHLAG: *Neutest. Theol.*, Die Liebe, ii. 459–462; BAUR: *Neutest. Theol.*, Die Liebe des Vaters zum Sohn und Gottes zur Welt, pp. 397–400; WENDT: *Teaching of Jesus*, Admonition to love in the Johannine farewell discourse, i. 357–362 (orig. pp. 287–292); MESSNER: *Lehre der Apostel*, Die Liebe, pp. 351–354; W G. BALLENTINE: Art. "*Lovest Thou me?*" in the *Bibliotheca Sacra* for July, 1889, pp. 524–542; E. A. PARK: Sermon on "God is love," in his *Discourses*, pp. 155–180.

THE principal passages which illustrate the idea of love as presented in our sources, are very familiar, and to a considerable extent have been already quoted. The passages have been fully tabulated by Westcott.[1] It will be sufficient for our purpose to give a brief *résumé* of his grouping. The passages are distributed into classes with reference to two points : (1) the term which is used to express the idea of love, and (2) the subject and object of the love that is predicated.

Two verbs meaning *to love* are frequently used in John's writings, ἀγαπᾶν and φιλεῖν. The noun ἀγάπη,

[1] *The Epistles of St. John*, pp. 130–133.

THE DOCTRINE OF LOVE 267

corresponding to ἀγαπᾶν, also occurs frequently, but φιλία, which would correspond to φιλεῖν, is not found.¹ The proper difference between these two verbs has been frequently defined by scholars with great care. I can therefore do the reader no better service than to quote two or three of these definitions. "'Αγαπᾶν properly denotes a love founded in admiration, veneration, esteem, like the Latin *diligere, to be kindly disposed to one, to wish one well;* but φιλεῖν denotes an inclination prompted by sense and emotion, Latin, *amare*; ut scires, eum a me non *diligi* solum, verum etiam *amari* (Cicero)."²

"Φιλεῖν denotes the love of natural inclination, affection, — love, so to say, originally spontaneous, involuntary; ἀγαπᾶν, on the other hand, love as a direction of the will. . . . The range of φιλεῖν is wider than that of ἀγαπᾶν, but ἀγαπᾶν stands all the higher above φιλεῖν on account of its moral import. It does not in itself exclude affection, but it is always the moral affection of conscious deliberate will which is contained in it, not the natural impulse of immediate feeling."³

"Φιλεῖν (*amare*) denotes a passionate, emotional warmth, which loves and does not care to ask why; the affection which is based on natural relationship, as of parents, brothers, etc. 'Αγαπᾶν (*diligere*) denotes

[1] This word occurs in the New Testament only once, — James iv. 4, "the friendship (φιλία) of the world."
[2] Thayer's *Lexicon*, sub voce, φιλέω.
[3] Cremer, *Biblico-Theological Lexicon*, sub voce, ἀγαπάω.

268 THE JOHANNINE THEOLOGY

a calm, discriminating attachment, which loves because of the excellence of the loved object; the affection which is based on esteem, as of friends. Φιλεῖν is the stronger, but less reasoning; ἀγαπᾶν the more earnest, but less intense."[1]

It is evident, if these definitions are correct, that ἀγαπᾶν is the word of loftier meaning; it is the word which expresses the ideas of choice, esteem, reverence, and the like, while φιλεῖν designates rather those natural or friendly relations which spring from the affections. Accordingly, love to God is always denoted in the New Testament by ἀγαπᾶν, and the noun for love in the religious sense is always ἀγάπη. Men are commanded to love their enemies with the love of benevolence or the love that seeks their true good (ἀγαπᾶν), not with the love of complacency or personal affection and attachment (φιλεῖν). It would, indeed, be incongruous to *command* love in the sense of φιλεῖν, but not in the sense of ἀγαπᾶν. From such examples of the usage it appears that ἀγαπᾶν relates rather to the judgment or the will; φιλεῖν rather to the emotional or sensuous nature.

In general these distinctions seem applicable in John. 'Ἀγαπᾶν is many times predicated of the love of the Father to the Son, e. g., "The Father loveth (ἀγαπᾷ) the Son, and hath given all things into his hand" (iii. 35, cf. x. 17; xv. 9; xvii. 23-26). It is once used of the love of God to the world: "God so loved (ἠγάπησεν) the world" etc. (iii. 16), and several

[1] Plummer, *Commentary*, on xi. 5.

THE DOCTRINE OF LOVE 269

times of his love to men (xiv. 21, 23; xvii. 23; I. iv. 10, 11). Once φιλεῖν is used to designate the love of the Father to the Son: "For the Father loveth (φιλεῖ) the Son, and showeth him all things that himself doeth" (v. 20). If the accurate distinction of the terms is here to be preserved, φιλεῖν must, in this case, refer to the intimate, personal relation of the Father and the Son (so Meyer, Godet, Weiss, et al.). In one passage also (xvi. 27) the love of the Father for the disciples of Christ is designated by φιλεῖν: "For the Father himself loveth (φιλεῖ) you," etc. Here, in the judgment of most interpreters, the thought is, The Father loves you as his children because of your love to me (Christ), and therefore hears and grants your requests. In these two cases where φιλεῖν is used of God's love to another it is not difficult to assign to it an appropriate force as designating the close attachment of personal affection.

Again, John applies ἀγαπᾶν to the love of the Son to the Father (xiv. 31), and to his love for his disciples, either individually or generally (xi. 5; xiii. 1, 34; xiv. 21); while φιλεῖν is also found to describe the love of Jesus for a disciple or friend (xi. 3, 36; xx. 2). The love of the Master for the "beloved disciple" is four times designated by ἀγαπᾶν (xiii. 23; xix. 26; xxi. 7, 20) and only once by φιλεῖν (xx. 2). This example of the use of φιλεῖν seems to show that John sometimes employs the words interchangeably, although it does not necessarily prove that they bear precisely the same shade of meaning. But in such cases the proper distinction of the words must not be overpressed. Another instance of an apparently interchangeable use of the words is found in the narrative of Jesus' relations with the family at Bethany. His love for Lazarus is designated by φιλεῖν (xi. 3, 36), while that for the three members of the family, who are named in succession, is expressed by ἀγαπᾶν (xi. 5). This usage is sometimes explained by saying that in verses 3 and 36 the sisters and the Jews, who speak of Jesus' love for Lazarus, naturally use the more emotional word, while the evangelist, who speaks in verse 5, uses the loftier and less impulsive word (so Plummer and Westcott). Others think that the higher word ἀγαπᾶν (in xi. 5) is chosen with great delicacy by John because the sisters, Martha and Mary, are also mentioned (so Meyer and Weiss). H. Holtzmann regards the two examples just cited (iii. 35, cf. v. 20; xi. 3, 36, cf. xi. 5) as proving that John uses the two verbs promiscuously.

The love of the disciples for Christ (viii. 42; xiv. 15 sq.) and for their brethren (xiii. 34; xv. 17 et al.) is generally designated by ἀγαπᾶν, although φιλεῖν is also found (xvi. 27; xxi. 15 sq.). The passage last cited is one of considerable interest and difficulty in its bearing upon the usage of the words. Jesus twice asks Peter: ἀγαπᾷς με; and Peter replies: φιλῶ σε. The third time the question is: φιλεῖς με; and Peter still answers: φιλῶ σε. The almost universal opinion of interpreters is that the change of words is intentional, and that the point of the conversation is largely lost by overlooking the distinction. The view generally adopted is that Jesus uses the loftier word expressing deliberate choice and devotion, and that Peter hesitates to claim such a love, but affirms the love of personal affection: $\phi\iota\lambda\hat{\omega}\ \sigma\epsilon$. Jesus then drops to the level of Peter's own assertion, and says: Are you sure that you love me even thus — $\phi\iota\lambda\epsilon\hat{\iota}s\ \mu\epsilon$; — alluding, probably, to Peter's previous denial of him, and, perhaps, asking the question three times because of the three denials. To this question Peter replies affirmatively, but without claiming more than the affection denoted by $\phi\iota\lambda\epsilon\hat{\iota}\nu$. Some have called in question the distinction upon which the foregoing interpretation proceeds, on the ground of the seemingly interchangeable use of the terms which we have already noticed. Even Weiss, who observes the natural distinction of the words in the other cases, thinks it doubtful whether it is applicable here. If Jesus had throughout employed $\dot{\alpha}\gamma\alpha\pi\hat{\alpha}\nu$, while Peter uniformly used $\phi\iota\lambda\epsilon\hat{\iota}\nu$, the recognition of the distinction would be, in my judgment, more natural than it now is. The supposition of an intentional change from $\dot{\alpha}\gamma\alpha\pi\hat{\alpha}\nu$ in the first two to $\phi\iota\lambda\epsilon\hat{\iota}\nu$ in the third question, is unnecessary to the sense and force of the passage, and seems somewhat over-subtle. Moreover, it must be remembered that this conversation, in all probability, was held in Aramaic, in which no such distinction as that between the two Greek verbs could have been marked. To this difficulty it is replied that we must deal with the Greek version of the event as we have it, and that by some additional words or gestures the Lord may have made such a distinction as the Greek has preserved.[1]

Whatever opinion be adopted respecting these few doubtful cases which we have just mentioned, there can, I think, be no reasonable doubt that the distinction between ἀγαπᾶν and φιλεῖν is, in general, applicable in the writings of John.[2] Even in those few instances where the two words appear to be used synonymously there is a certain presumption that a difference of meaning is really implied. In any case, we have here to do with love in the distinctively moral and religious sense, which is specially denoted by ἀγαπᾶν and ἀγάπη. It is necessary next to notice what is affirmed of the subjects and objects of this love, and then to inquire into its nature and significance.

When God is the subject of this love there are

[1] So Schaff, in *Lange on John, in loco.*

[2] Dr. W. G. Ballentine, in an elaborate article on the subject (*Bibliotheca Sacra*, July, 1889), not only denies that there is any distinction between ἀγαπᾶν and φιλεῖν in John xxi. 15 *sq.*, but contends that the distinctions commonly made between them are not applicable in the New Testament generally. His evidence is drawn almost wholly from the Septuagint, where he shows that the words are often used without discrimination. A promiscuous use of the terms in the New Testament would not necessarily follow from such a use in the Septuagint, nor would a few cases in which the distinction between them is doubtful suffice to prove that the New Testament writers in general used the words synonymously.

THE DOCTRINE OF LOVE

three objects upon which it is said to terminate, the Son (iii. 35 *et al.*), the world (iii. 16), and the disciples of Christ (xiv. 21, 23). In I. iv. 10, 11, John speaks of the love which God has shown to his readers in sending Christ as the propitiation for their sins. This passage refers, therefore, to God's love to them while they were yet sinners, and belongs, practically, with iii. 16, which speaks of his love to the world (ὁ κόσμος). Of similar import is I. iii. 1, 16: "Behold what manner of love the Father hath bestowed upon us," etc. While, therefore, the love of God to the sinful world is not often explicitly mentioned, it is several times referred to, and is assumed in many passages besides those just cited. The Son is said to love the Father (xiv. 31), and his disciples (xiii. 1; xiv. 21). Christians are spoken of (I. v. 1, 2) in contrast to non-Christians (v. 42; I. ii. 5), as loving God, and still more frequently as loving Christ (xiv. 21–28) and one another (xiii. 34, 35; I. iii. 10–14). Over against this true religious love to God and man stands the love of darkness (iii. 19), or of the world (I. ii. 15).

It will be seen that the love which is so central in John's conception of religion is a personal relation between man and God, on the one hand, and among men themselves, on the other. The apostle reaches his highest point of contemplation in placing the seat of love in the very nature of God himself. The duty of men to love one another springs from the nature and source of love. It is a divine principle, a quality of God's own nature and action; nay, it is a name for God's ethical nature itself. The life of true love is therefore a divinely imparted life. It is derived from God and involves fellowship with him. Whence it follows : " He that loveth not knoweth not God ; for God is love" (I. iv. 8). For the mind of John the ethical nature of God determines the nature and demands of the Christian life. To be like God is the sum of all Christian obligations. " If we love one another, God abideth in us, and his love is perfected in us " (I. iv. 12). " God is love ; and he that abideth in love abideth in God, and God abideth in him " (I. iv. 16).

It should not, of course, be supposed that in saying " God is love" the apostle intended to construct a scientific definition of the moral nature of God. In the very nature of the case, love scarcely admits of accurate and exhaustive definition. The analysis of the divine attributes to which we in modern times are accustomed did not engage the minds of the New Testament writers, who spoke in popular language and for practical religious ends. But while it is impossible to maintain that John had ever proposed to himself to construct a precise conception of love which should answer the demands of scientific thought, he has, nevertheless, given us a concise statement of God's moral nature upon which theological thought cannot improve. It is, at any rate, quite unjustifiable to treat his statement as if it meant only that God, as a matter of fact, *has* love for men, or that he has

THE DOCTRINE OF LOVE 275

chosen — though he might have done otherwise — to love his creatures, on the theory that love is only a subordinate attribute of God which it is optional with him to exercise or not. Whatever be the scope or content of love, as John uses the word, it certainly represents to his mind an essential and constituent element in the divine nature, and theology has never been able to construct a better definition of the ethical perfection of God than is contained in the apostle's words: " God is love." [1]

I am persuaded that no proposition could be more directly contrary to the fundamental principles of John's teaching than that which has been so commonly affirmed in theology that justice is *the* central and all-determining attribute of God, to which love is only subordinate and secondary. This is the formula

[1] " The saying of the apostle, ' God is love,' is the best compendium of the Christian idea of God." — Van Oosterzee, *Christian Dogmatics*, i. 269. " Love is the supreme, the only adequate definition of the essence of God." — Dorner, *System*, i. 454. "God himself is good only as he is love, and his holiness and righteousness depend upon his love." — Müller, *The Christian Doctrine of Sin*, i. 113. "God is love, the perfect, the absolutely good and only good Being, so that no attribute or activity can be ascribed to him which cannot be derived from his love." — Nitzsch, *System*, p. 145. " In the Old Testament love is an attribute of God, one of many exercised in particular relations. In the New Testament first love can be shown to be the very Being of God as answering to the revelation in Christ; and we may see a certain fitness in the fact that this crowning truth is brought out in the latest of the apostolic writings." — Westcott, *The Epistles of St. John*, p. 168.

which a rigorous, formal logic has sought to apply in theology, upon the assumption that God is a judge rather than a Father, and that the world which he has made is a legal rather than a moral world. Some show of justification for this view may be found in the legalism of the Old Testament, although an appeal in support of it to the Talmud, which represents the later religious thought of Judaism when juridical conceptions had wellnigh supplanted moral ones, would be far better warranted. It may seem to be favored by the survival in Paul of some traces of Pharisaic thought, but with both the language and spirit of John it is in irreconcilable contradiction. This subject will meet us again when we come to consider the relation of love to righteousness.

John neither gives us a definition of love, nor furnishes the material for a formal definition. What his conception of love is, we are left to infer from the qualities which are ascribed to it and the actions which flow from it. The more important of these we will enumerate.

(1) Love is a personal relation of communion or fellowship, or, at least, looks forward to the constitution of such a relation. The intimate fellowship of the Father and the Son illustrates the highest form of love. It involves perfect fellowship of sympathy and interest, and the perfect mutual delight of each subject in the object of love. John presents this perfect communion as the type of love among men : " Even as the Father hath loved me, I also have loved

you: abide ye in my love. . . . This is my commandment, that ye love one another even as I have loved you" (xv. 9, 12). Here the love of the Father for the Son is the norm of the Son's love for his disciples, and this love, in turn, is the type and measure of all true love among brethren. Love is a personal life-union involving reciprocal delight, interest, and attachment.

This relation is sometimes described as an indwelling, or abiding, of one person in another. This mode of expression is doubtless chosen in order to emphasize the closeness of the relation. Love involves a certain "oneness" of those whom it unites. Each is at once the subject and the object of love. Love is mutual, or, at least, naturally tends to become so. A community of feeling, thought, and interest springs up where love binds persons together. Jesus prays that his disciples "may be one" even as he and the Father are one, and explains in what follows that this unity of which he speaks is a unity which is born of love: "I in them, and thou in me, that they may be perfected into one, that the world may know that thou didst send me, and lovedst them, even as thou lovedst me" (xvii. 23).

Love is, therefore, the true unifying bond among men. It is the principle which leads each to make the interest of all his care. From this consideration it appears, as John says, that "love is of God" (ἐκ τοῦ θεοῦ, I. iv. 7); it is a principle essentially divine. The capacity to love is implanted in man by him in whose image he is made. As God is the ground of all unity and harmony in the universe, so God-likeness among men, that is, love, is the true bond of brotherhood. Selfishness is the principle of isolation; love alone binds men together in helpful and happy relations. All love among men is a reflection of the divine nature in them, and a trace of the presence in human life of him who is ever seeking to reconcile men to himself, to one another, and to their true destiny; to solve the contradictions and abolish the discords of life, and to unite men in the kingdom of love and peace.[1]

(2) It follows from what has been said that love is by its very nature a social virtue. Love carries us out of ourselves. It is essentially inconsistent with the indifferent temper. It is an active, forthputting quality whose very nature is violated by the hermit-spirit. Love implies mutual relations and common interests. It is the social principle in man. Mutual service and helpfulness, which spring out of love, make social life possible. If these were wholly wanting, society would revert to barbarism, which is simply extreme individualism involving utter disregard of others or of the general weal. Love is therefore the only principle on which a true civilization can be built.

This idea is involved in the doctrine which John so often presents,— that love is the true basis of union

[1] For an ample discussion of "uniting love," see Sartorius on *The Doctrine of Divine Love*, pp. 260-309.

THE DOCTRINE OF LOVE

in the kingdom of God. One brotherhood knit together by love is the ideal society. The kingdom of God is realized among men in proportion as they live the life of love, that is, in proportion as they love one another as Christ has loved them. As the provisions of redemption proceed from the divine love, so the realization of its results in the life of the world must be brought about by the reign of love in mankind. The divine love is redeeming the world into itself. Salvation springs from love and man is saved unto love. This is but to say that God in redemption is bringing men to himself, and uniting them into a brotherhood through their common likeness to himself. Here again we see illustrated a peculiarity of John's thought which we have more than once observed, — the tendency to ground the whole nature and all the requirements of the religious life in the being of God. Love must be the true principle of fellowship in the divine kingdom and the law of Christian duty, since God is love. Religion is man's fellowship with God, and involves fellowship among men, and neither is, in its best sense, possible except upon the basis of ethical likeness to God.

(3) The possession of love is the guaranty of righteous living. The life of love and the life of sin are essentially incompatible. The apostle puts this principle forward in the sharpest possible form when he says: "Whosoever is begotten of God" — that is, has entered the life of love — "does not commit sin (ἁμαρτίαν οὐ ποιεῖ), because his seed abideth in him:

and he cannot sin, because he is begotten of God"
(I. iii. 9). Love and sin are contrary, that is, love is
essentially righteous. Many other passages presuppose this idea. Brotherly love is a quality of those
who abide in the light, that is, live the life of love in
fellowship with God, while hatred of one's brother is
a work of darkness, that is, a mark of the sinful life
(I. ii. 10, 11). Love of the world — supreme attachment to the pleasures and possessions of this outward,
passing order of things — is inconsistent with love to
the Father, which implies fellowship of life with God,
and moral likeness to him (I. ii. 15–17). Again, the
bestowment of the Father's love upon men, and the
answering love of the human heart makes men children of God, and as such the sinful world does not
know them. Their lives are ruled by love, and the
world has no just appreciation of that sort of life.
As the world in its selfish isolation from God does
not, in an ethical sense, know him, so does it not
know those who have entered into the divine life of
love, since love and sin are opposites (I. iii. 1). The
same thought is amplified in the verses which follow.
Childship to God involves the hope of increasing likeness to him (or to Christ). " Every one that hath
this hope (of becoming like the divine ideal) set on
him (Christ), purifieth himself, even as he (Christ) is
pure" (I. iii. 2, 3).

The centrality of love in the Christian life is explained by the fact that the apostle has a comprehensive and profound view of the nature of love. It so

THE DOCTRINE OF LOVE

includes or involves all the moral perfections of God that it can be made the law and measure of all his commandments. Love is therefore central in religion because it is central in God; and as it is central in his nature, so is it central in his action and requirements. The limitation of the meaning of love by which it is made a name for benevolence or good-nature, and is then set in sharp contrast to righteousness and made secondary and inferior to it, is a procedure in theology which can find no warrant in John's conception of the subject. To his mind, love and righteousness are inseparably intertwined; in fact, they are essentially one. Love is holy in its very nature; the life of love is the righteous life. Over and over the apostle insists that the sinful acts of men spring from lack of love. To do righteousness, that is, to live the righteous life, and to love are synonymous (I. iii. 10). Cain's murder — a representative sinful deed — illustrates the violation of the principle of love which from the beginning of Christ's teaching had been the substance of the gospel message (I. iii. 11, 12). The absence of love is moral death; the possession of love is eternal life (I. iii. 14). Love to God begets pity and compassion. The apostle contends that a man cannot be a Christian and refrain from pitying and helping a brother in distress (I. iii. 17); yet it is gravely argued in theology that it is optional with God to withhold mercy or grace from his creatures without the impairment of his perfection. It would be denied by none that the exercise of pity, compassion, or grace, is good. Yet it is held to be optional with God whether to be good to that extent, or not. It has been claimed that what is false in philosophy may be true in theology. This appears to be the only principle on which the theological *dictum* to which we have just referred can be justified. I have more than once referred to it in order that it might be looked at from different sides and tested by the various expressions of the apostle, which illustrate his conception of love. If it is true in dogmatic theology, it is certainly false in John's whole philosophy of revelation and life. It affirms a possible disposition or mode of action on God's part which, according to John, would vitiate the character of a Christian man. The argument which John's writings furnish against the *dictum* in question might be briefly summed up in saying: God is Christian; that is, Christ is, in his character and commands, the interpreter of the nature and action of God, and the import of his message is that God is love, and that love is in its very nature pitying, generous, and forgiving.

At the risk of some possible repetition let us follow out the conceptions of God as love and of the essential unity of righteousness and love, which we find in John. Love is essential and constituent in God's nature. If God is love, he must act as love. A quality or attribute without which God would not be the perfect Being he is, cannot be merely subordinate in his nature, and cannot be conceived of as merely passive or quiescent. Love has been eternally operative within the internal relations of the Deity. In these relations it is not only constitutive but it operates from an ethical necessity springing from the nature of God. Let us apply the subject to created spirits who have never sinned. If love moved God to create them and to sustain them in life, is it rational to suppose that God *can* withhold his love from them, — that in the case which we have supposed love is a purely optional attribute? To me this seems quite inconceivable, it being understood that the necessity to love of which I speak is a purely moral necessity springing, not from any source outside the Deity, but from his own immanent perfections. If love is a quality so essential in God that without it he would not be God, it is surely no presumption to say that God must love, at least, his sinless creatures, since love cannot be essential and constituent in his nature and purely optional as to its exercise.

It is needless to follow out in detail the application of the *dictum* in question to the subject of redemption. It is sufficient for our purpose to show that the theory that retributive justice is superior to and independent of love in God, and that there springs from his very nature a necessity that he should be just, but no necessity that he should be gracious or generous, is incongruous with the teaching of the apostle John. We may, however, add that since, as all admit, God has always loved even sinners, it is probably according to his nature to do so. If love were only secondary and subordinate to justice, it would be unlikely that the lower attribute would always prevail. If, as Calvinistic theology has so urgently asserted, there is a conflict in the Divine Being between love and justice, it is certainly strange that the supreme attribute whose exercise is absolutely necessary did not triumph over the subordinate and optional quality, and exclude the sinful world from salvation altogether. This theology really lays no logical ground for a plan of grace for sinners. It is inconceivable that a work of gracious salvation could ever be begun if God were what this theory defines him to be.

Respecting the attitude of God as love toward sinful men, it is important not to confound two widely different conceptions, that of any obligation on God's part to love sinners as such, and that of his obligations to himself as the perfect Being. There is nothing, of course, in the sinful man *as such* which can make a *claim* upon God's mercy or constitute a basis of obligation, but there is an obligation to show mercy which is grounded in the Divine Being himself as morally perfect, that is, as uniting in his own nature all possible excellences. When it is argued that as men must be righteous but may or may not be kind, so God must be just, but may or may not be merciful, the premises should be carefully tested. Suppose a man chose not to be kind. Is he, in that case, the sort of a man which he *ought* to be? Is he as good, as morally excellent, as he would be if he were kind? Certainly not, unless one denies that kindness is a

THE DOCTRINE OF LOVE

virtue. A man even is under obligation to be kind. How preposterous to claim that God is less obligated to perfection of life than man. His obligation to possess and to exercise all virtuous attributes is absolute, but it is founded in nothing above or outside himself, but in his own eternally perfect ethical nature.

The view that love can be a passive, quiescent, or potential quality only, is contrary to the very idea of love. Love is an active power, an energizing affection. To conceive of it as possibly quiescent or non-operative in the perfect Being is to misconceive its nature. Such a conception cannot be applied even in human relations, to say nothing of its inapplicability to God in his relations to his creatures. What would be said of a man who maintained that he was at liberty, at will, to love his fellow-men or not? The character of the strictly and merely just Shylock who felt that it was optional with him whether he should be kind or merciful, and who chose not to be so, has not been generally admired. It is amazing that theological speculation should ever have held that such a disposition may be regarded as conceivable and possible for the God of all grace.[1]

[1] *Cf.* my review, in the *New Englander* for June, 1888, of Dr. A. H. Strong's *Philosophy and Religion*, — a work in which it is maintained that holiness and love are essentially different; that holiness is the fundamental and determining attribute of God, and that justice, therefore, *must be* exercised, while benevolence or love — the self-imparting impulse in God — *may be* exercised or *not*. "As we may be kind but must be righteous, so God, in whose image we are made, may be merciful, but must be

(4) Love is presented in John as the giving impulse in God, the motive of his self-communication. "God so loved the world that he gave" (iii. 16), is the keynote of John's doctrine of love in this aspect of it. The gift of the Son for the salvation of the world is the supreme expression and proof of God's love for the world. As this greatest of his gifts is born of love, so also are all his benefactions and self-impartations. It is the very nature of love to give and to bless, and this giving is, in the last analysis, self-giving. "Behold what manner of love the Father hath given to us (δέδωκεν ἡμῖν), that we should be called children of God" (I. iii. 1), exclaims the apostle. God bestows his life upon us; he imparts his own nature to us in making us his children. We become children of God by a divine birth, by an impartation from God himself. Thus he who is love bestows his love upon us so that we abide in love, that is, abide in God, and God in us (I. iv. 16). So too the gift of Christ to the world is God's gift of himself to us, since Christ shares eternally in the Father's nature and comes forth from the bosom of

holy. Mercy is optional with him" (page 196). The same view underlies the whole soteriology of this author's *Systematic Theology*, as it does that of Dr. Shedd's *Dogmatic Theology*. I venture also to refer to my reviews of both these works in the *New Englander* for January, 1887, and for February, 1889, respectively. See, also, Dr. E. A. Park's sermon (on the text: "God is love"): *All the Moral Attributes of God are comprehended in his Love*, in the volume entitled, *Discourses on some Theological Doctrines*, etc., Andover, 1885.

the Father. Creation, redemption, and providence are all grounded in the essential and eternal love of God. Love is the bond of intercommunion in the immanent and eternal relations which are involved in the equal deity of Father, Son, and Holy Spirit. These eternal relations within the Deity ever give scope to the exercise of love, so that, even apart from creation, it is rightly defined as the transitive attribute of the divine nature. "Love can be described as a need that can be satisfied only by giving. . . . Love is no external attribute, needing created relations in order to its exercise, for it was before creation, and creation was through it; and it is no attribute of pure immanence, for though it lives within Deity, and has there the necessary conditions of its life, yet it ever strives from within outwards, — struggles, as it were, towards creation."[1]

(5) Love is the motive of sacrifice and service. "Greater love hath no man than this, that a man lay down his life for his friends" (xv. 13). A passage in the First Epistle closely akin to this seems to indicate the sense in which Jesus speaks of laying down his life: "Hereby know we love, because he laid down his life for us: and we ought to lay down our lives for the brethren" (I. iii. 16). We have seen in an earlier chapter (pp. 172-175) that the *laying down* of life here spoken of is not naturally understood, as some scholars hold, to refer to the *paying down* of life as a ransom-price. The term seems rather to

[1] Fairbairn, *The Place of Christ in Modern Theology*, p. 411.

bear a general ethical import. Christ's giving of his life is here spoken of in the most comprehensive possible sense. His whole work of self-giving, culminating in his death, is the product of love. The expiatory idea is not necessarily excluded from such expressions, but it is not directly signified. Such a special idea is lost in the general conception. It is as if John had said: The Saviour's labors and sufferings on behalf of men, whatever their import, were the language of love, and they teach us how Christian love should express itself among brethren. The comprehensiveness of the terms used is noticeable. The giving of life seems to include much more than the experience of death, since Christians are to give their lives for one another as Christ gave his for them. All the forms in which Christ gave himself in serving love to men, seem fairly included in that laying down of his life of which the apostle here speaks.

(6) Love involves faithful devotion to its object. This thought is pictorially presented in the description of the scene in the familiar home at Bethany where Mary anoints the feet of Jesus with precious spikenard and wipes them with her hair (xii. 3). This is a picture of the grateful love of the disciple for the Master. With equal vividness is the love of the Lord for his disciples depicted on the occasion when he takes a towel and girds himself, and, pouring water into a basin, proceeds to wash the disciples' feet (xiii. 3–5). The event has its permanent significance as a picture of devotion and of service. The

THE DOCTRINE OF LOVE

disposition which it illustrates is the offspring of love, since it was the consciousness of divinity out of which sprang the impulse and effort to bless and serve, which the scene depicts. It was because Jesus knew that he came forth from God and was going again to God that he girded himself for this service (verse 3). Here again we see how this devotion was grounded in the very nature of that essential divinity whose moral perfection consists in love. That love is the true motive of personal devotion is assumed in the words of Jesus: "If ye love me, ye will keep my commandments" (xiv. 15, *cf.* verses 21, 24). The principle of love is one that can be securely trusted. The possession of true love is the best guaranty that the obligations of the Christian life will be discharged. Love is the germ which produces of its own nature the fruits of Christian devotion and service.

CHAPTER XII

THE DOCTRINE OF PRAYER

Literature. — No writer on the Theology of John, so far as I have observed, has discussed the doctrine of prayer as a distinct subject; but certainly the interest and importance of the theme, and the special difficulties which are connected with the references to it in John, entitle it to careful consideration. For the discussion of the points involved, I must refer the student to the critical commentaries on the passages to be reviewed. The following references will be found useful in respect to certain phases of the subject: WEISS : *Johann. Lehrb.*, Der erhöhte Christus, pp. 270–280, and *Bibl. Theol.*, The Church of the Disciples, ii. 398–404 (orig. 654–658); WESTCOTT : *The Epistles of St. John*, The Divine Name, pp. 243–245; EZRA ABBOT: *Critical Essays*, The Distinction between αἰτέω and ἐρωτάω, pp. 113–136 (reprinted from the *North American Review*, Jan., 1872); BERNARD : *The Central Teaching of Jesus Christ, passim;* F. W. Robertson's sermon on Prayer (Am. ed. pp. 644–651). The general subject is discussed in most treatises on Doctrinal Theology and Christian Ethics.

THE subject of prayer as presented in the Johannine writings may be naturally divided into four sub-topics: (1) The words by which prayer is described; (2) The references which are made to the prayers of Christ; (3) Indications respecting the nature and spirit of prayer on the part of the disci-

THE DOCTRINE OF PRAYER 291

ples; and (4) assurances in regard to the answering of prayer.

It is noticeable that John does not employ the words δεῖσθαι and προσεύχεσθαι, which are so commonly used in the New Testament in reference to prayer. Instead of these he uses two words both of which properly mean *to ask*: αἰτεῖν, to ask in the sense of making a request, and ἐρωτᾶν, to ask in the sense of interrogating. In the New Testament, however, this latter word frequently bears the non-classical meaning, *to request* or *to beseech*; and in John it is several times applied to the making of requests to God in prayer. This New Testament sense of ἐρωτᾶν is, no doubt, connected with the Septuagint use of that verb as a translation for שׁאל, *to ask*, which often means to ask in the sense of making a request.

The question as to the distinction between αἰτεῖν and ἐρωτᾶν in John's usage, where the latter means *to request* or *beseech*, has been much disputed among scholars. It is observed that the word ἐρωτᾶν is regularly applied to the prayers of Jesus,[1] while αἰτεῖν is used in describing the prayers of his disciples. A few typical examples may be given: "I will pray (ἐρωτήσω) the Father," etc. (xiv. 16); "I pray (ἐρωτῶ) for them; I pray (ἐρωτῶ) not for the

[1] In the judgment of some interpreters ἐρωτᾶν is once applied to the prayers of Christ's disciples: "In that day ye shall ask (ἐρωτήσετε) me nothing" (xvi. 23). This point we shall consider later.

world," etc. (xvii. 9); "Neither for these only do I pray" (ἐρωτῶ), etc. (xvii. 20). The usage of αἰτεῖν, on the other hand, may be illustrated thus: "And whatsoever ye shall ask (αἰτήσετε) in my name, that will I do," etc. (xiv. 13); "If ye shall ask (αἰτήσετε) anything of the Father, he will give it you in my name" (xvi. 23); "And whatsoever we ask (αἰτῶμεν), we receive of him," etc. (I. iii. 22).

It is certainly quite natural, in view of the peculiar uniformity with which John applies these two words to the prayers of Jesus and to those of his disciples respectively, to seek for the distinction between the words in some difference between the relation which Jesus bears to God and that which others bear to him. Such an explanation was put forward by Archbishop Trench[1] and has been accepted, apparently on his authority, by many other scholars. He explains the difference between the words as follows: —

"Αἰτέω, the Latin *peto*, is more submissive and suppliant, indeed the constant word for the seeking of the inferior from the superior. . . . Ἐρωτάω, on the other hand, is the Latin *rogo ;* or sometimes *interrogo*, its only meaning in classical Greek, where it never signifies *to ask*, but only *to interrogate*, or *to inquire.* Like *rogare*, it implies that he who asks stands on a certain footing of equality with him from whom the boon is asked, as king with

---

[1] *New Testament Synonyms*, § xl. Trench's explanation of the distinction between the words has been more or less fully adopted by Wordsworth, Lightfoot, Alford, and Westcott.

king, or, if not of equality, on such a footing of familiarity as lends authority to the request.

"Thus it is very noteworthy, and witnesses for the singular accuracy in the employment of words, and in the record of that employment, which prevails throughout the New Testament, that our Lord never uses αἰτεῖν or αἰτεῖσθαι of himself, in respect of that which he seeks on behalf of his disciples from God; for his is not the *petition* of the creature to the Creator, but the *request* of the Son to the Father. The consciousness of his equal dignity, of his potent and prevailing intercession, speaks out in this, that often as he asks, or declares that he will ask, anything of the Father, it is always ἐρωτῶ, ἐρωτήσω, an asking, that is, as upon equal terms, never αἰτέω or αἰτήσω."

This theory of the distinction is certainly attractive, and seems plausible in view of the fact which we have observed, that in the usage of John ἐρωτᾶν is applied to Christ's prayers and αἰτεῖν to those of his disciples. The assertions of Trench, however, that ἐρωτᾶν implies "a certain footing of equality" between the one making the request and the object of the request, and that αἰτεῖν is used "for the seeking of the inferior from the superior," rest on no known etymological distinction between the terms, and cannot be maintained unless supported by unquestionable usage. Dr. Ezra Abbot has shown that the distinction breaks down utterly when this test is applied.[1] The student need only consult the

---

[1] "*The Distinction between* αἰτέω *and* ἐρωτάω," *North American Review*, January, 1872, reprinted in *Critical Essays*, pp. 113–136.

passages reviewed by Dr. Abbot to be convinced that Trench's distinction will hold neither in the New Testament in general, nor even in John's writings in particular. In order to show that no "footing of equality" is necessarily implied in the word ἐρωτᾶν, it is sufficient to point out that the request of the Syrophœnician woman that Jesus would cast the demon out of her daughter (Mark vii. 26) is expressed by that verb. The centurion also asked (ἐρωτῶν) Jesus to heal his servant (Luke vii. 3), and the Gerasenes besought (ἠρώτησαν) him to depart from them (Luke viii. 37). In these requests certainly there can be no tone of authority or assumption of equality between the persons concerned.

If the uses of ἐρωτᾶν in the Gospel of John (outside of the passages where it is applied to the prayers of Jesus) be carefully considered, it will be found that they do not bear out the idea that ἐρωτᾶν refers to an asking "upon equal terms." The disciples besought (ἠρώτων) Jesus to take food (iv. 31); the Samaritans besought (ἠρώτων) him to remain with them (iv. 40), and the nobleman of Capernaum besought (ἠρώτα) him to come and heal his son (iv. 47). These are but a few of the instances in which the definition of ἐρωτᾶν as denoting an asking on equal terms, or with a tone of authority, is inapplicable. It is also found that there are many cases where αἰτεῖν cannot be shown to express "the seeking of the inferior from the superior," such as Luke

i. 63, xii. 48; Acts xvi. 29; 1 Pet. iii. 15; and Deut. x. 12 [Septuagint]: "What doth the Lord thy God require (αἰτεῖται) of thee?"

Although Trench's theory of the distinction between the words in question is certainly disproved, it is still a noteworthy fact that the prayers of Jesus are referred to in John by ἐρωτᾶν, and not by αἰτεῖν,[1] and that, as Trench says, the former word "is in no single instance used in the New Testament to express the prayer of man to God, of the creature to the Creator." While the fact that in John ἐρωτᾶν is frequently used of the petitions which various persons addressed to Christ, is fatal to Trench's general theory, it still seems to be a fact requiring explanation that this term alone is used of the prayers of Jesus, and is not used of the prayers of men addressed to God, while αἰτεῖν is frequently so used. Dr. Abbot's explanation of the difference is as follows:—

"The main distinction appears to be this: Αἰτέω is, in general, to ask for something which one desires to *receive*, something to be *given*, rarely for something to be done; it is therefore used when the *object sought*, rather than the person of whom it is sought, is prominent in the mind of the writer; hence also it is very rarely employed in exhortation. Ἐρωτάω, on the other hand, is to request or beseech a person to *do* something, rarely to give some-

[1] In one passage (xi. 22) Martha uses αἰτεῖν of Jesus' prayers, a fact to which Trench appeals as showing "her poor, unworthy conception of his person."

thing; it refers more directly to the *person* of whom the favor is sought, and is therefore naturally used in exhortation and entreaty."[1]

On this view of the difference between the words, the application of ἐρωτᾶν to the prayers of Jesus might, perhaps, be naturally explained by saying that his perfect fellowship and trust, and his knowledge of the Father, gave his prayers more of a reference to the Father's *person* and were more of a committing of himself to the Father's will and action than are the prayers of others, who ask rather that specific things be given them. The prayers of other men are more of the nature of petition, while those of Jesus are more of the nature of resignation and self-commitment to the Father. If this view be taken, it is obvious that ἐρωτᾶν, as applied to prayer, has a higher quality than αἰτεῖν. Cremer regards the difference as formal rather than material, αἰτεῖν expressing the desire of the will and ἐρωτᾶν marking the *form* of the request as a desire expressed to God in prayer.[2] Even in this view ἐρωτᾶν would suggest a certain closeness of fellowship and naturalness of relation between the worshipper and God which would not be associated with αἰτεῖν.

The distinction in usage which is observable in John can scarcely be accidental. There seems to be an element of truth in Trench's too broad and sweeping generalizations. Some higher import and asso-

[1] *Critical Essays*, p. 127.
[2] *Bibl.-Theol. Lex.*, sub voce, αἰτέω.

THE DOCTRINE OF PRAYER

ciations appear to be implied in ἐρωτᾶν than in αἰτεῖν, although it is difficult confidently and sharply to define the distinction. In I. v. 16 both verbs are used of prayer to God: "If any man see his brother sinning a sin not unto death, he shall ask (αἰτήσει) and God will give him life for them that sin not unto death. There is a sin unto death: not concerning this do I say that he should make request" (ἐρωτήσῃ). Here the two terms may be used synonymously, but it seems to me likely that αἰτεῖν denotes the making of a petition that something be granted, while ἐρωτᾶν is more general and refers rather to the appeal of the subject in question to God's will and wisdom. As Cremer suggests, ἐρωτᾶν seems here merely to characterize the form of prayer more precisely and to stand as the tenderest, finest expression for praying. If this distinction is here legitimate, it evidently accords with the view which we have taken of the usage in the Fourth Gospel. Αἰτεῖν is the more specific and more urgent word; it suggests the idea of petition for some definite gift; ἐρωτᾶν is more general, and is the higher and finer word, suggesting, as it does, the reference of the matter in hand to God's wisdom with the confidence of perfect trust. The latter verb is, therefore, more naturally used of the prayers of Jesus, while the former is applied to the asking of gifts and favors from God by others. I would not claim that this distinction can always be clearly and sharply made, but only that as applied to prayer to God in John's writings it is at least generally observable.

Let us now turn to our second topic, — the references in the Fourth Gospel to the prayers of Christ. The principal relevant passages are found in chapters xiv., xvi., and xvii. Jesus describes the sending of the Holy Spirit as following upon his praying the Father to send him (xiv. 16). He also speaks of a time when he will tell them plainly of the Father, and adds: "In that day ye shall ask in my name: and I say not unto you that I will pray the Father for you; for the Father himself loveth you, because ye have loved me, and have believed that I came forth from the Father" (xvi. 26, 27). Jesus will pray, on behalf of the disciples, that the Comforter be sent to them; when he is come he will, as it were, take the place of Christ, continue his work, and interpret his truth. The Comforter will come in Christ's name (xiv. 26); that is, the sphere and aim of Christ's work and those of the Comforter's work will be the same. Now, in this day of the Spirit, this time of fuller revelation, he will, through the Spirit, speak to his disciples concerning God more fully and frankly than he had done before. Previous to this time of greater enlightenment they had asked nothing in his name (xvi. 24); that is, the real spiritual purport and aim of his work which the "name" connotes had not been disclosed to them; but when the Spirit comes he will come in Christ's name, — that is to say, will disclose him more fully; and those who possess the Spirit will consequently ask in that name, — that is, with the right spirit and with adequate knowledge. The Spirit who represents and interprets Christ will, so to speak, initiate them into Christ, so that they will both ask and receive from God in his name (xiv. 13; xvi. 23). Through the possession of the Spirit, he says, my intercession on your behalf will be rendered unnecessary; you will come direct to God in the illumination which the Spirit will bestow, and asking in my name, holding all your desires and requests subject to the spirit and purpose of my work for you, will receive from God the fullest answers to your prayers. The question concerning the relation between the statement (xvi. 26) "In that day ye shall ask in my name" and the assertion in a preceding verse (23), "In that day ye shall ask me nothing," will meet us at a later stage of our discussion. It may here be noted that the idea which is presented in the last half of verse 26, that Jesus has no need to speak of his intercession for them in the dispensation of the Spirit, may be adjusted to his assertion in xiv. 16 and xvii. 9, that he prays for them, on the view that these passages are general and refer to the time prior to the gift of the Spirit, while the prayer referred to in xvi. 26, which, it is said, will be rendered unnecessary by the Spirit's illumination, is specific intercession, the ends of which will be accomplished by the Spirit's work in believers.

It remains to notice, under this head, the intercessory prayer of Jesus for his disciples in chapter xvii. In that prayer he prays specifically for those who have believed (xvii. 9), and for them who shall believe through the word of those who are already disciples (xvii. 20). He desires, not that they should be taken out of the evil world by death, as he himself is soon to be, but that they may be kept by the Father from the power of the evil one who is the prince of this world. In the quality of their life they are not akin to the evil world, as he himself is not; they share his own life and spirit. Jesus asks that they may be set apart and kept in the power and possession of the truth which they have received from him. This truth of his, the truth which he perfectly embodies and reveals, is their proper life-element, as opposed to the false and sinful world. When thus consecrated in and through the power of the truth they will be fit media for conveying the same truth to others and for communicating to them the life which corresponds to truth. Hence Jesus adds: "As thou didst send me into the world, even so sent I them into the world" (xvii. 18.) The same living truth which he has given to them, they are to bear on to others. He has set himself apart to this great work of bringing light and truth to men in order that those who receive it should, in turn, become bearers of light and channels of truth to others. Consecration through the power of the truth, the embodiment of the truth in life, and the expression of it through personal example and influence, — this is the first great desire for his disciples which Jesus expresses in his intercessory prayer.

THE DOCTRINE OF PRAYER

He then prays for the unity of all believers: "That they may all be one; even as thou, Father, art in me, and I in thee, that they also may be in us: that the world may believe that thou didst send me" (xvii. 21). Perfect harmony and fellowship among his disciples, like that which exists between the Father and himself, would, he implies, be effective in convincing the world of his divine mission. If his spirit could heal the divisions and harmonize the discords of earth, such a result would prove the most convincing possible evidence of the divineness of his work. He came to bring to the world the true principle and bond of brotherhood among men, — love. The work of love bears within itself its own attestation. Wherever men make it the guiding light of their lives, it commends itself to all with irresistible power as divine in its source and as divinely adapted to secure the best good for man. From the idea of unity among men through his indwelling in them (xvii. 23) the thought of Jesus mounts up to dwell upon their perfect union with him and with the Father through love, reaching its culmination in the words: "that the love wherewith thou lovedst me may be in them, and I in them" (xvii. 26).

This intercession was special in its import and purpose. It does not have in view the world in general: "I pray not for the world, but for those whom thou hast given me" (xvii. 9). He asks blessings for them which, in the nature of the case, could not be received by the world. He commends his disciples to God for special guidance and favor since they have shown a disposition to receive the truth and to live righteously. They have special needs, special capacities, and special claims upon the paternal sympathy of God. The exclusion of the world from this particular intercession has the effect to emphasize the higher relation in which those who have received the Son and his message stand to the Father. It does not imply any limit in the love and interest of Christ for the world. In the same prayer he expresses the desire that through the consecration and unity which he is now seeking for his disciples the world may be led to believe (xvii. 21). Just as earnestly as Jesus here seeks special grace for those who had responded to his call, would he at other times pray for the conversion of the world which he had come to save (i. 29; iii. 16; iv. 42; xii. 47).

Our third theme is, the prayers of the disciples. The first inquiry which arises is, What is meant by prayer in Christ's name? We have already observed how Jesus said: "Hitherto," that is, previous to the gift of the Spirit, "have ye asked nothing in my name" (xvi. 24). He then proceeds to assure them that in the dispensation of the Spirit they shall ask in his name (xvi. 26). Clearly, therefore, prayer "in his name" involves some higher element, and this element is the result of the gift and illumination of the Spirit. It is a part of that fuller blessing which the Spirit is to bring, and which makes it

THE DOCTRINE OF PRAYER

expedient that Jesus should go away in order that the Spirit may come to apply and perpetuate his work (xvi. 7). The capacity to pray to the Father in Christ's name results from that fuller enlightenment and more profound experience in Christian life to which Jesus refers in saying that the Spirit will bear witness of him, will guide the disciples into all the truth, and will take of his and declare it unto them (xv. 26; xvi. 13, 14). Further light is thrown upon the expression in question by the statement that (according to the best text) the Father gave to Jesus his own "name" to make known to the world; "in thy name which thou hast given me" (ἐν τῷ ὀνόματί σου ᾧ δέδωκάς μοι, xvii. 11); "I made known unto them thy name, and will make it known" (xvii. 26, cf. 6). The "name" of God is, according to a Hebrew method of thought, a symbol for God's nature. The Father gives to the Son his name to manifest to men in the sense that he commissions the Son to reveal himself as he truly *is*, to disclose his nature, thought, and feeling more adequately than they had ever been disclosed. This manifestation of God Christ makes to the world in his own person. He reveals to men, through the whole power and spirit of his life and work, the grace, the love, and the fatherliness of God.

What, then, is the force of the sayings, "If ye shall ask [me] anything in my name, that will I do" (xiv. 14); "That whatsoever ye shall ask of the Father in my name, he may give it you" (xv. 16)?

Place beside these assurances another in which different terms are used: "If ye abide in me, and my words abide in you, ask whatsoever ye will, and it shall be done unto you" (xv. 7). To ask in Christ's name must, therefore, be practically equivalent to asking while abiding in him, and while his words are abiding in the petitioner, that is, to ask *in him*, in his spirit, in accord with the whole aim of his work for and in the believer.[1] It should be noted, in addition to what has been said, that the Spirit himself who, through his teaching and guidance, leads believers into that experimental knowledge of Christ and his work which enables them to pray in his name, is said to be sent in his name (xiv. 26), and also that God is said to answer prayer in Christ's name: "If ye shall ask anything of the Father, he will give it you in my name" (xvi. 23). Thus it is seen that the phrase which we are considering is very comprehensive. The Spirit is sent, prayer is offered, and the answer is given in Christ's name. The person and work of Christ sum up in themselves the whole gracious purpose and proceeding of God for man's salvation and spiritual growth. All that God does for us is held within the scope of that revelation of God and communication of divine life to men which Jesus accomplishes. The perpetu-

[1] The import of the term "name" as a symbol in the Fourth Gospel may be more fully tested by consulting the following passages: i. 12; ii. 23; iii. 18; v. 43; x. 25; xii. 13; and xx. 31.

ation of the work of salvation in the world through the ministry of the Spirit and the fostering and strengthening of spiritual life through answers to prayer, stand in direct connection with Christ's person and work. The significance and end of his work are normative for all divine action in redemption and sanctification. As applied to prayer, therefore, the phrase "in his name," implies a right appreciation of Christ as revealing God to man and as revealing man to himself, and a right relation to this saving work. Bishop Westcott has this comment: "The meaning of the phrase 'in my name' is 'as being one with me, even as I am revealed to you.' Its two correlatives are *in me* (vi. 56; xiv. 20; xv. 4 *sq.*; xvi. 33; *cf.* I. v. 20), and the Pauline *in Christ*. . . . Augustine remarks that the prayer in Christ's name must be consistent with Christ's character, and that he fulfils it as Saviour, and therefore just so far as it conduces to salvation."[1]

The question now arises, How can we adjust the statements that in the day of the Spirit the disciples shall ask in his name (xvi. 26), and that if they shall ask him anything in his name he will do it (xiv. 14), with the assertion that in the day when he has departed and the Spirit is come they shall ask him nothing (xvi. 23 *a*). It is noticeable that in this last passage it is the verb ἐρωτᾶν which is used to describe the *asking* of the disciples. The Greek is: καὶ ἐν ἐκείνῃ τῇ ἡμέρᾳ ἐμὲ οὐκ ἐρωτήσετε οὐδέν. The

[1] *Commentary, in loco,* xiv. 13.

common view is that the word ἐρωτᾶν in this passage has its proper classical signification (frequent also in John and in the New Testament generally), *to inquire, to ask a question;* and that the meaning of the statement is: In the time when you become enlightened by the Spirit you will ask me no such questions as you have been doing: " How know we the way ? " (xiv. 5.) " Whither goest thou ? " (xvi. 5.) " What is this that he saith, A little while ? " (xvi. 18.) Others understand it to mean, *to make request of me in prayer.* On the former view the statement stands directly connected with verse 19: " Jesus perceived that they were desirous to ask him (ἤθελον αὐτὸν ἐρωτᾶν), and he said unto them, Do ye inquire among yourselves concerning this, that I said, A little while, and ye behold me not, and again a little while, and ye shall see me ? " With this meaning corresponds also the use of ἐρωτᾶν in verse 30. This view avoids the difficulty of applying ἐρωτᾶν in this one passage to the prayers of the disciples, whereas elsewhere in John it is applied to the prayers of Jesus only. Another consideration favoring the meaning *inquire* rather than *request* in our passage is that otherwise the statement here seems to clash with that found in xiv. 14, especially in case the pronoun *me* (μέ) is genuine, as it probably is. In the case just supposed we should have in xvi. 23 the statement that in the dispensation of the Spirit the disciples should address no prayer to Jesus, while in xiv. 14 he says that if they ask him anything in his name, he will do it.

THE DOCTRINE OF PRAYER 307

On the more common interpretation of ἐρωτήσετε the meaning of verses 23, 24 is well given in Godet's paraphrase: "You will no longer address your questions to me, as when I was visibly with you; and in general I declare to you that, as to what you may have need of, you will be able, because of the communion established henceforth through the Holy Spirit between yourselves and the Father, to address yourselves directly to him." [1]

To this interpretation of ἐρωτήσετε it is, however, objected that it unduly separates the two parts of verse 23. Trench, indeed, affirms that "every one competent to judge is agreed that 'ye shall ask' of the first half of the verse has nothing to do with 'ye shall ask' of the second." [2] But it is certainly unusual for the two parts of a verse to "have nothing to do with" each other, especially where a certain definite subject is being consecutively presented. Moreover, it is observed that in the sentence under review the pronoun *me* (ἐμέ) is emphatic both in form and by position. This emphasis seems to imply that it stands in contrast with some other personal term. What, then, is its correlative? On the former interpretation, which separates the two parts of the verse, no antithesis is expressed. It may be supplied in some such way as this: In the time of the Spirit ye shall ask *me* no questions, but *the Spirit* will teach you; or, you shall, instead of asking me, have direct

[1] *Commentary, in loco,* xvi. 23.
[2] *Synonyms of the New Testament,* p. 143.

access to the *Father* in prayer. But it is urged that by assigning to ἐρωτήσετε the meaning *ye shall request*, the two parts of the verse are brought into natural connection, and the correlative to the emphatic pronoun *me* of 23 *a* is found in *the Father* of 23 *b*. In that case the verse would mean: In that day you shall indeed make no requests of *me*, as you have been doing during my visible presence with you, but you may go direct to *the Father*, and he will give you whatever you need in my name. Dr. Ezra Abbot also raises, on behalf of this view, this question: Why should our Saviour say that when he was gone from earth and the Spirit had come, they should *ask him no questions?* Why should he tell them that they would not do what, in the nature of the case, was impossible?[1]

These considerations seem to me to be overbalanced by those which favor the former interpretation. It might be said of the disciples that they would ask him no such questions in that day as they had been asking, if the meaning were that they would not

---

[1] The student may be interested to see how modern commentators stand divided on the interpretation of ἐρωτήσετε. I have accordingly made a list of representative scholars on either side. In favor of the meaning *ask no questions*, are Tholuck, Lücke, DeWette, Alford, Trench, Lange, Meyer, Godet, Westcott, H. Holtzmann, and Plummer. Favoring the meaning *make request*, are E. Abbot, Weizsäcker, Weiss, O. Holtzmann. The views of older interpreters and of lexicographers are given in Dr. Ezra Abbot's article on "*The distinction between* αἰτέω *and* ἐρωτάω," in his *Critical Essays*.

THE DOCTRINE OF PRAYER 309

harbor them in their minds, or that they would not bring them to him in prayer. Moreover, the emphasis on the pronoun *me* may be naturally explained in the words of President Dwight: "The real force of this emphatic ἐμέ is this, that their permanent joy was to be connected with a new intercourse with the Divine Being, not that of questions presented to *him*, but of prayers offered to *God the Father* in his name." [1] If, then, the meaning *ask no questions* (such as you have been asking) be assigned to ἐρωτήσετε the passage xvi. 23 *a* will furnish no special difficulty when set alongside of the clear implication in xvi. 14 that, after his departure from earth, his disciples will *make requests* of him. It should also be noticed that the word for "ask" in xvi. 23 *b* is αἰτεῖν. This fact, I think, lends probability to the view that in the first part of the verse ἐρωτᾶν has a sense specifically different from αἰτεῖν in the second part. Otherwise the change of verbs would have no apparent motive, while if ἐρωτᾶν in 23 *a* means *to ask questions*, the use of different words in the two clauses is naturally explained. On neither interpretation of ἐρωτήσετε is there any conflict with xvi. 26. If the *asking* in the two passages is specifically different, there can be no conflict, because there is no direct *relation*. If, on the other hand, the *asking* is the same in kind in the two cases, there is no inconsistency, because in xvi. 23 *a* an asking *from Christ* (as contrasted with the Father) is

[1] Notes appended to Godet's *Commentary, in loco*, xvi. 23.

denied, while in xvi. 26 an asking directly from the Father is affirmed.

In conclusion, let us observe the terms of the assurances which are given that prayer will be answered. The language in which these assurances are expressed is very strong, and might seem, at first sight, to imply that whatever is asked will be given. But it is to be noticed that the asking is required to be in Christ's name : " Whatsoever ye shall ask in my name, that will I do, that the Father may be glorified in the Son. If ye shall ask me anything in my name, that will I do" (xiv. 13, 14). Moreover, the answering of prayer is also said to take place in Christ's name: "If ye shall ask anything of the Father, he will give it you in my name" (xvi. 23). It is quite certain that in this passage the phrase "in my name" should be connected with the phrase "he will give" instead of with the phrase "if ye shall ask." The other order, which is found in the Textus Receptus, is opposed to the reading of the best manuscripts, and is probably due to a tendency to conform this passage to xiv. 13 and xv. 16. Prayer, then, is to be offered, as it will be answered, in Christ's name. This phrase involves certain conditions and limitations affecting prayer. It implies that we are to ask in Christ's spirit, — the spirit of submission and trust, — and in accord with the nature and aim of Christ's work for us. It excludes the idea that human desires can give the law to the divine order and that the human will can become determining for the divine. The import

THE DOCTRINE OF PRAYER 311

of prayer in Christ's name is well indicated in such passages as I. v. 14: "If we ask anything according to his will, he heareth us," and xv. 7: "If ye abide in me, and my words abide in you, ask whatsoever ye will, and it shall be done unto you."

The assurances that whatsoever is asked shall be given are conditioned upon abiding in Christ, that is, upon the possession of a spirit in prayer like that which characterized him. Prayer for him was submission to God's will. "Not my will, but thine, be done," is the epitome of all his requests. His was the prayerful *life*, and to the test of that life we must bring all our ideas on the subject. The promise that God will give whatsoever we ask, is applicable within the sphere of Christ's work for us. So far as prayer is "in his name" it shall be answered; so far as the petitioner "abides" in Christ, he shall receive his requests. The whole practical import of Jesus' teaching concerning prayer which John has preserved, is well reflected in the words of the collect which asks that the Lord will hear the prayers of his servants, and adds: "and that they may obtain their petitions, make them to ask such things as shall please thee."

CHAPTER XIII

THE DOCTRINE OF ETERNAL LIFE

Literature. — WENDT: *Teaching of Jesus*, Eternal life in the Johannine discourses, i. 242–248 (orig. pp. 188–193); WEISS: *Johann. Lehrb.*, Der Begriff des ewigen Lebens, pp. 1–11, and *Bibl. Theol.*, Christ the Life of the World, ii. 347–352 (orig. pp. 614–618); REUSS: *Hist. Christ. Theol.*, Of Life, ii. 492–505 (orig. ii. 549–564); WESTCOTT: *The Epistles of St. John*, The idea of Life, pp. 214–218; BAUR: *Neutest. Theol.*, Das ewige Leben als Gegenwart und Zukunft, pp. 403, 404; BEYSCHLAG: *Neutest. Theol.*, Himmelreich und ewiges Leben, i. 262–264.

THE passages and topics which are to be considered under the heading "Eternal Life" are closely akin to those which we have already studied under the title, "The Origin and Nature of the Spiritual Life" (chapter X). It has seemed to me, however, that there was enough that was distinctive in the teaching concerning eternal life to entitle it to a separate treatment.

"Eternal life," or "life" in the absolute sense, is a name for the heavenly good which Jesus brings to men in the gospel; it is conferred upon men upon condition of faith in him. It is noticeable that in the Johannine writings it is usually described as a

THE DOCTRINE OF ETERNAL LIFE 313

present possession of believers. In the Synoptic Gospels, in which the term is less frequently used, it has a future reference, as in Mark x. 30, and the parallel passage, Luke xviii. 30, where "eternal life" stands in contrast to "this time": "He shall receive a hundredfold now in this time, . . . and in the world to come eternal life." In John, however, emphasis is laid upon the view that the believer already *has* eternal life, — an idea which, in other forms, is abundantly recognized in the Synoptists. We read, for example, in the Fourth Gospel: "He that heareth my word, and believeth him that sent me, hath eternal life, and cometh not into judgment, but hath passed out of death into life. Verily, verily, I say unto you, the hour cometh, and now is, when the dead shall hear the voice of the Son of God; and they that hear shall live" (v. 24, 25). And again: "He that believeth hath eternal life" (vi. 47); "He that eateth my flesh and drinketh my blood hath eternal life; and I will raise him up at the last day" (vi. 54). From passages like this just quoted, however, (*cf.* vi. 40) we see that eternal life, though a present possession of the Christian, looks forward to the "last day" for its completion; and thus we find in John a combination of present and future references which corresponds substantially to the twofold representation by the Synoptists of the kingdom of God as both present and future.

What, now, is this great gift, this heavenly benefit, which is called "eternal life"? In the opinion of many interpreters we find in xvii. 3 a description of its nature: "And this is life eternal, that they should know thee the only true God, and him whom thou didst send, even Jesus Christ." Weiss says that this passage states "wherein the essence of eternal life consists," and Westcott affirms that "the definition is of the essence of eternal life," and the same general position is taken by the great majority of commentators. But those who hold that we have here a definition of eternal life are not wholly agreed as to what it is defined to be. One point of difference concerns the force of ἵνα, κ. τ. λ., rendered, "that they should know," etc. The two scholars just quoted take different views of this phrase. Weiss argues that just because the clause "that they should know," etc., describes the nature of eternal life, it is impossible that the connective (ἵνα) can have the telic force. The clause in question, he contends, states the *content* of eternal life, and cannot, therefore, be a clause of purpose. Westcott, however, ingeniously says: "Eternal life lies not so much in the possession of a completed knowledge as in the striving after a growing knowledge. The *that* (ἵνα) expresses an aim, an end, and not only a fact. So, too, the tense of the verb (γινώσκωσι) marks continuance, progress, and not a perfect and past apprehension gained once for all." I cannot but regard this view of Westcott as oversubtle, and, in general, on the force of ἵνα in such

THE DOCTRINE OF ETERNAL LIFE 315

passages (*cf.* iv. 34; vi. 29, 39, 40; xv. 12; xviii. 39) I prefer the view of Weiss.[1]

But apart from this point, and on the assumption that eternal life consists in the knowledge of God and of Christ, there is room for considerable difference of view on the question, What is the nature of this knowledge which *is* eternal life ? How much does it include ? Is it to be understood as being absolutely synonymous with eternal life, or as being its root or subjective principle, as Lücke and Meyer maintain ? This last mode of viewing the passage is but a step removed from a second general method of interpretation which sees in it, not a statement of the *nature* of eternal life, but an assertion of the *condition* on which eternal life is attained. We find that John frequently represents Jesus as identifying a result with the means or agent by which it is obtained. Accordingly, he *is* the resurrection and the life (xi. 25), that is, the means whereby these are secured to men. Similarly he is said to be the way, the truth, and the life (xiv. 6), and his "words" and "commandment" are said to be eternal life (vi. 63; xii. 50), where the meaning must be that they are the means or condition of securing eternal life. In view of this Johannine "pregnant mode of expression" Wendt infers that "Jesus is not there (xvii. 3) stating wherein eternal life consists

[1] *Cf.* Burton, *New Testament Moods and Tenses*, § 213. The views of Weiss and Westcott are quoted from their Commentaries on xvii. 3.

316   THE JOHANNINE THEOLOGY

as to its essence, but wherein lies *the means of obtaining it.*[1]

A similar view of our passage is maintained by Beyschlag, who holds that it would have been incongruous for Jesus to define the nature of eternal life in his intercessory prayer, while the phrase is frequently used elsewhere in his teaching without formal definition. He therefore holds that the words, "that they may know thee," etc., are intended to indicate in what way and by what means Jesus imparts eternal life, and that the phrase "this is eternal life" is used in the sense of "thereupon rests," or "thereby is mediated eternal life." He further holds that the nature of eternal life required no formal definition, since it is made sufficiently evident by its contrast with death (v. 24) and destruction (iii. 16), and by the figures by which its bestowment is described, such as "the bread of life" and "living water" (vi. 35; iv. 10-14; vii. 37), and concludes: "The life is just that true, perfectly satisfying, blessed life which flows into the soul of man from communion with God."[2]

[1] *Teaching of Jesus*, i. 244 (orig. p. 190).

[2] *Neutest. Theol.*, i. 263, 264. In a note appended to the passage summarized above, Beyschlag characterizes Weiss's view, that in xvii. 3 the nature of eternal life is defined as consisting in the knowledge of God, thus: "An erroneous conception, which is carried so far that he (Weiss) says (*Bibl. Theol.*, p. 663, Eng. tr. ii. 411), with reference to v. 26 and vi. 57: 'As the Father and the Son are one, because there is common to them the life of the complete knowledge of God,'" etc., — an interpretation which, naturally enough, leads Beyschlag to exclaim: "Die volle Gotteserkenntniss Gottes?"

While it seems to me improbable that Jesus intended, in the passage under review, to give a definition of the nature of eternal life, it is none the less true, as Beyschlag affirms, that eternal life and the knowledge of God are closely related conceptions. If this knowledge is thought of as a condition of possessing eternal life, it is still vitally and essentially related to that life. It is necessary, therefore, in seeking the meaning of "eternal life," to determine as accurately as possible what this knowledge of God and of Christ fairly includes. The question has already been touched upon in our discussion of the idea of God and of the way in which God is known (pp. 65-67).

It seems to me certain that by the knowledge in question is meant a vital and practical apprehension of God in his true character as he is revealed in Christ. It is not a mere intellectual conviction, but an appropriation of God to the heart and life by the whole nature; it is such a spiritual intuition of God, such a laying hold upon the revelation of him as disclosed in Christ, as makes him the supreme object and determining power in life. In this view most interpreters of John are substantially agreed; it accords with a quality of John's thinking which we noticed in our opening chapter, — that is, the tendency to contemplate all the powers of the individual in their unity, and so to regard the total man as involved in all his acts and choices. Weiss admits the view stated above, but stops short of conceding Luther's claim that the idea of inward fellowship (*innere Gemeinschaft*) is involved in the term.[1] This seems to be an effort to make a distinction where there is no real difference. If, as Weiss says, this knowledge is "a spiritual beholding, a sinking of one's self into the highest object of knowledge by means of which it is inwardly appropriated and elevated so as to become the determining central point of the whole spiritual life,"[2] it must involve an inward fellowship with God. The simplest way of testing the correctness of this opinion is to review some of the more important passages in John, where he speaks of the knowledge of God or of Christ.

Let us first notice several passages in which the possession of this knowledge is denied, and observe the class of persons who are said *not* to have it, and the grounds on which they are so described. The "world" is said not to have known the true light which was shining in its darkness, and this saying is illustrated and enforced by reference to the rejection of Christ by the Jews (i. 10, 11). Jesus tells the hostile and wicked Jews that they have not known God, and adds, "but I know him" (viii. 55). It is obvious that as his is the knowledge of personal intimacy or fellowship, so their lack of the knowledge of God is due to their moral unlikeness to God and want of sympathy with his will. In xiv. 7 Jesus says to the disciples: "If ye had known me,

[1] *Commentary*, in loco, note (p. 544).
[2] *Commentary*, in loco.

ye would have known my Father also," and the conversation which ensued shows very clearly that it is through the deeper apprehension of his person and through closer unity with his life that they were to know the Father. In this connection the Spirit is promised, who shall unveil Christ and his truth to them that they may thereby know God. But some, he says, have no affinity for the Spirit. The world cannot receive him, "for it beholdeth him not, neither knoweth him: ye know him; for he abideth with you, and shall be in you" (xiv. 17). The Jews will persecute the disciples, said Jesus, "and these things will they do, because they have not known the Father, nor me" (xvi. 3). The sinful world knew not God, but Jesus knew him and made him known to men, and will continue to make him known; and what is the aim of that knowledge? "That the love wherewith thou lovedst me may be in them, and I in them" (xvii. 26). These passages show how inseparable is the knowledge of God from the life of love in fellowship with God. Several passages in the First Epistle emphasize the same connection of ideas: "For this cause the world knoweth us not, because it knew him not" (I. iii. 1). "He that loveth not knoweth not God; for God is love" (I. iv. 8).

So far, therefore, as eternal life consists in, or is dependent upon, a knowledge of God, there is involved in it a spiritual fellowship with God. It makes little practical difference whether we regard

xvii. 3 as a formal definition of eternal life or as a statement of the method of its attainment. The conditions of entering the kingdom of God are also conditions of continuing to participate in its benefits. Humility, meekness, hunger and thirst after righteousness, and kindred qualities are as truly characteristics of the member of the kingdom as they are conditions of his becoming such. What, then, is eternal life ? It is the fulfilment of man's true destiny in fellowship with God as revealed in Jesus Christ; it is life after the divine pattern, — Christ-like life. It is the correspondence of man to his true idea, the realization of that sort of character of which Christ is the type. After a careful collation of all the passages in which John presents the idea of life, Bishop Westcott sums up their significance in the following statement: —

"If now we endeavor to bring together the different traits of ' the eternal life,' we see that it is a life which, with all its fulness and all its potencies, is *now ;* a life which extends beyond the limits of the individual, and preserves, completes, crowns individuality by placing the part in connection with the whole ; a life which satisfies while it quickens aspiration ; a life which is seen, as we regard it patiently, to be capable of conquering, reconciling, uniting the rebellious, discordant, broken elements of being on which we look and which we bear about with us ; a life which gives unity to the constituent parts and to the complex whole, which brings together heaven and earth, which offers the sum of existence in one thought. As we reach forth to grasp it, the revelation of God is

THE DOCTRINE OF ETERNAL LIFE

seen to have been unfolded in its parts in Creation; and the parts are seen to have been brought together again by the Incarnation."[1]

This general view of the nature of eternal life may be further tested by reference to those discourses in chapters v. and vi. of the Gospel, to which for another purpose we have already referred (pp. 156–164). If the interpretation of these discourses which we adopted be correct, we may find in them a strong confirmation of the mystical conception of eternal life. The moral blindness, pride, and obduracy of the Jews are depicted as the reason why they will not come to Christ that they may have life (v. 37–40). Had they possessed a humble and teachable spirit, had they penetrated to the real truth of the Scriptures and lived the life of obedience and fellowship with God which corresponds to that truth, they would have had eternal life.

Still more explicitly in the discourse on the bread of life does Jesus represent eternal life as dependent upon spiritual fellowship with himself. He is himself the bread that possesses and gives life. This bread must be eaten; that is, his own person, his very spirit and life, must be appropriated in order that eternal life may be secured. "He that eateth my flesh and drinketh my blood hath eternal life; and I will raise him up at the last day. He that eateth me, he also shall live because of me" (vi. 54, 57). There is a passage in the First Epistle

[1] *The Epistles of St. John*, pp. 217, 218.

which, though not very plain in its grammatical form, is clear in its bearing upon the nature of eternal life: "And we know that the Son of God is come, and hath given us an understanding, that we know (ἵνα γινώσκομεν) him that is true [God], and we are in him that is true, in his Son Jesus Christ. This one [God] is the true God, and eternal life" (I. v. 20). The essential thought of the passage is that Christ has disclosed God to men in his real character so that they may truly know him, and they do thus know him by being in him as they are in Christ. Union with Christ involves union with God, and this true God to whom we are united through Christ becomes eternal life to us. In the knowledge and fellowship of God we realize the true life. This "knowledge rests on fellowship and issues in fellowship" (Westcott).

Our inquiries have thus far led us to a generic conception of "eternal life" in John's writings. It remains, however, to examine more particularly the force of the phrase so far as it is dependent upon the word "eternal" (αἰώνιος). The phrase "eternal life" occurs seventeen times in the Gospel and six times in the First Epistle. In none of these cases does there appear to be any distinctive emphasis upon the word *eternal*, and in but few instances is the phrase so used as to throw any light upon the force of that word. There are five passages, however, which should be noticed in this connection. In two places eternal life is contrasted with perishing or

THE DOCTRINE OF ETERNAL LIFE 323

destruction (ἀπώλεια): "God so loved the world, that he gave his only begotten Son, that whosoever believeth on him should not perish (μὴ ἀπόληται), but have eternal life" (iii. 16); "And I give unto them eternal life; and they shall never perish" (οὐ μὴ ἀπόλωνται), etc. (x. 28). The idea contained in the word *perish* is probably that of an ethical destruction, the loss of man's true destiny as a child of God; the opposite of this idea, "eternal life," would not, in that case, emphasize primarily the continuance of existence, but the attainment of the true goal of man's being in fellowship with God. It lies, no doubt, in the very idea of this life that it is imperishable or endless, but the stress of thought does not lie upon its perpetuity, but upon its nature or content. The same will be found to be the case where eternal life is contrasted with death: "He that heareth my word, and believeth him that sent me, hath eternal life, and cometh not into judgment, but hath passed out of death into life" (v. 24). It is quite certain that the *death* here spoken of is the moral death of sin, the state from which it is the mission of the Son to raise men (*cf.* verse 21). Here, too, the spiritual life which is bestowed is eternal, not primarily in the sense of being endless, but in the sense of being akin to God, as the closing words of the passage intimate: "He that heareth, etc., hath passed out of *the* death [ἐκ τοῦ θανάτου, the death which is really such] into *the* life" [εἰς τὴν ζωήν, the life which is truly life].

In two other passages the certainty of resurrection is affirmed in close connection with the promise of eternal life: "This is the will of my Father, that every one that beholdeth the Son, and believeth on him, should have eternal life; and I will raise him up at the last day" (vi. 40); "He that eateth my flesh and drinketh my blood hath eternal life; and I will raise him up at the last day" (vi. 54). In these passages, however, the assurance of resurrection does not appear to stand in special connection with the word *eternal*, but with the whole idea which is covered by the phrase "eternal life," which is declared to be spiritual fellowship with Christ. It is apparent from the associations of the word *eternal* in the phrase "eternal life" that it is a qualitative rather than a quantitative term; it emphasizes the source and nature of the life which it describes, rather than its continuance. We cannot trace the genesis or development of John's idea of the life that is *eternal*, but it seems as if he had derived the content of the word *eternal* from associating it with God as the source and type of true life: "For as the Father hath life in himself, even so gave he to the Son also to have life in himself" (v. 26); therefore, "as the Father raiseth the dead and quickeneth them, even so the Son also quickeneth whom he will" (verse 21). It is a reasonable conjecture that John's conception of eternal life stands closely connected with his idea of the nature of God. That idea is qualitative or ethical. The apostle seems to carry every truth of religion up beyond all associations of time and space, and to ground it in the very essence of God. Now, since it is not the perpetuity of God's existence, but his moral perfection, which chiefly constitutes his glory, it would follow that the dignity of the life which springs from union with him is found, not primarily in its continuance, but in its Godlike quality.

I may, in passing, indicate the way in which the Johannine teaching concerning eternal life may be made to bear upon the doctrine of "conditional immortality." If *death* or *destruction*, with which eternal life is set in contrast, be understood, not merely or chiefly in the ethical sense, but also in the sense of cessation of existence, and if the emphasis in the phrase "eternal life" be laid upon the idea of continuance, it would follow that eternal life in Christ involves immortality for those only who believe on him. This life, we are told, is in his Son (I. v. 11), and in iii. 15 the correct text most naturally yields the translation found in the Revised Version: "that whosoever believeth may in him have eternal life" (so Meyer, Weiss, Westcott, and Plummer). Eternal life in Christ will therefore mean immortality through union with Christ if the terms are taken in what I have called a quantitative, rather than a qualitative sense, — that is, as referring to perpetuity, as contrasted with cessation of being. It does not seem to me, however, that this application of the passages in question is naturally suggested by their language or context, or by the apostle's methods of religious thought. *Life* seems to denote, for his mind, fulness and richness of being, the realization of man's true destiny through union with God and likeness to Christ. Such a life is, of course, by its very nature, imperishable. Death can claim no dominion over it: "If a man keep my word, he shall never taste of death" (viii. 52); that is, he shall pass through physical death unharmed; "though he die, yet shall he live" (xi. 25; *cf*. vi. 50, 51, 58). This last group of passages, which assert continuance of life for the believer, may seem to justify the inference that for unbelievers there is no continuance of being. There is, however, no indication that the apostle himself associated this inference with his doctrine of life, and the actual statements which he makes or reports seem to show that for his mind the perpetuity of the true life is incidental to its nature. The direct contrast to eternal life, therefore, would not be extinction, but depravation, loss, moral destruction.

But if persistence of being is not the primary idea which John associates with life considered as *eternal*, how shall we define the notion which that word adds to the noun which it qualifies? I think no better answer can be given than that of Bishop Westcott: Eternal life "is not an endless duration of being in time, but being of which time is not a measure. We have indeed no powers to grasp the idea except through forms and images of sense.

THE DOCTRINE OF ETERNAL LIFE 327

These must be used; but we must not transfer them as realities to another order."[1] Reuss sums up the meaning of "eternal life" in three ideas: (1) "the idea of a real existence, an existence such as is proper to God and to the Word; an imperishable existence, — that is to say, not subject to the vicissitudes and imperfections of the finite world;" (2) "the idea of power, an operation, a communication, since this life no longer remains, so to speak, latent or passive in God and in the Word, but through them reaches the believer;" and (3) the idea "of satisfaction and happiness, . . . direct results of union with Christ."[2]

[1] *Epistles of St. John*, p. 215.
[2] *Hist. Christ. Theol.*, ii. 496 (orig. ii. 553, 554).

CHAPTER XIV

THE JOHANNINE ESCHATOLOGY

Literature. — WEISS: *Johann. Lehrb.*, Die Eschatologie, pp. 179-191, and *Bibl. Theol.*, The Last Day, ii. 416-421 (orig. 667- 671); WENDT: *Teaching of Jesus*, Coming again to the disciples according to the Johannine discourses, ii. 294-303 (orig. 565-573); REUSS: *Hist. Christ. Theol.*, Of Judgment, ii. 446- 454 (orig. ii. 498-508); BEYSCHLAG : *Neutest. Theol.*, Das Weltgericht, Die Auferstehung und das ewige Leben, i. 287-293, and Die letzten Dinge, ii. 464-466; FROMMANN : *Johann. Lehrb.*, Das Gericht, u. s. w., pp. 660-701; BAUR: *Neutest. Theol.*, Die Eschatologie, u. s. w., pp. 404-407; NEANDER: *Planting and Training*, Resurrection and Judgment, etc., ii. 48-53; MESSNER : *Lehre der Apostel*, Die Vollendung, pp. 357-360.

THOSE themes of religious thought which are commonly comprehended under the term "eschatology" are less prominent in John than in most of the New Testament writers. This fact is naturally explained by his tendency to contemplate religion as a present possession and experience. We have seen a conspicuous illustration of this tendency in our study of his doctrine of eternal life. A mystical theology like John's dwells with special fondness upon such truths as union with Christ and spiritual fellowship with God, — truths which are independent

THE JOHANNINE ESCHATOLOGY

of time, and which tend to make the mind which is absorbed in them relatively indifferent to future events and changes. In the judgment of some scholars we find almost no eschatology at all, in the ordinary sense, in John's writings. Reuss is one of these. He says: "The current eschatological ideas of primitive Christianity are not found in the Gospel of John, or, at the most, if they are adverted to in some popular forms of expression, they are so isolated that they in no way affect the system as a whole. . . . Of all the facts of eschatology, the only one of which passing mention is made, is the resurrection of the dead."[1]

These statements we shall have occasion to test in the course of our inquiries. We will, however, forewarn the reader that we shall often find in John a close association of mystical ideas, such as that of a spiritual coming of Christ and that of a spiritual resurrection, with those of current eschatology, such as the idea of a visible second advent and that of a resurrection from the dead. This apparent commingling of two sets of notions will often make it difficult, and, perhaps, sometimes impossible, to draw a clear line of division between the literal and the spiritual. There are three themes in connection with which the eschatology of John can best be studied. They are: (1) the second advent, (2) the resurrection, and (3) the judgment.

The term *advent* or *coming* (παρουσία), which is

[1] *Hist. Christ. Theol.*, ii. 498, 499 (orig. ii. 556, 558).

so frequently used by Paul to denote the personal return of Christ to raise the dead and judge the world, is used but once in our sources: "And now, my little children, abide in him; that, if he shall be manifested, we may have boldness, and not be ashamed before him at his coming" (ἐν τῇ παρουσίᾳ αὐτοῦ, I. ii. 28). Reuss admits that this passage expresses the expectation of the second coming, but regards it as an illustration of the imperfectly developed mysticism of the First Epistle, which finds its completion only in the Fourth Gospel. The Epistle, he maintains, differs widely in this respect from the Gospel, "and makes use of many theses borrowed from ordinary eschatology."[1]

An obvious general allusion to the approaching end of the age is found in the words, "It is the last hour" (I. ii. 18). The bearing of I. iii. 2, 3 is not quite certain. The statement in the first part of verse 2, "It is not yet made manifest (οὔπω ἐφανερώθη) what we shall be," may be regarded as favoring the translation of the last part which is found in the margin of the Revised Version: "We know that, if it [that is, what we shall be] shall be manifested (ἐὰν φανερωθῇ), we shall be like him," etc. On this construction of verse 2 the "hope" which is spoken of in verse 3, as set on God or Christ, would refer directly to the expectation of being like God or Christ. If, however, the subject of "shall be manifested" (φανερωθῇ) is supposed to be Christ

[2] *Hist. Christ. Theol.*, ii. 503 (orig. ii. 561).

THE JOHANNINE ESCHATOLOGY

(so both our English versions), then the "hope" of verse 3 would refer, at least indirectly, to the anticipation of his advent. It is impossible to decide confidently between these two possible renderings, but I think the balance of probability favors the rendering found in our English versions. But whatever view be taken of this doubtful passage, it will be seen from the other two just quoted that the idea of a literal second coming of Christ is not absent from John's Catholic Epistle.

The passages of principal interest and difficulty, however, which bear upon our topic, are found in chapters xiv. and xvi. of the Gospel. I shall examine these passages, and try to ascertain their natural meaning by a study of the language and context. The effort will be to interpret what our author has written; the task of determining by conjecture the precise words and meaning of Jesus himself, in the utterance, sixty years or more before they were written down, of those discourses which John had reported, I shall not attempt.

The first passage which we have to consider is xiv. 3: "And if I go and prepare a place for you, I come again ($\pi\acute{a}\lambda\iota\nu$ $\check{\epsilon}\rho\chi o\mu a\iota$), and will receive you unto myself; that where I am, there ye may be also." There are four interpretations of the words "I come again" which deserve notice: (1) Some refer them to the coming of Christ to the believer at death, by which he is taken to the Saviour's heavenly abode (so Tholuck, Lange, Reuss, H.

Holtzmann). (2) Many apply the words to a spiritual coming of Christ to his disciples, either specifically, through the descent of the Paraclete (so Neander, Lücke, Godet), or — in accordance with a tendency to identify Christ and the Spirit — generally, to Christ's own spiritual presence with his disciples (so Wendt and Beyschlag). (3) Several interpreters suppose that the words "I come again" are to be taken in a pregnant or manifold sense. This view is thus defined by Alford: "This ἔρχομαι is *begun* in his resurrection (verse 18), *carried on* (verse 23) in the spiritual life (xvi. 22 *sq.*), *further advanced* when each is fetched away by death to be with him (Phil. i. 23), *fully completed* at his coming in glory." The interpretation of Westcott is similar: "Though the words refer to the last 'coming' of Christ, the promise must not be limited to that one 'coming' which is the consummation of all 'comings.' Nor again must it be confined to the 'coming' to the Church on the day of Pentecost, or to the 'coming' to the individual either at conversion or at death, though these 'comings' are included in the thought. Christ is, in fact, from the moment of his resurrection, ever coming to the world, and to the Church, and to men as the risen Lord" (*cf.* i. 9).[1] This view is shared by Stier, Lange, Reynolds, and Plummer. (4) The language is regarded as referring to Christ's second coming. This is the view of Hofmann, Ewald, Meyer, Luthardt, and Weiss.

[1] *Commentaries, in loco.*

To review all these opinions in detail and give the points which may be urged for and against each of them, would unduly extend the limits of this chapter. The language of the verse and the context most strongly favor, in my judgment, the last opinion cited. Christ's coming again seems to be set over against his going away to heaven and preparing a place for the disciples. To receive them unto himself seems most naturally to mean to take them to this heavenly abode; and to these *local* conceptions the idea of his personal coming best corresponds. Nor is there any strong presumption against this application of the words, in view of the references to the "last day" (vi. 39, 40; xi. 24) and to the advent (xxi. 22; I. ii. 28). The strongest objection to this view is derived from the apparently different meaning of the "comings" of Christ which are spoken of in the following verses (xiv. 18, 23, 28) of the same discourse. These verses may well make us hesitate to decide by what sort of a "coming" Jesus may originally have spoken of receiving his disciples unto himself, but they do not avail to cast doubt upon the meaning of the words of xiv. 3, as they stand. If they are not referred to the parousia, they should probably be understood as a figurative method of describing the blissful death of believers.

We must now examine the later verses of the chapter, which speak of a "coming" of Christ. In verse 18 we read: "I will not leave you desolate [orphans]: I come to you." What "coming" is this?

The connection seems to me to make it practically certain that this coming refers to the gift of the Spirit. In the preceding verse (17) the abiding presence of the Spirit is promised, and in the following (19) Jesus says: "Yet a little while, and the world beholdeth me no more; but ye behold me: because I live ye shall live also." The world has only physical sight, and when I am no longer present in bodily form, the world has no more knowledge of me; but ye, through the Spirit's illumination and teaching, continue, in a spiritual sense, to see me. Our communion is a fellowship of life. I shall still exist for you, my disciples; I shall still come to you and abide with you through the presence and power of the Spirit. The great majority of recent interpreters agree in referring this passage to the coming of Christ in the Spirit.[1] Others have referred the words to Christ's appearances after his resurrection;[2] others to the parousia;[3] and still others have given to the words a double sense and applied them both to his corporeal and to his spiritual return.[4] Westcott gives the words a continuous sense: "*I come*, ever and at all times I am coming." The application of the words to the Spirit is, however, confirmed by the subsequent verses.

In xiv. 23 Jesus seems clearly to speak of a spirit-

---

[1] So Lücke, Meyer, Godet, Reynolds, Plummer, Dwight.
[2] So Ewald and Weiss.
[3] So Hofmann and Luthardt.
[4] So DeWette, Ebrard, Lange, H. Holtzmann.

THE JOHANNINE ESCHATOLOGY 335

ual "coming" of both the Father and himself to those who love him: "If a man love me he will keep my word: and my Father will love him, and we will come unto him, and make our abode with him;" and what he afterwards says in xiv. 28 can hardly be meant in a sense specifically different: "Ye heard how I said to you, I go away and I come again to you." Since his departure from earth and the sending of the Spirit are counterparts (xvi. 7), it would follow that his "coming" to them after his departure would be most naturally understood to refer to his coming in the gift of the Paraclete.

In chapter xvi. Jesus speaks of his disciples and himself as *seeing* each other after his departure: "A little while, and ye behold me no more; and again a little while, and ye shall see me" (verse 16). "Ye therefore now have sorrow: but I will see you again, and your heart shall rejoice, and your joy no one taketh away from you" (verse 22). The interpretation which is adopted for xiv. 18 will have considerable influence in the effort to determine the meaning of these passages. Some, however, who do not refer xiv. 18 directly or solely to Christ's appearances after his resurrection, understand the *seeing*, which is here spoken of, as occurring in connection with those appearances.[1] While, as we intimated, the *spiritual* sense of xiv. 18 would probably be found to be supported by a majority of modern commentators, the same cannot be said of xvi. 16, 22. These

[1] So Lange and Ebrard.

verses have been more commonly referred to the reunion of Christ with his disciples after his resurrection.[1] Some have applied them to the parousia,[2] and still others have understood them to relate to a process or series of "comings,"[3] in accordance with the "perspective view" of such prophecies. The choice seems clearly to lie between the reference to the appearances after the resurrection and that to the spiritual vision of Christ. The whole context, especially verses 23, 25, and 26, seems to me to speak strongly for the latter view. Spiritual fellowship in the dispensation of the Spirit ("that day," verses 23, 26), a completer apprehension and appropriation of himself, is the theme of the discourse. Jesus assures the disciples that, though he will soon withdraw his bodily presence from them, he will, through the Spirit, even more fully disclose himself to them, so that he and they shall spiritually see and speak to one another. This interpretation will be found in the writings of Lücke, Meyer, Reuss, Godet, and Dwight.

One further passage remains to be considered. After Jesus had given to Peter the charge, "Feed my sheep" (xxi. 17), he speaks to him of the martyrdom which awaits him in his old age, and then adds, "Follow me" (verse 19). Peter thereupon sees the beloved disciple John following, and at once inquires

[1] So Luther, Hengstenberg, Ewald, Weiss.
[2] So Augustine, Hofmann, Lechler.
[3] So Alford and Westcott.

THE JOHANNINE ESCHATOLOGY 337

in regard to his fate. To this Jesus replies: "If I will that he tarry (μένειν) till I come (ἕως ἔρχομαι), what is that to thee? Follow thou me" (verse 22). This saying, adds the narrator, gave rise to the report that John was not to die, — that is, that he should survive till Jesus came. Interpreters have found it no easy task to determine what "coming" is here alluded to. Some have thought of Christ's coming to John "in a gentle and natural death."[1] It is held that this idea alone forms a natural antithesis to the martyrdom which Peter is to experience; but this view involves the implication that Jesus comes at death only to those who die naturally or without violence. This contrast would represent him as coming to John in death, but not to Peter. Others think the reference to be, primarily, to the coming of Christ in the fall of Jerusalem, though some of these writers regard this catastrophe as the beginning of a series of "comings" which are implied in the expression.[2] This theory aims to escape the difficulty that Jesus could have intimated the possibility of John's surviving his second advent, — a thing which was, as a matter of fact, impossible. Since all the disciples, however, thought of the parousia as near, they would naturally interpret the words of Jesus as alluding to it. This reference of the words, however, seems far-fetched, and since

---

[1] So Ewald, Olshausen, Lange.

[2] So, with some variations, Luthardt, Godet, Alford, and Westcott.

John outlived the destruction of Jerusalem by many years, not much is gained by this view in the way of harmonizing the possibility suggested with the actual fact.

It seems, on the whole, preferable to refer the words "till I come" to the parousia,[1] and carefully to observe the hypothetical form in which they are set. Peter is to suffer a violent death before the parousia; he is actuated, perhaps by sympathy (Weiss, Godet, Plummer), or possibly by curiosity (Bengel, De Wette), or by jealousy (Lücke, Meyer), to ask the fate of John. Jesus replies to Peter that he need not concern himself about that; if it be his will that John should live till his coming, that can make no difference with his own divinely appointed course. This hypothetical statement easily became transformed into a categorical assertion, — though without warrant; for Jesus did not say: He shall live till I come, but only: *If* I will that he do so, that does not concern thee.[2]

It will be seen that, according to the interpreta-

---

[1] So Lücke, De Wette, Meyer, Weiss, H. Holtzmann.

[2] Dr. A. P. Peabody, in his essay on the Fourth Gospel, referred to in the Preface, presents the view that the words *follow* and *come* in the conversation really related only to remarks concerning local movements, which the disciples partially overheard, and "not unnaturally connected with the profoundly solemn subjects on which he had, no doubt, been talking with them as with Peter, and they imagined that by 'staying till I come back' he meant 'living till my second coming.'" See p. 111 of the volume of essays entitled, *The Fourth Gospel*.

tions which I have preferred, there are but four passages in our sources which can be pointed to as referring directly to the second coming of the Lord. We have also to remember that many scholars dispute this reference in the case of three out of these four passages. In the order of the certainty with which they refer to the parousia, I should arrange them as follows: I. ii. 28; xiv. 3; I. ii. 18; xxi. 22. Cautious as one's conclusions must be in dealing with passages of such peculiar difficulty as these and others kindred to them, two or three results seem clear: (1) The Johannine writings, as well as the Synoptic Gospels and the Epistles, express the expectation of the near parousia of the Lord. (2) The expression *I come, I am coming*, is not always used in the same sense. Jesus is represented as predicting "comings" which cannot be identified with the parousia. (3) We are thus led to observe a fact of capital importance for the study of the New Testament doctrine of the parousia in general. If Jesus actually spoke of various "comings," some of which were spiritual revelations or crises, may it not be that he really referred to some such manifestations of himself in his kingdom, where he is represented in the Synoptists as predicting his coming (apparently conceived of by the writers as personal and visible) in connection with such events as the mission of the twelve (Matt. x. 23; *cf*. xxiv. 13, 14), and the destruction of Jerusalem (Matt. xxiv. 29 *sq*. Mark xiii. 24; Luke xxi. 32), and that, too, during the lifetime of persons then living (Matt. xvi. 27, 28; xxvi. 64; Mark ix. 1; xiii. 20; Luke ix. 27; xxi. 32)?

In close connection with the allusions to the parousia, and as showing the association of the resurrection and the judgment with it, stand certain references to the "last day." In the discourse on the bread of life, the statement is four times repeated that Christ will "raise up at the last day" those who have been renewed through faith in him and fellowship with his life (vi. 39, 40, 44, 54). In xi. 24 Martha speaks of the resurrection of her brother "at the last day." This "day" is, therefore, the day of resurrection; that it is also the day of judgment is evident from xii. 48: "The word which I spake, the same shall judge him in the last day;" and I. iv. 17: "Herein is love made perfect with us, that we may have boldness in the day of judgment." Although the language in John is less explicit than in the Synoptists and in Paul respecting the relations of the parousia, resurrection, and judgment, there can be no reasonable doubt that they are conceived of as occurring in close connection, in the order named, at the nearly approaching end of the present age.

We turn next to John's teaching concerning the resurrection. The passages which we have just noticed (vi. 39, 40, 44, 54) in connection with the expression "the last day," clearly assert a future resurrection of the believer from the state of death, though they do not define the nature of it. Reuss regards the words "I will raise him up" as only a popular form of saying that "to the believer there is no death" (xi. 25).[1] But while there is a certain kinship between these two ideas, the former is too definitely expressed to permit of identification with the latter. A passage of much interest and importance for our present theme is v. 19-29. The idea of resurrection is here three times presented, in verses 21, 25, and 29, and is again indirectly referred to in verse 24. Verse 21 reads: "For as the Father raiseth the dead and quickeneth them, even so the Son also quickeneth whom he will." These words were spoken just after the healing of the impotent man at the pool of Bethesda. The Son, we are told, has wrought this miracle on the Father's authority and in accord with the Father's own beneficent activity (verse 19), but the Son will do even greater works than such miracles are (verse 20), for he will raise the dead and quicken them (verse 21). What sort of a resurrection is here meant? Before attempting to decide, let us follow the discourse a few steps farther. Jesus explains that judgment, as well as resurrection, belongs to the Son, who is entitled to equal honor with the Father (verses 22, 23) and continues: "Verily, verily, I say unto you, He that heareth my word, and believeth him that sent me, hath eternal life, and cometh not into judgment, but hath passed out of death into life. Verily,

[1] *Hist. Christ. Theol.*, ii. 500 (orig. ii. 558).

verily, I say unto you, the hour cometh, and now is, when the dead shall hear the voice of the Son of God; and they that hear shall live" (verses 24, 25). Then he speaks of the Father as the absolute source of life, and the Son as the mediate source of life, and the bearer of judgment, and continues: "Marvel not at this: for the hour cometh in which all that are in the tombs shall hear his voice, and shall come forth; they that have done good, unto the resurrection of life; and they that have done ill, unto the resurrection of judgment" (verses 28, 29).

Shall we regard this whole passage as literal throughout, or as figurative throughout, or as partly literal and partly figurative? It has been interpreted in all three ways; I unhesitatingly follow the great majority of modern interpreters in deciding for the third view. In that case we may either regard verse 21 as introducing the conception of spiritual resurrection, which is found also in verses 24 and 25,[1] or we may suppose that Jesus' life-giving work in both its spiritual and its physical aspects is presented, and that verses 24, 25, and verses 28, 29, respectively, set forth these two sides of his salvation.[2] This is a minor point of difference, and the language of verses 21-23 is not decisive. But since this language is very general and is intended to describe the "greater works" (verse 20) than miracles of healing which the Son shall do, it

[1] So Lücke, De Wette, Olshausen, Meyer, Plummer.
[2] So Tholuck, Godet, Weiss, Westcott.

THE JOHANNINE ESCHATOLOGY

seems to me most natural to take verses 21–23 as a comprehensive description of Christ's life-bringing and judicial mission, which is described in the verses that follow both on its ethical or spiritual (verses 24–27) and on its physical side (verses 28, 29). In any case, the language of verses 24, 25 cannot, without violence, be made to refer to anything but a spiritual resurrection, and just as little can that of verses 28, 29 refer to anything but a physical resurrection. In the former passage Jesus is speaking of the believer as already possessing eternal life, and declares that the hour when the dead shall hear the voice of the Son of God is already present. A spiritual quickening from moral death which is already taking place must be meant. But in verses 28 and 29, the dead who are "in the tombs" are spoken of, and they are described as coming forth to a resurrection, either of life or of judgment, according as they have done good or ill. Here only physical resurrection can be meant.

What we see, then, in this passage is not, as Reuss says, a comparison between the spiritual resurrection and the physical, with a declaration of the superior importance of the former (*cf.* μείζονα ἔργα, verse 20),[1] but a juxtaposition of the two ideas which, taken together, illustrate the greatness and completeness of the Saviour's life-giving mission. We must now look more closely at verses 28 and 29, and place alongside of them the few other passages

[1] *Hist. Christ. Theol.*, ii. 499 (orig. ii. 558).

which illustrate the idea of physical resurrection in John. In verse 29 it is said that they that have done good shall come forth unto the resurrection of life (εἰς ἀνάστασιν ζωῆς), and they that have done ill unto the resurrection of judgment (εἰς ἀνάστασιν κρίσεως). The genitives "of life" and "of judgment" may be understood as conveying the idea of *belonging to*, and so may designate, respectively, a resurrection which results in life in the Messiah's heavenly kingdom, and a resurrection which issues in a condemnatory judgment.[1] These words are also taken as defining and limiting the terms on which they depend, so that the sense would be: a resurrection which results from the possession of life, and a resurrection which results from the judgment which is already outstanding against those who have rejected Christ (iii. 18).[2] I can see no reason why both ideas may not be involved. Those who possess the true life enter upon its completion at the resurrection; those who, by reason of sin and unbelief are already judged, find that sentence confirmed and ratified in the final assize. When it is said that unbelievers are judged already, that believers do not come into judgment, and that those who have done ill come forth to a resurrection of judgment, the word "judgment" is used in the sense of an unfavorable or condemnatory judgment, so that the idea of a judgment for the righteous in the sense of a favorable sentence pro-

---

[1] So Lücke, Meyer, Godet.
[2] So Luthardt, Weiss, H. Holtzmann.

nouncing their acquittal and acceptance is not excluded. It will be seen that our passage — in contrast to Paul — explicitly asserts the resurrection of all men; but there is no hint of a separation in time between the resurrection of life and the resurrection of judgment (as Meyer holds). Only the former resurrection, however, carries with it the idea of the fulness of life and blessedness which characterizes John's conception of salvation.

We find nothing further in John bearing directly upon the resurrection, except the references to it in connection with the death and raising of Lazarus. When Jesus said to Martha: "Thy brother shall rise again" (xi. 23), she replied: "I know that he shall rise again in the resurrection at the last day" (verse 24); to which Jesus answered: "I am the resurrection and the life: he that believeth on me, though he die, yet shall be live: and whosoever liveth and believeth on me shall never die" (verses 25, 26). It is evident that Martha is here represented as cherishing a belief in a resurrection at the end of time. Reuss says that, in his reply to her, Jesus does not exactly negative this idea, but "deprived it of all theological value, in comparison with that other belief, that life and resurrection begin even now, triumphing over death in him who receives both directly from the Saviour."[1] But the contrast between the thought of Jesus and that of Martha is not the contrast between spiritual and physical resur-

[1] *Hist. Christ. Theol.*, ii. 500 (orig. ii. 558).

rection, but that between a far-off resurrection day and the present power of resurrection which resides in himself: "I *am* the resurrection and the life" (xi. 25). Jesus would call her thoughts away from the "last day" to himself, as the One who has abolished death for those who believe in him, and has brought in eternal life. Resurrection is included in the larger thought of *life*, which does not, indeed, exclude physical dissolution, but which deprives it of all power over the believer. Probably the saying, "I am the resurrection," etc., was also intended to point forward to the raising of Lazarus which followed. In any case, Jesus wishes to direct Martha's thoughts to *himself*, as a present life-giving power, and to indicate the wide scope of that *life* which he brings to men, according to which it includes, rather than abrogates, the idea of physical resurrection. It need only be added that the raising of Lazarus (xii. 1, 9, 17) and the resurrection of Jesus himself (xx. 1 *sq.*), which John narrates in detail, are quite inconsistent with the views that the idea of corporeal resurrection is only present by suggestion in John. Moreover, all the references to the subject are in the Gospel. There is not one in the Epistle, where, according to Reuss's theory of the imperfect mysticism and cruder eschatology of the Epistle, as compared with the Gospel, they should be found.

We turn to the doctrine of the judgment. Just as the life-giving work of the Son is presented chiefly in its present aspect, so John emphasizes the process of judgment which is continually taking place more than he does the final judgment at the end of the present world-period. And as the future resurrection seems to be viewed as an element, and, in some sense, as the consummation of the Son's bestowment of life upon mankind, so the future judgment appears to be regarded as the culmination of a process of judgment which is inseparably connected with the presence and effect of divine light and truth in the world.

There are several distinctions which need to be carefully kept in mind in seeking to construct from the scattered notices in John a doctrine of the judgment. They are such as these: (1) the distinction between judgment when it stands in contrast to salvation, and judgment in the sense of the moral testing of men according to their acceptance or rejection of the truth; (2) the distinction between judgment in the neutral and in the condemnatory sense; (3) the contrast between present and future judgment, and the relation of Christ to each.

I have already (pp. 63, 64) pointed out the solution of the apparent contradiction between certain passages which deny that Christ judges men and certain others which represent him, not only as actually judging them, but as coming into the world for that purpose. I will briefly call attention to them again. The principal passages are: "I judge no man" (viii. 15); "And if any man hear my sayings and keep them not, I judge him not: for I came not to judge the world, but to save the world" (xii. 47);

"For God sent not the Son into the world to judge the world; but that the world should be saved through him" (iii. 17). Yet Jesus says in immediate connection with the first of these passages: "Yea and if I judge, my judgment is true" (viii. 16); and elsewhere: "As I hear, I judge: and my judgment is righteous" (v. 30), and again: "I have many things to speak and to judge concerning you" (viii. 26); and even: "For judgment came I into this world" (ix. 39). The doctrine which results from these apparently inconsistent statements is, that the direct and primary purpose of Jesus' mission was to save and not to condemn the world, but that his revelation of the truth to men inevitably tests them and separates them according to their acceptance or rejection of it. This principle is stated in the passage: "This is the judgment, that the light is come into the world, and men loved the darkness rather than the light; for their works were evil" (iii. 19). Light cannot but test those to whom it comes; truth judges by its very nature, and its discriminations are absolutely "true" and "righteous" (viii. 16; v. 30). In this sense (not in the sense of condemnation) Jesus says: "For judgment came I into this world" (ix. 39), that is, for the purpose of testing men and determining what attitude they would take toward divine truth, as he immediately proceeds to say: "That they which see not [that is, those who are conscious of their need of light and guidance; *cf.* verse 41] may see; and that they which see [that is, those who, in their spiritual pride, say 'we see,' verse 41] may become blind."

Closely akin to these passages are others which more directly describe a present process of judgment. That process is the moral testing which is inseparably connected with the revelation of God in Christ, and in so far as the work of Christ secures the salvation of the world, this judgment involves the condemnation and dethronement of the powers of evil: "Now is the judgment of this world: now shall the prince of this world be cast out" (xii. 31). The Son conducts this judgment: "For neither doth the Father judge any man, but he hath given all judgment unto the Son; that all may honor the Son even as they honor the Father" (v. 22, 23); "and he (the Father) gave him (the Son) authority to execute judgment, because he is the Son of man" (v. 27). But even here the saying of Jesus that he judges no man, if properly understood, is applicable. He does not personally judge men; his personal attitude toward mankind is solely that of Saviour. It is rather his work, his word, his truth, which is represented as judging men in the sense of pronouncing condemnation against them both here and hereafter. The judgment is that light is come; men's attitude toward the light involves their judgment; the light judges them, or — if the statement will not be misunderstood — they judge themselves. "He that believeth is not judged;" his attitude toward the truth carries in its very nature his acquittal; he that believeth not hath been judged already, because he hath not believed on the name of the only begotten Son of God " (iii. 18, 19); his judgment is involved in his attitude toward the truth which Jesus embodies and reveals. The Saviour does not come to judge him, but to save him, but by his rejection of salvation he turns the saving message itself into a judgment.

This distinction must, I think, be the key to the understanding of a passage where Jesus disclaims even the exercise of condemnatory judgment in the last day upon those who reject him and receive not his sayings: "If any man hear my sayings and keep them not, I judge him not: for I came not to judge the world, but to save the world. He that rejecteth me, and receiveth not my sayings, hath one that judgeth him: the word that I spake, the same shall judge him in the last day." (xii. 47, 48). Only the two-fold distinction (1) between judgment as moral testing and as condemnation, and (2) between Christ's direct personal work (salvation) and the judicial effect of his truth (if rejected), can enable us to adjust this passage to those which describe Christ as judging. He is *not* the judge in the sense that his personal desire and the whole direct aim of his mission contemplate salvation; yet he *is* the judge in so far as his truth necessarily tests and separates men, and pronounces condemnation against those who reject it. His "word" shall judge men at the last day, as it is constantly judging those to whom it comes.

Having seen in what sense Christ is both the present and future judge of men, we naturally ask, What is the import of the saying that the Father judges no man, but hath committed all judgment to the Son, and especially of the further statement that the Father has given the Son "authority to execute judgment because he is the Son [or a son] of man" (v. 22, 27)? On this passage Beyschlag has this suggestive comment: "The eternal love condemns no one because he is a sinner; as such it does not at all condemn; it leaves it to men to judge themselves, through rejection of the Saviour who is presented to them. 'The Son of man' is the judge of the world just because he presents the eternal life, the kingdom of heaven, to all, and urges all to the eternal decision, and thus urges those who continue unbelieving to a continuing self-judgment."[1] Much here turns upon the saying that Jesus executes judgment "because he is Son of man." Many have supposed this to mean that he does this as Messiah, since judgment is a part of Messiah's work; but in New Testament usage both terms have the article where the phrase "the Son of man" refers to Jesus as Messiah. It is noticeable that here the title is υἱὸς ἀνθρώπου. Meyer supposes the title to point specifically to the incarnation. As incarnate Son he is judge, because in the economy of redemption he was appointed to do his work through becoming man. This view seems to ground his judicial function too much in an "economy" or decree, and too little in

[1] *Neutest. Theol.*, i. 290.

his nature as Son of man. Beyschlag thinks that judgment is here attributed to the Son because he is the ideal man, the true standard of humanity. To me that view seems preferable which finds a thought here akin to that of Heb. ii. 17, 18 and iv. 15, which speak of the necessity that Christ should share man's nature and enter into his life and experience in order to fulfil his work. Weiss expresses this idea by saying that Christ judges "so far as he is a Son of man, and can in human form bring near to men the life-giving revelation of God."[1] Westcott interprets thus: "The prerogative of judgment is connected with the true humanity of Christ (*Son of man*), and not with the fact that he is the representative of humanity (*the Son of man*). The Judge, even as the Advocate (Heb. ii. 18) must share the nature of those who are brought before him. The omission of the article concentrates attention upon the nature and not upon the personality of Christ."[2]

The passage in which it is said that the Paraclete, "when he is come, will convict the world . . . of judgment, because the prince of this world hath been judged" (xvi. 8, 11) has already been considered in its general import (pp. 210 *sq.*). So far as it bears upon our present inquiry it is closely akin to xii. 31: "Now is the judgment of this world: now shall the prince of this world be cast out." These words

---

[1] *Johann. Lehrb.*, p. 224.

[2] *Commentary, in loco.* This general view of the passage — with variations — is illustrated in the expositions of Augustine, Luther, Baur, Holtzmann, Plummer, and many others.

THE JOHANNINE ESCHATOLOGY   353

express the sense of Christ's triumph in his redemptive work, the certainty of the overthrow — seen as already accomplished — of Satan's kingdom. They resemble the saying of Jesus upon hearing the report of the successful work of the seventy disciples: "I beheld Satan falling as lightning from heaven" (Luke x. 18).

The passages which we have thus far examined illustrate, almost exclusively, the idea of a process of judgment going on continuously in this world, and constituting the reverse side of the work of redemption. Several of the terms, however, which are used in connection with the teaching respecting the resurrection, such as "resurrection of judgment" and resurrection "at the last day," prepare us to find that judgment is also represented as a future event. Accordingly, we read not only of resurrection but of judgment "in the last day" (xii. 48). Thus the two events are coupled together. In like manner, the parousia is associated with these events where the apostle exhorts his readers to abide in Christ, "that, if he shall be manifested, we may have boldness, and not be ashamed before him at his coming" (I. ii. 28). That the prospect of judgment is here associated with Christ's coming is evident from the language of the passage, and is confirmed by the kindred expression, "that we may have boldness in the day of judgment" (I. iv. 17).

It will thus be seen that there are only a few passages in John which directly speak of the future judgment. There are as many more, however, which clearly imply the idea of such a judgment. While, therefore, it is impossible to maintain by legitimate exegesis that the common eschatological conception of the judgment is not present in John, it is equally certain that the emphasis of the apostle's thought rested rather upon that of a continuous process of judgment coincident with the work of salvation. The final judgment appears to be regarded as the climax of the moral process of testing which goes on through the operation of the truth upon the minds of men. The idea of the judgment which the apostle presents suggests the saying of Schiller: "The history of the world is the judgment of the world."[1] The conceptions of a present and of a future judgment are not inconsistent. The latter presupposes the former, and ratifies and completes it. It is quite natural that John, according to his mystical method of thought, should lay chief emphasis upon the moral process, since for him the whole work of redemption, both in its direct and remote effect, is viewed from the stand-point of inward experience and moral development. He sees the future as already implicit in the present; eternal life as already begun here; the physical resurrection as a part of the Son's complete bestowment of life, which has already taken place for the believer, and the future judgment as but the crisis of a process which is going forward constantly in the life of every man.

[1] "Die Weltgeschichte ist das Weltgericht."— *Resignation*.

CHAPTER XV

THE THEOLOGY OF PAUL AND OF JOHN COMPARED

Literature. — REUSS: *Hist. Christ. Theol.*, Paul and John, ii. 513–536 (orig. ii. 572–600); LECHLER: *Apostolic and Post-Apostolic Times*, John and Paul, ii. 250–259 (orig. pp. 516–524); LANGE: *Das apostolische Zeitalter*, Das Stadium und der Typus der Lehre des Johannes, ii. 603–613; FROMMANN: *Der Johann. Lehrb.*, Verhältniss der johanneischen Christologie zu der anderweitigen neutestamentlichen Lehre, pp. 480–547; MESSNER: *Lehre d. Apostel*, Vergleichung der apostolischen Lehrbegriffe, pp. 381–421; VAN OOSTERZEE: *Bibl. Theol. of the New Test.*, The Harmony of the Apostles with each other, pp. 253–260: BAUR: *Neutest. Theol.*, Verhältniss zum Paulinismus, pp. 393–395; SCHAFF: *Apostolic Christianity* (vol. i. of his *History of the Christian Church*), The Theology of the Apostolic Church, pp. 510–564; MURPHY: *The Scientific Bases of Faith*, Paul and John on the Person of Christ, pp. 391–418.

PAUL and John represent the two most distinctive types of apostolic doctrine. Their marked differences in personality and in methods of thought make a comparison of the types which they represent at once a difficult and a fascinating task. Paul is the representative Christian schoolman of his time; he is practised in analysis and argument. John illustrates rather the meditative and intuitive order of mind. Paul is always seeking to argue out the

356   THE JOHANNINE THEOLOGY

truth, and to prove it from the Old Testament and from experience. John simply *sees* the truth and declares it, as if confident that those who have an eye for it will also see and accept it. Paul's method is more inductive; John's more deductive. The former is illustrated in the piling up of proofs of the doctrine of justification by faith in Romans. The undeniable corruption of the heathen world, the equal depravity of the Jews, and the multiform testimony of the Old Testament, are proofs which combine to show that salvation can only be by grace, never by merit. For John, however, the work of salvation seems to flow naturally from the very nature of God as love. Paul is more analytic, John more synthetic. Although Paul's religious conceptions are capable of combination and simplification, the apostle has kept them to a great extent apart, and has dealt with them separately. His doctrines of faith, of works, of sin, and of the law, are sufficient illustrations. All John's religious ideas are, on the contrary, comprehended in a few elementary principles, which are never lost sight of. The whole life of Christ flows out from his nature as the eternal Light of the world. The whole gospel, with all its various duties and obligations, is grounded in the nature of God as light and love. Sin is simply darkness, or the absence and opposite of love. Salvation is not conceived of as a process by which, upon certain terms, acquittal from a sentence of condemnation is secured (as with Paul), but as a welcoming of the light, and walking in it,— in short, as a life of fellowship with God.

With these hints respecting certain generic differences in the modes of religious thought which the two apostles illustrate, let us briefly review the principal doctrines which they have in common, and note such points of difference and of likeness as may present themselves.

1. *The Idea of God.* — Both apostles have an intense sense (characteristic of the Jewish mind) of the direct efficiency of God in all things. For both, the will of God is sovereign, and definite particular events are regarded as necessarily happening in order that specific Old Testament predictions may be fulfilled. In both writers we observe the Jewish mode of thought respecting God and the way in which he makes known his will in the Old Testament and accomplishes his purposes of mercy; but in Paul the Jewish type of thought is much more pervading and determining. In him God is conceived of in a more legal way than in John; he is a judge on the throne of the world. The problem of religion is, how man may appear before him so as to be accepted and acquitted. To John, God appears rather as the Being in whom all perfections are met. The problem of religion is, whether men will desire and strive to be like him. For Paul, God is certainly essentially gracious as well as essentially just, yet he has nowhere comprehended the ethical perfections of God in a single conception such as John's, — "God is light," or, "God is love."

There is unquestionably a fundamental unity between Paul's and John's doctrine of God. In the teaching of both writers, creation, revelation, and redemption are accordant with the divine nature and flow out from it, but this conception is much more explicitly presented in John than in Paul. When the separate elements of Paul's doctrine are gathered up and combined, it is obvious that holy love would best define for him the moral nature of God; but, owing to his more Jewish, legal method of thought, he has less closely unified the divine attributes than has John. Paul emphasizes more the will of God, John more his nature. Paul thinks it enough to ground events in the choices or acts of God; John goes farther and grounds them in his essence. I have no question that these standpoints ultimately meet and blend. Paul's view, when carried back to the farthest point to which thought can reach, conducts us to the conception of John. It is, however, significant that Paul, with all his argument and reasoning, only comes into a distant view of those loftiest heights of contemplation concerning God, where John habitually dwells as if they were the natural home of his spirit. With keen and just discrimination, therefore, did the ancient Church accord to John the name *theologian*, since he, of all early Christian teachers, penetrated most profoundly into the depths of the divine nature.

2. *The Person of Christ.* — Both writers emphasize the pre-existence of Christ and his exaltation to heavenly glory; both emphasize his relation to the

universe at large in the work of revelation and redemption; both ascribe creation mediately to him. For Paul, all fulness of divine life and power dwell in Christ, and the scope of his redeeming love is as wide as the universe. But while this lofty character and work are by Paul ascribed to Christ, it will be noticed that he contemplates the Saviour chiefly in his historic manifestation. He designates him generally by titles which refer to him as a historic person, such as "Christ." It remains for John to seek out some term which shall designate his essential, eternal nature. This term is *the Logos*, by which the apostle would express the nature of One who sustains an inner, changeless relation to God which underlies the incarnation and saving work of the Redeemer. John seems to advance beyond the idea of a voluntary humiliation of the Son of God for man's salvation, and to conceive of the incarnation as a certain special method of manifestation which the Logos adopted quite in accordance with his nature. He is the perpetual medium of revelation; the bringer of life and light to men. It is true that it is almost impossible to determine where the line runs in the prologue between the acts of the Logos before and after the incarnation. Probably the apostle intended no such line to be sharply drawn; he conceives the revelation of the Logos in humanity merely as a historic illustration of his eternal nature and action. The historic is set on the background of the eternal, and after the description of the historic manifestation of the Logos is clearly introduced, the thought still recurs, now and again, to the universal truths which that manifestation illustrates. In the opening verses (i. 1-4) the absolute nature and action of the Logos are described, ending with the statement, "and the life was the light of men." Then the description enters the sphere of history and the shining of the light of the Logos in the world's darkness is depicted (verse 5), and then comes John's witness in preparation for the coming of the true Light (verses 6, 8). This Light now appears, but the description of it uses the broadest terms. He was coming into the world and lighting every man; he was from the beginning in the world which he had made (verses 9–10). The Logos is for John the universal principle and agent of revelation; he has been perpetually operative in the world. In every time he has touched the lives of men, and his revelation of himself in the incarnation is grounded in what he essentially is, and in those relations which he has ever borne to the world which he has made and in which he has dwelt. While, therefore, both apostles have the same general conception of the exaltation of Christ's person, John develops more distinctly than Paul the idea of the eternal personal pre-existence of the Son, and of his perpetual activity since the beginning of time in revealing the divine light to men, and in blessing and saving those who received it.

3. *The Work of Christ.* — Both apostles agree in

ascribing a sacrificial significance to the saving mission of Christ. For Paul his death on the cross is the central point of his work, and for John he is the Lamb of God whose death takes away the world's sin, and the propitiation for the sins of the world. But John appears to conceive of the idea of sacrifice more comprehensively than Paul. For Paul, Christ's death is a ransom-price by which men are redeemed. Some kind of equivalence is assumed to exist between the Saviour's sufferings and the penalty due to human sin. The sufferings of Christ in some way meet the ends of the remitted punishment; they vindicate God's holy displeasure against sin as fully as the punishment of sin would do, and thus they stand in stead of that punishment, and make it morally possible for God to withhold the penalty of sin from all who trust in the Redeemer.

This Pauline method of thought respecting redemption clearly has its roots in the Old Testament and in Jewish thought. As in the sacrificial system, the animal which is slain in sacrifice is regarded as a victim which suffers vicariously in the place of the sinful man, so the Saviour is regarded as suffering in the sinner's stead, and as bearing in some real sense the penal consequences of the world's sin. Christ's death is vicarious in the sense that his sufferings are substituted for sin's punishment, and they serve the ends of that punishment by vindicating the righteousness of God as fully as the punishment of sin would have done.

While John is much less explicit than Paul in his references to the method of redemption, he appears to contemplate the Saviour's sacrificial work as an example of the operation of a universal law. He likens his death to the dying of the grain of wheat, which must itself perish in order that the germ within it may unfold and the larger product appear. Men, too, are to give their lives for one another as Christ gave his life for them. Such expressions of John seem to rest upon the idea that the law of self-giving, of dying in order to fuller life, is impressed upon the whole universe, and is, perhaps, founded in the very nature of God. "God so *loved* the world that he *gave*," seems to be the key-note of this Johannine conception of sacrifice. Love is essentially vicarious, and the universe is built on the principle of sacrifice. Lower forms of life are perpetually giving themselves to sustain higher forms; they die and rise again in a larger and richer life. John seems to conceive of Christ's giving of his life not so much as an act of suffering and death as a process of self-giving, and the appropriation of its benefits is by him described as a partaking of Christ's body and blood. John's expressions upon the subject are mystical, and their precise meaning difficult to grasp and define; but they illustrate a mode of thought which it is extremely interesting to follow out, and one which has fascinated many of the profoundest minds of Christendom. The few hints which he has given us in his writings form but scanty material for a doctrine of the atonement, but I am persuaded that his idea of vicariousness is rooted in his idea of God as love. In love as the giving, sympathizing, burden-bearing quality of God's nature lies the starting-point of John's thought respecting the method of redemption. The idea of outward substitution and transfer, which is still observed in Paul, is lost in John, because the whole subject is carried to a higher standpoint and seen in a higher light. The essential vicariousness of love is the principle which, in John, carries the notion of substitution up out of the sphere of outward, legal relations, and places it in the very bosom of God. Satisfaction does not represent an act of appeasing God's righteousness *ab extra*, but a process within the divine perfection whereby love — which is God's perfect moral nature — finds its satisfaction in giving and suffering for others.

The standpoints of Paul and John are not really inconsistent. The Johannine idea of God, if made the premise of Paul's argument, would lead him along the path which conducts to John's conception of salvation. It is Paul's more legal method of thought concerning God, and his less perfectly unified conception of the divine nature, which makes him seem to follow a different track of thought from John. But in the last analysis the two types of doctrine meet and blend. Paul teaches that in the suffering and death of Christ God exhibited his righteousness so that he might be just in justifying the believer. But when we inquire, What *is* God's righteousness, and how does God exhibit it? we can find no rational answer except that God's righteousness is the self-respect of perfect love, and that all the perfections of God are exhibited by their exercise. God satisfies his perfections only by revealing them and by realizing in the universe the ends which accord with them. If God is love, the doctrine of Paul as well as of John carries us in all reflection upon the atonement out of the realm of temporal substitution and satisfaction into the realm of those truths which are esssential and eternal in God.

4. *The Doctrine of Sin.* — In the main features of this doctrine there is an obvious agreement between Paul and John. Sin is for both universal and guilty. Paul connects sin in its origin and diffusion with the transgression of Adam, while John — so far as he intimates any view of sin's origin — appears to ascribe its introduction into the world to Satan. Both ideas rest upon the narrative of the fall in Genesis, and coincide so far as the idea of the primal source of temptation is concerned. The forms in which the two writers speak of sin are, in some cases, similar; in some, different. Both represent sin as a bondage or slavery, in contrast to the true freedom which is the boon of the Christian man; both depict it as a state of moral death, — the opposite of the true life of the soul. But Paul's characteristic conception of sin is that of a world-ruling power or personified principle which makes men its

captives, shuts them up in prison, and pronounces condemnation upon them. John, in accordance with a peculiar dualistic method of thought, is more accustomed to speak of sin as darkness in contrast to light, or as hate as contrasted with love. The true life consists in walking in the light, while the sinful life consists in walking in darkness. Light is for John the symbol of goodness or God-likeness; darkness the synonym of evil or unlikeness to God.

The contrast between flesh and spirit which has so important a connection with Paul's doctrine of sin is quite incidentally presented in John, and does not carry the same associations which it has in Paul. In Paul's writings "the flesh" is the sphere of sin's manifestation, and thus comes to be used in an ethical sense and almost to be identified with sin itself. "The spirit" in man is what we should call his religious nature, in which he is allied to God, — the highest element of his personality, which leads him to aspire after holiness. Between the flesh and the spirit there goes on in the natural man a constant conflict, with the result that the flesh keeps its supremacy. It is only when Christ is received in faith that the victory of the spirit is achieved. John has essentially the same doctrine, but he does not develop it in this form. "Flesh" and "spirit" represent for him two contrasted orders of being, — the sphere of the lower or outward to which we are related by our natural life, and the higher realm of reason and spirit with which our begetting from God sets us in relation.

5. *The Method of Salvation.* — In describing the way of salvation Paul's great words are, *justification*, and *righteousness*; John's are, *birth from God*, and *life*. In no other particular are the characteristic differences of the two apostles so clearly illustrated. Paul, in accordance with his Jewish training and as a result of his controversies with Pharisaic opponents, wrought out the doctrine of salvation in juridical forms. God is a judge whose sentence of condemnation is out against sinful man; Christ by his death provides for the annulling of the sentence. Faith is the condition on which this effect could be secured; that condition being met, the claim is cancelled and a decree of acquittal is issued. Righteousness for Paul is the *status* of a man so acquitted. The process by which the result is reached is called justification. Not that all this is conceived of by Paul as a *mere* court-process. It has its ethical counterpart in the spiritual transformation of the justified man, but the legal idea determines the *form* of the doctrine. With John the case is quite different; he has relinquished the forms of Jewish legalism. No controversy with Judaizing opponents requires him to meet them upon the plane of their own conceptions. Salvation is not thought of as the result of a divine declaration, but as the result of a divine impartation of life. It is not described as a legal status, but as a condition or character.

But even here, sharp as the formal difference is, there is an underlying unity; both apostles have at the heart of their teaching the same profound mysticism; for both, the Christian life is realized in union with Christ. To be in Christ, to abide in him, to feed upon him, are terms which represent equally the profoundest thoughts of both writers. Both coincide perfectly in making the divine grace the source of salvation, and a self-renouncing acceptance of that grace the condition of appropriating it.

6. *The Doctrine of Faith.* — In this article the apostles closely coincide. For both, faith is more than mere belief; it involves personal relation and fellowship. With Paul it is associated with such ideas as are expressed in the phrases "in Christ," "dying with Christ," and "newness of life." With John it is associated with "abiding in Christ," "living through Christ," and "eating the flesh and drinking the blood of the Son of man." In both, therefore, there is a pronounced mystical element. Faith is life-union with Christ. It is no mere possession of truths which lie dead and cold in the mind; it is a vital alliance with Christ, the hiding of our life with him in God. By both apostles equally is faith regarded as the very opposite of a meritorious achievement which saves by its inherent excellence; it is the correlative of grace, and therefore involves the explicit renunciation of merit before God. Faith has its power and value, not in itself as an exercise of the human powers, but in its

object, Christ, to which it links us. The saving power of faith lies in the fact that it joins our life to Christ. It is, therefore, not so much an achievement as an acceptance.

It does not follow, however, that faith is a mere passive receptivity. The very nature of faith, as an acceptance of a divine life, involves the possession of a new moral energy. Faith works by love. In faith a new life-force is received and new powers stir within the Christian man. It would be equally out of harmony with Paul and with John to regard faith as a mere act standing at the beginning of the religious life but isolated from it. Faith penetrates the whole Christian life; it is an active, energetic principle. If it carries us out of ourselves, it does so in order that it may bring us under the power of new spiritual forces which shall inspire and ennoble our whole nature, and impart an unwonted energy to our every faculty.

7. *The Doctrine of Love.* — Both apostles magnify the idea of love and give it a central place in their conceptions of religion. Although John is often, and properly, called the apostle of love, there is no passage in his writings which lays greater stress upon the duty of love and upon its centrality in the gospel than does that sublime "Psalm of Love," the thirteenth chapter of First Corinthians. It would be an interesting and instructive study to compare this chapter in detail with the First Epistle of John, where his doctrine of love is most fully developed.

PAUL AND JOHN COMPARED

In both, love is made the sum of all goodness. For Paul, love best summarizes "that which is perfect;" it best represents spiritual maturity in contrast to all such partial gifts and graces as knowledge, or the power to prophesy or to speak with tongues. Love is the quality which gives unity and worth to all other virtues; it is the very essence of goodness without which all outward acts which are commonly esteemed to be good are really without value in the sight of God.

In like manner in John love is the "commandment," at once old and new, which comprehends all specific duties and obligations. But John also urges that this principle is true both in Christ and in his disciples (I. ii. 8), that is, it is the law of the divine nature as well as of the human,—a universal principle or law of being. Hence he urges that as Christ out of love "laid down his life for us," so "we ought to lay down our lives for the brethren" (I. iii. 16). It follows from this conception that "every one that loveth is begotten of God, and knoweth God" (I. iv. 7) since "God is love" (verse 8). In love we enter into fellowship with God and become like him, since his moral nature is itself love. "God is love; and he that abideth in love abideth in God, and God abideth in him" (I. iv. 16).

It will thus be seen that John carries his doctrine of love one step further than Paul, and that this step is a most important and significant one. Paul applies the principle of love to the mutual duties and relations of men, but he does not show, at least, not explicitly, that the application of this principle among men is grounded in the very nature of God. This step is taken by John; or rather, it would be more exact to say that he starts from this conception of God's nature and finds in it the divine law which ruled in the life and work of Jesus, in which men must also find the ideal for their own lives. In this difference between the two ways in which the apostles deal with the same great principle, we find a conspicuous illustration of John's more abstract and deductive method of thought, as contrasted with Paul's more concrete and inductive method. It can hardly be doubted that the statements of Paul respecting love in the thirteenth chapter of First Corinthians would, if carried out, inevitably lead to the great conclusion (which to John, however, was rather a presupposition) that God's nature is essentially love, and that love is the highest duty and the most comprehensive virtue, because the ideal of all goodness and the law of all duty must always lie in the very being of God.

It appears to me, therefore, that the two apostles, notwithstanding the formal differences in the development and application of their ideas of love, are essentially one, and that if we should carry up the law of love which Paul so eloquently describes as the sum of virtue, we could find no other source or seat for it — no other ground for its authority and value — than that to which John refers it when he says:

"Let us love one another: for love is of God" (I. iv. 7).

From the brief comparative sketch which we have given of the teachings of Paul and of John, it will be evident that the latter furnishes us to a much smaller degree than the former with the elements of a *system* of thought. Paul has to a great extent put together for us the various elements of his teaching so as to give them a certain completeness of form. John has given us only single truths, a series of glimpses into great depths which he has made no effort to explore in detail. We can hardly speak of a Johannine *system* at all, and we are left to correlate as best we can the *disjecta membra* of doctrine which John has left us in his writings. The two great Christian teachers, however, in many ways supplement each other, and both illustrate and enforce with peculiar power the great truths of God's love and grace which constitute the changeless substance of the gospel of Christ.

BIBLIOGRAPHY[1]

I. TREATISES ON THE JOHANNINE THEOLOGY.

B. WEISS, *Der Johanneische Lehrbegriff in seinen Grundzügen untersucht.* Berlin, 1862.

K. FROMMANN, *Der Johanneische Lehrbegriff in seinem Verhältnisse zur gesammten biblisch-christlichen Lehre.* Leipzig, 1839.

K. R. KÖSTLIN, *Der Lehrbegriff des Evangeliums und der Briefe Johannes, u. s. w.* Berlin, 1843.

A. HILGENFELD, *Das Evangelium und die Briefe Johannes nach ihrem Lehrbegriffe dargestellt.* Braunschweig, 1849.

E. H. SEARS, *The Fourth Gospel the Heart of Christ.* Boston, 1872.

J. J. LIAS, *The Doctrinal System of St. John considered as evidence for the date of the Gospel.* London, 1875.

O. HOLTZMANN, *Das Johannesevangelium untersucht und erklärt.* Darmstadt, 1887.

E. HAUPT, *Der erste Brief des Johannes, ein Beitrag zur biblischen Theologie.* Colberg, 1870. English translation. Edinburgh, 1879.

---

[1] New Testament Introductions, Commentaries on the writings of John, and treatises on the literary and historical questions connected with these writings (with the exception of two or three such works which are largely Biblico-theological in method), are omitted from this list, since they do not strictly belong to the subject of the Johannine Theology. Ample references to these branches of literature may be found in Gloag's *Introduction to the Johannine Writings* (London, 1891), in Schaff's *History of the Christian Church*, Vol. I. (New York, 1882), and in Watkins's Bampton Lectures for 1890 on *Modern Criticism considered in its relation to the Fourth Gospel* (London, 1890).

374 BIBLIOGRAPHY

W. W. PEYTON, *The Memorabilia of Jesus, commonly called the Gospel of St. John.* London and Edinburgh, 1892.

J. H. SCHOLTEN, *Das Evangelium nach Johannes.* Translated from Dutch into German. Berlin, 1867.

F. D. MAURICE, *The Gospel of St. John,* a Series of Discourses; also *The Epistles of St. John,* a Series of Lectures on Christian Ethics. London and New York, 1893.

II. WORKS ON MORE COMPREHENSIVE SUBJECTS, WHICH INCLUDE A TREATMENT OF THE JOHANNINE THEOLOGY.

B. WEISS, *Lehrbuch der biblischen Theologie des Neuen Testaments.* 5 Aufl. Berlin, 1888. Translation from the third edition. 2 vols. Edinburgh, 1882–83.

H. H. WENDT, *Der Inhalt der Lehre Jesu,* Göttingen, 1890. English translation under the title, *The Teaching of Jesus.* 2 vols. Edinburgh and New York, 1892.

E. REUSS, *Histoire de la Théologie chrétienne au Siècle apostolique.* 2 vols. Strasbourg and Paris, 1864. English translation. 2 vols. London, 1872.

W. BEYSCHLAG, *Neutestamentliche Theologie.* 2 vols. Halle, 1891; also *Die Christologie des Neuen Testaments.* Berlin, 1866.

W. F. ADENEY, *The Theology of the New Testament.* New York, 1894.

C. F. SCHMID, *Biblische Theologie des Neuen Testaments.* 5 Aufl. 1886. Translation from the fourth edition. Edinburgh, 1877.

H. EWALD, *Revelation; Its Nature and Method.* Edinburgh, 1884. *Old and New Testament Theology.* Edinburgh, 1888. These volumes are translations of parts of the work, *Die Lehre der Bibel von Gott, u. s. w.* 4 vols. Leipzig, 1871–76.

F. C. BAUR, *Vorlesungen über neutestamentliche Theologie.* Leipzig, 1864.

H. MESSNER, *Die Lehre der Apostel.* Leipzig, 1856.

J. P. THOMPSON, *The Theology of Christ from his own Words.* New York, 1870.

BIBLIOGRAPHY 375

J. J. VAN OOSTERZEE, *The Theology of the New Testament.* Translated from the Dutch by M. J. Evans. London, 1870; also by G. E. Day. New Haven, 1871.

A. IMMER, *Theologie des Neuen Testaments.* Bern, 1877.

A. NEANDER, *History of the Planting and Training of the Christian Church, etc.* English translation. 2 vols. London (Bohn ed.). Revised translation by E. G. Robinson. New York, 1869.

J. P. LANGE, *Das apostolische Zeitalter*, Braunschweig, 1853-54.

G. V. LECHLER, *Das apostolische und das nachapostolische Zeitalter.* 3 Aufl. Leipzig, 1885. English translation. 2 vols. Edinburgh, 1886.

C. WEIZSÄCKER, *Das apostolische Zeitalter der christlichen Kirche.* 2 Aufl. Freiburg, i. B., 1890. English translation. 2 vols. New York, 1894.

O. PFLEIDERER, *Das Urchristenthum, seine Schriften und Lehren, in geschichtlichem Zusammenhang.* Berlin, 1887.

F. W. FARRAR, *The Early Days of Christianity.* Various editions. London and New York.

P. SCHAFF, *History of the Apostolic Church.* New York, 1853. *History of the Christian Church.* Vol. I. New York, 1882.

P. J. GLOAG, *Introduction to the Johannine Writings.* London, 1891.

O. CONE, *The Gospel and its Earliest Interpretations, a Study of the Teaching of Jesus and its Doctrinal Transformations in the New Testament.* New York, 1893.

III. TREATISES OR ESSAYS ON SPECIAL TOPICS.

A. H. FRANKE, *Das alte Testament bei Johannes, ein Beitrag zur Erklärung und Beurtheilung der Johanneischen Schriften. Göttingen*, 1885.

T. D. BERNARD, *The Central Teaching of Jesus Christ, a Study and Exposition of the Five Chapters of the Gospel according to St. John*, XIII *to* XVII *inclusive.* London and New York, 1892.

J. C. HARE, *The Mission of the Comforter.* Boston, 1854; also, London and New York.

B. F. WESTCOTT, *The Revelation of the Father, short lectures on the titles of the Lord in the Gospel of St. John.* London and New York.

H. KÖHLER, *Von der Welt zum Himmelreich, oder die Johanneische Darstellung des Werkes Jesu Christi synoptisch geprüft und ergänzt.* Halle, 1892.

T. HÄRING, *Gedankengang und Grundgedanke des ersten Johannesbriefes,* in *Theologische Abhandlungen Carl von Weizsäcker gewidmet.* Freiburg, i. B., 1892.

A. HARNACK, *Ueber das Verhältniss des Prologs des vierten Evangeliums zum ganzen Werk,* in the *Zeitschrift für Theologie und Kirche,* 1892, pp. 189–231.

H. HOLTZMANN, *Der Logos und der eingeborene Gottessohn im vierten Evangelium* in the *Zeitschrift für wissenschaftliche Theologie,* 1893, pp. 385–407.

INDEX OF TEXTS

OLD TESTAMENT BOOKS.

Reference	Page
Gen. ii. 7	201
iii. 1 sq.	141
iii. 8	83
iv. 3 sq.	141
vi. 2	143
xv. 1–6	32
Ex. xii. 46	27, 169
xiii. 2	178
xxii. 28	34
xxviii. 30	176
xliv. 27	182
xlv. 19	182
Num. v. 8	182
ix. 42	27, 169
xxi. 8.	25, 180
xxvii. 21	176
Lev. v. 18	182
xxv. 9	182
Deut. x. 12	295
xv. 19	178
xvii. 6	33
xviii. 15	31
xix. 15	33
2 Sam. vii. 14	105
1 Kings viii. 27	48
2 Kings v. 18	182
Job xi. 19	183
xxviii. passim	78
Ps. xxii. 18	27
xxv. 11	182
xxxiii. 4	78
xxxiii. 6, 9	77
xxxiv. 20	27, 109
xlv. 6	34
lxv. 4	182
lxix. 4	26
lxix. 9	33
lxxviii. 38	182
lxxix. 9	182
lxxxii. 6	34
xc. 2	89
cxix. 89	78
cxxx. 4	182
cxlvii. 15	77
Prov. viii. 1–4	79
viii. 22–30	79
viii. 32–36	79
xix. 6	183
Isa. ii. 1	87
vi. 9, 10	26
xliv. 3	26
liii. 1	26
liii. 7	169, 170
liii. 10–12	170
liv. 13	25
lv. 1	26
lv. 10, 11	77
lviii. 11	26
Jer. xxiii. 29	78
Ezek. xlv. 17	182
Dan. ix. 9	182
Hos. vi. 2	40
xi. 1	105
Zech. vii. 2	183
xii. 10	28

GOSPEL OF JOHN.

Reference	Page
i. 1	88, 90, 91–93
i. 1–10	360
i. 1–18	88 sq.
i. 2	88
i. 3	89, 93
i. 4	3, 15, 61, 99, 128, 257
i. 4, 5	94
i. 5	15, 99, 128, 131, 138
i. 6–9	94
i. 7	99, 228, 236
i. 9	15, 61, 99, 257, 332
i. 10	15, 66, 93, 94, 134
i. 10, 11	318
i. 11	24, 94, 131, 242
i. 12	107, 226, 242, 243, 304
i. 12, 13	71, 94, 233, 251
i. 13	242, 243
i. 14	95, 103, 106
i. 14–18	95
i. 15	96, 236
i. 16	96
i. 17	23
i. 18	48, 49, 70, 90, 103, 106, 107, 108, 236
i. 29	136, 138, 161, 167, 168, 180, 185, 186, 302
i. 32	236
i. 34	236
i. 36	180, 185
i. 47–51	221
ii. 11	226
ii. 16	33
ii. 17	33
ii. 19	40
ii. 21	38 sq.
ii. 22	220
ii. 23	304
ii. 23, 24	222, 233
ii. 23–25	207
iii. 3	246
iii. 3–8	242, 243, 245, 248 sq.
iii. 5	14, 249
iii. 6	129
iii. 11	236
iii. 12	228
iii. 13	108, 117
iii. 14	25, 161, 180, 185, 186
iii. 15	180, 228, 325
iii. 16	57, 103, 110, 113, 138, 164, 226, 268, 273, 302, 316, 323
iii. 17	63, 113, 164, 348
iii. 18	103, 110, 226, 304, 344, 350
iii. 18–21	164
iii. 19	133, 138, 273, 348, 350
iii. 19–21	64, 90, 131, 132
iii. 20, 21	236
iii. 21	10
iii. 31	109, 117
iii. 35	55, 70, 103, 109, 268, 270, 273
iii. 36	226
iv 10–14	316
iv. 20–24	42, 43
iv. 22	24, 36, 138, 165
iv. 23	47, 70
iv. 24	46
iv. 31	294
iv. 34	315
iv. 39	233
iv. 39–42	222
iv. 40	294
iv. 42	165, 302
iv. 44	138
iv. 47	294
v. 2–20	62
v. 16, 17	37
v. 17	55

INDEX OF TEXTS

Text	Page	Text	Page	Text	Page
v. 17 sq.	70	vii. 20	139	xii. 3	288
v. 18, 19	110	vii. 22	33	xii. 9	346
v. 19	38, 114, 157	vii. 37	316	xii. 13	304
v. 19-21	235	vii. 38	25	xii. 16	209
v. 19-27	60, 156 sq.	viii. 12	61, 99, 128, 132	xii. 17	346
v. 19-29	341 sq.	viii. 12-30	223	xii. 24	179
v. 20	55, 111, 157	viii. 15	63, 157, 347	xii. 25	180
v. 21	111, 157, 269, 270, 323, 324	viii. 16	64, 348	xii. 26	180
v. 22	111, 157, 349, 351	viii. 17	33, 35	xii. 31	134, 216, 349, 352
v. 23	64, 157, 349	viii. 21	136	xii. 32	180, 185, 186
v. 24	157, 316, 323	viii. 23	134	xii. 33	180
v. 24, 25	313	viii. 24	136	xii. 34	180
v. 26	59, 157, 316, 324	viii. 26	348	xii. 35	99, 128, 132
v. 27	64, 157, 349, 351	viii. 28	180, 186	xii. 36	99, 132
v. 28	111, 158	viii. 30-32	223	xii. 38-41	26
v. 30	64, 348	viii. 32	135	xii. 41-43	237
v. 30-47	237	viii. 33-36	135	xii. 44	226
v. 34	138, 165	viii. 34	136	xii. 44-46	227
v. 35	36	viii. 42	8, 270	xii. 46	99, 128, 132, 133, 138
v. 37 sq.	31, 50	viii. 43	8	xii. 47	63, 133, 138, 157, 164, 302, 347, 350
v. 37-40	321	viii. 44	140, 141		
v. 38-40	43, 44	viii. 45, 46	220	xii. 48	340, 350, 353
v. 42	273	viii. 47	8, 256	xii. 50	315
v. 43	304	viii. 48	139	xiii. 1	269, 273
v. 44	51	viii. 52	139, 326	xiii. 2	139
v. 45	36	viii. 53	121	xiii. 3	15, 289
v. 45-47	30, 31	viii. 55	66, 318	xiii. 3-5	288
v. 46	31	viii. 56	32, 121	xiii. 4	172
v. 46, 47	220	viii. 58	89, 113, 117, 120-122	xiii. 10	13
vi. 1-14	158 sq.			xiii. 19	228
vi. 22-65	111, 112	ix. 2, 3	137	xiii. 23	209
vi. 26-31	158	ix. 5	99	xiii. 34	269, 270
vi. 28, 29	228	ix. 39	63, 64, 135, 348	xiii. 34, 35	273
vi. 29	315	ix. 41	64, 348	xiii. 37	173
vi. 31-34	161	x. 8	36	xiii. 37, 38	172
vi. 32	159	x. 9	105	xiv. 1	226, 232
vi. 32 sq.	230	x. 11	172, 174	xiv. 3	331 sq., 339
vi. 33	227	x. 15	24, 172	xiv. 5	306
vi. 35	159, 227, 233, 316	x. 16	156	xiv. 6	192, 266, 315
vi. 38	117	x. 17	56, 172, 268	xiv. 7	318
vi. 39	315, 333, 340	x. 18	172	xiv. 9	4, 49, 114
vi. 40	226, 227, 313, 315, 324, 333, 340	x. 20	139	xiv. 9, 10	237
		x. 25	304	xiv. 11	103, 114, 224
vi. 41	159, 162	x. 28	323	xiv. 13	292, 299, 310
vi. 44	159, 340	x. 30	4, 103, 114	xiv. 14	303, 305, 306, 310
vi. 45	25, 159, 227, 236	x. 34	35	xiv. 15	283
vi. 46	103, 112, 236	x. 34-36	34	xiv. 15 sq.	270
vi. 47	159, 227, 228, 233, 239, 313	x. 37, 38	220	xiv. 16	190, 191, 194, 291, 298, 299
		x. 38	115, 224	xiv. 17	134, 191, 195, 319, 334
vi. 50	227, 326	xi. 3	269, 270		
vi. 51	159, 160, 171, 174, 186, 227, 326	xi. 5	268-270	xiv. 18	193, 199, 262, 333, 335
		xi. 22	295		
		xi. 23-26	345, 346		
vi. 52-59	261	xi. 24	333, 340	xiv. 19	194, 199, 262, 334
vi. 53	159, 161	xi. 25	315, 326, 341	xiv. 20	260, 262, 263, 305
vi. 54	159, 313, 324, 340	xi. 27	133, 219	xiv. 21	269, 273, 289
vi. 56	159, 305	xi. 34	172	xiv. 21, 22	263
vi. 57	60, 114, 316	xi. 36	269, 270	xiv. 21-23	68, 273
vi. 58	326	xi. 47-53	175 sq.	xiv. 21-28	273
vi. 62	117	xi. 48	168	xiv. 23	58, 269, 333, 334
vi. 63	130, 315	xi. 49-52	255, 256	xiv. 24	289
vi. 70	139	xi. 51	185	xiv. 26	190, 194, 196, 204, 205, 207, 298, 304
vii. 19	36	xii. 1	346		

INDEX OF TEXTS

	Page		Page		Page
xiv. 28	110, 333–335	xvii. 20	292, 300	ii. 8–10	100, 132
xiv. 30	134	xvii. 21	115, 220, 301, 302	ii. 10, 11	280
xiv. 31	269, 273	xvii. 22	116, 261	ii. 12	186
xv. 1 sq.	230, 259, 260	xvii. 23	58, 261, 269, 277,	ii. 13, 14	123
xv. 2	168		301	ii. 15	273
xv. 4 sq.	305	xvii. 23–26	268	ii. 15, 16	8, 134
xv. 5	260	xvii. 24	55, 90, 116, 133	ii. 15–17	280
xv. 7	304, 311	xvii. 25	63, 134, 171	ii. 16	130
xv. 9	56, 268, 277	xvii. 26	301, 303, 319	ii. 18	145, 148, 206, 330, 339
xv. 12	277, 315	xviii. 14	176	ii. 20	22, 206
xv. 13	172, 173, 177, 185,	xviii. 18	300	ii. 21	10, 206
	287	xviii. 36	134	ii. 22	145, 219, 234
xv. 16	70, 303, 310	xviii. 37	10	ii. 23	148
xv. 17	270	xviii. 39	315	ii. 24	258
xv. 18, 19	135	xix. 24	27	ii. 27	207
xv. 19	115	xix. 26	269	ii. 27, 28	194, 202, 258
xv. 24	27	xix. 31	168	ii. 28	333, 339, 353
xv. 25	24, 35	xix. 36	27, 169	ii. 29	12, 64, 65, 244
xv. 26	190, 191, 192, 194,	xix. 37	28	iii. 1	57, 70, 71, 254, 273,
	195, 196, 197, 205,	xix. 38	168		280, 286, 319
	207, 303	xix. 41	172	iii. 2	254, 280
xv. 27	197	xx. 1 sq	346	iii. 2, 3	203, 330, 331
xvi. 3	319	xx. 2	172, 269	iii. 3	280
xvi. 5	306	xx. 13	172	iii. 4	127, 136
xvi. 7	190, 195, 196, 206,	xx. 15	172	iii. 5	107, 168
	208, 214, 303, 335	xx. 22	194, 201, 203	iii. 6	13, 137, 259
xvi. 8	196, 197, 216, 352	xx. 23	136	iii. 6–9	171
xvi. 8, 9	135, 138	xx. 24–29	225	iii. 7	10, 13, 65, 265
xvi. 8–11	210 sq.	xx. 29	207	iii. 8	8, 136, 140, 141
xvi. 11	352	xx. 31	100, 105, 219, 304	iii. 9	13, 136, 137, 244, 280
xvi. 12	209	xxi. 7	269	iii. 9, 10	71
xvi. 13	196, 197, 205, 206,	xxi. 15 sq.	270–272	iii. 10	8, 140, 254, 281
	207	xxi. 17	336	iii. 10–14	273
xvi. 13 sq.	192, 303	xxi. 19	336	iii. 11, 12	281
xvi. 14	195–197	xxi. 20	269	iii. 14	138, 281
xvi. 14, 15	195, 205	xxi. 22	333, 337, 339	iii. 16	172, 173, 178, 185,
xvi. 16	194, 197, 200, 335				273, 286, 287, 369
xvi. 17	195, 197			iii. 17	281
xvi. 18	306	**FIRST EPISTLE OF**		iii. 19	8, 10
xvi. 19	306	**JOHN.**		iii. 19, 20	68–70
xvi. 22	335			iii. 21	192
xvi. 22 sq.	332, 336	i. 1	89, 100, 122	iii. 22	292
xvi. 23	70, 291, 292, 299,	i. 1, 2	99	iii. 24	260
	304, 305–310	i. 1–4	61	iii. 28	203
xvi. 23, 24	307	i. 2	3, 67, 123	iv. 2	95, 234
xvi. 24	298, 302	i. 3	67, 260	iv. 3	145, 148
xvi. 26	195, 197, 298, 299,	i. 5	3, 5, 47, 60, 61, 100,	iv. 4	8, 116
	302, 305, 310		132	iv. 5	8, 116
xvi. 27	58, 269, 270, 298	i. 5 sq.	5	iv. 6	8, 192
xvi. 28	116, 117, 133	i. 6	10, 128, 132	iv. 7	52, 67, 244, 277, 371
xvi. 30	306	i. 7	100, 132, 166–168, 176,	iv. 7, 8	6, 66, 369
xvi. 33	305		186	iv. 7–21	5
xvii. 3	51, 66, 239, 315	i. 8	166	iv. 8	47, 52, 54, 274 sq.,
xvii. 5	90, 107, 113, 116,	i. 8–10	13		319
	117, 119, 120, 133	i. 9	64, 65, 136, 137, 166, 186	iv. 9	103
xvii. 6	303	i. 10	137	iv. 9–11	57
xvii. 9	292, 299, 300	ii. 1	70, 170, 185, 192	iv. 10	161, 181, 184, 185,
xvii. 11	63, 303	ii. 2	181, 184, 185		269, 273
xvii. 12	24	ii. 4	10	iv. 11	269, 273
xvii. 14	134	ii. 5	273	iv. 12	49, 260, 274
xvii. 15	168	ii. 5, 6	258	iv. 13	166, 259
xvii. 17	179	ii. 7–11	5	iv. 14	138, 165
xvii. 19	178, 179, 186	ii. 8	108, 128, 369	iv. 15	166, 219, 234

INDEX OF TEXTS

	Page
iv. 16	52, 55, 239, 259, 274
	sq., 286, 369
iv. 17	340, 353
iv. 19	58
v. 1	219, 243, 245, 251
v. 1, 2	254, 273
v. 1–4	235
v. 4	218, 234, 245
v. 5	234
v. 6	146
v. 7	192, 207
v. 8	238, 249
v. 9	234
v. 10, 11	239
v. 11	325
v. 12	228, 233, 234
v. 14	311
v. 16	297
v. 16, 17	136, 145, 149 sq.
v. 18	243, 246
v. 19	134, 138
v. 20	51, 305, 322

SECOND EPISTLE OF JOHN.

	Page
2	95
3, 4	70
4	10, 192
7	145, 146, 148

THIRD EPISTLE OF JOHN.

	Page
3, 4	10

OTHER NEW TESTAMENT BOOKS.

	Page
Matt. v. 12	118, 119
vi. 20	118
x. 23	339
xi. 27	112
Matt. xii. 31 sq.	152
xvi. 16	105
xvi. 27, 28	340
xx. 28	172
xxiv. 13, 14	339
xxiv. 29 sq.	339
xxv. 34	119
xxvi. 61	40
xxvi. 63	105
xxvi. 64	340
Mark i. 4	250
i. 8	250
iii. 22 sq.	152
vii. 18	209
vii. 26	294
ix. 1	340
x. 30	313
xiii. 20	340
xiii. 24	339
xiv. 58	40
Luke i. 63	295
vii. 3	294
viii. 37	294
ix. 27	340
ix. 54	210
x. 18	144, 353
x. 22	112
xii. 10	152
xii. 48	295
xviii. 13	182
xviii. 30	313
xxi. 32	339, 340
Acts vi. 13, 14	41
vii. 35	85
xxi. 29	295
Rom. i. 17	235
x. 9	204
1 Cor. v. 7	169
xii. 3	204, 234
2 Cor. v. 16	225
Gal. iii. 9	140
iii. 19	85
iii. 29	140
Eph. i. 3 sq.	205
v. 2	178
Phil. i. 23	332
ii. 8, 9	181
Col. i. 16, 17	93
2 Thess. ii. 3, 6, 7	147
1 Tim. ii. 6	172
1 Tim. iii. 6	144
v. 22	246
Heb. i. 2, 3	93
ii. 2	85
ii. 17	182
ii. 17, 18	352
iv. 15	352
vi. 1	187
vi. 4–8	154
x. 26–31	154
James i. 27	246
iv. 4	267
1 Pet. i. 19	170
iii. 15	295
2 Pet. ii. 4	142
Jude 4	142, 143
14 sq.	143
Rev. v. 12	170
vii. 14	170
xiii. 1 sq.	147
xx. 2	141

APOCRYPHAL BOOKS.

	Page
Wisdom of Solomon vi. 22,	81
vii. 21	81
vii. 24	81
vii. 25–29	82
viii. 4	81, 82
Ecclus. i. 1, 4, 9, 20	80
xxiv. 3–10	80, 81
Fourth Esdras vii. 28 sq.	105
xiii. 37 sq.	105
xiv. 9	105
Enoch xii. 4	143
xv. 3	143
lxiv. 2	143
cv. 2	105

GENERAL INDEX

ABBOT, E., cited, viii, 108, 290; on the words for prayer in John, 293, 296, 308.
Abiding in Christ, 258 *sq*.
ADAM OF ST. VICTOR, hymn commonly attributed to, cited, 211.
Adeney, W. F., cited, 374.
Alexandrian Philosophy, see *Philo*.
ALFORD, H., cited, 246, 250, 292, 308, 332, 336, 337.
Antichrist, doctrine of, in John, 145 *sq*.
AUGUSTINE, cited, 150, 160, 199, 336, 352.

BALLENTINE, W. G., cited, 266; on the words meaning *to love* in John, 272.
BAUR, F. C., cited, 46, 74, 75, 127, 156, 189, 241, 266, 312, 328, 352, 355, 374.
"Beast," the, in Revelation, how different from "Antichrist" in John, 147.
Begetting, the divine, 242 *sq*.; born of water and Spirit, 249 *sq*.
Benevolence, its relation to justice in God, 53, 54.
BENGEL, cited, 150.
BERNARD, T. D., cited, 189, 290, 375.
BEYSCHLAG, W., cited, 1, 22, 46, 76, 90, 92, 102, 104, 127, 133, 156, 189, 218; on the doctrine of faith in John, 231, 232; cited, 242, 252, 266, 312, 316, 328, 332; on the judgment, 351, 352, 374.
BEZA, cited, 152.

Bibliography, 373; cf. Preface, p. xi.
Birth from above or from God, see *Begetting*.
Blood, of Christ, theories respecting the meaning of, in ch. vi., 159-164.
BURTON, E. D., cited, 315.

CAIAPHAS, his view of Jesus' death, 175, 176, 255.
CALVIN, cited, 152, 249, 256.
CHARLES, R. H., his edition of the Book of Enoch, cited, 143.
Children of God, outside Judaism, 255.
Childship to God, 251-255.
CHRIST, his work grounded by John in his person, 3, 4; God's love for, 55-57; the doctrine of his person in the prologue of John's Gospel, 88 *sq*.; creation ascribed to, 93; incarnation of, 95; his union with the Father, 102 *sq*.; meaning of the title *Son of God* as applied to, 102 *sq*.; meaning of "only-begotten Son," 106 *sq*.; his pre-existence, 115-122; charged with using demoniacal power by the Pharisees, 139; as the giver of life, 156 *sq*.; as the Lamb of God, 168-170; his death on behalf of men, 171-177; "sanctifies himself" for men, 178, 179; his lifting up from the cross, 180, 181; as a propitiation for sin, 181-188; sends the Holy Spirit, 190 *sq*.; abiding in, 258 *sq*.; eating the flesh of, &c., 261; fellowship with, 262 *sq*.; the prayers of,

298 sq.; eternal life derived from, 314 sq.; his "coming," 331 sq.; his function of judgment, 346 sq.
CONE, O., cited, viii, 1, 175.
Comforter, see Spirit.
CREMER, H., on the sonship of Christ, 126, 182: cited, 267; on the difference between αἰτεῖν and ἐρωτᾶν, 296.
Cross, Christ lifted up upon the, 180, 181.

"Day, the last," 340.
DAVIDSON, S., cited, viii.
Death, of Christ, on behalf of men, 171-179.
Demoniacal Possession, in John and in the Synoptics, 139.
DE WETTE, cited, 69, 91, 152, 167, 178, 201, 250, 257, 308, 334, 338, 342.
DODS, M., cited, 189.
DORNER, I. A., on the theological significance of the idea of love, 275.
DRUMMOND, J. cited, 75.
Dualism, in John, the nature of, 129 sq.; supposed bearing of, upon the authorship of the Fourth Gospel, 132, 133.
DÜSTERDIECK, F., cited, 150.
DWIGHT, T., cited, ix, 70, 154, 155; on the conviction concerning sin wrought by the Spirit, 215; cited, 257; on the meaning of xvi. 23, 309; cited, 334.

EBRARD, J. H. A., cited, 69, 150, 153, 199, 335.
Ecclesiasticus, doctrine of wisdom in, 80 sq.
Enoch, Book of, its bearing upon the doctrine of the fall of Satan, 143 sq.
Eschatology, the Johannine, 328 sq.
"Eternal," meaning of the term in John, 322 sq. See *Life*.
EWALD, H., cited, 189, 332, 334, 336, 337, 374.

FAIRBAIRN, A. M., on the theological significance of the idea of love, 287.
Faith, Doctrine of, in John, 218; in the sense of believing that a thing is true, 219, 220; gradation in, 221-226; constructions which express the idea, 226-228; various opinions respecting the nature of, 228-235; its grounds, 235-238; doctrine of, in Paul and in John, compared, 367 sq.
Fall of Satan, whether taught in New Test., 142 sq.
FARRAR, F. W., cited, 1, 155.
Fellowship with Christ, 260 sq.
Flesh, contrasted with Spirit, in John, 129 sq.; "flesh and blood," of Christ, to be eaten and drunken, 158-164, 261.
FRANKE, A. H., cited, 22, 375.
FROMMANN, K., cited, 74, 102, 127; on John's doctrine of Satan, 144, 145, 156, 201, 218; on faith in John, 231; cited, 328, 355, 373.

GESS, W. F., cited, 107.
God, his ethical nature, 5; meaning of the phrase, "to be of God," 8; idea of, in John's writings, 46 sq.; as spirit, 46-48; as invisible, 48-50; "the true," 50, 51; as love, 52-55; his love for the Son, 55-57; for the world, 57, 58; for believers, 58, 59; as the giver of life to men, 59, 60; as light, 60-62; as righteous, 63; his retributive justice, 63-65; knowledge of, how attained, 65-68; the representation of him in I. iii. 19, 20, 68-70; his Fatherhood, 70-73; idea of, in Paul and in John, compared, 357 sq.
GODET, F., cited, 22, 75, 76, 91, 160, 168, 179, 199, 201, 250, 256, 257, 262, 269, 307, 308, 332, 334, 337, 342, 344.
GLOAG, P. J., cited, 1, 74.

HÄRING, T., cited, 376.
HARE, J. C., cited, 189; on the relation of the Spirit's work to faith in Christ, 208; cited, 213, 376.
HARNACK, A., cited, 76; on the relation of the prologue to the Fourth Gospel as a whole, 101, 159, 376.
HAUPT, E., cited, 1; on John's conception of history, 11; on God as light and as love, 60; cited, 67, 69, 70, 152, 167, 246, 373.
HEINZE, M., cited, 75.
HENGSTENBERG, cited, 336.
HILGENFELD, A., cited, 255, 373.
HOFMANN, J. C. K., cited, 199, 332, 334, 336.
HOLTZMANN, H. J., cited, viii, 67, 149, 154, 159, 178, 199, 201, 246, 250, 256, 270, 308, 332, 334, 338, 344, 352.
HOLTZMANN, O., cited, 22; on the Logos doctrine of John, 99, 100; cited, 308, 373.
HORTON, R. F., cited, 1.
HUTHER, J. E., cited, 67, 69, 70, 152, 167, 246.
HUTTON, R. H., cited, ix.

JEWS, their relation to the Messianic salvation, 24; their view of the Sabbath law, 37, 38; their real ignorance of Scripture, 43 sq.
JOHN, the theology of, its peculiarities, 1 sq.; its tendency to group its thoughts around central truths, 2 sq.; regards man as a unit, 8 sq.; the breadth of its ideas, 9 sq.; its realism, 11; its antitheses, 12; its idea of religion, 12 sq.; on the relation of the temporal and the eternal, 13, 14; its spiritual character, 14, 15; compared with Paul's theology, 16 sq.; its bearing on the union of doctrine and life, 18 sq.; its bearing on Christian unity, 20, 21; his view of the Old Test., 22 sq.; his doctrine of God, 46 sq.; his doctrine of the Logos, 74 sq.; his teaching respecting the relation of the Son to the Father, 102 sq.; his doctrine of Christ's pre-existence, 115 sq.; his doctrine of sin, 127 sq.; his "dualism," 129 sq.; his doctrine of salvation, 156 sq.; his teaching concerning the Holy Spirit, 189 sq.; his symbol the eagle, 210; his doctrine of faith, 218 sq.; his doctrine of the spiritual life, 241 sq.; his practical religious conceptions, 263-265; his doctrine of prayer, 290 sq.; his idea of "eternal life," 312 sq.; his eschatology, 328 sq.; his doctrine of the "coming" of Christ, 331 sq.; of the resurrection, 340 sq.; of the judgment, 346 sq.; his theology and Paul's compared, 355 sq.
Judgment, the, doctrine of, in John, 346 sq.

KEIL AND DELITZSCH, cited, 28.
KEIM, T., cited, viii, 201.
Knowledge of God and of Christ, as connected with "eternal life," 314 sq.
KÖHLER, H., cited, 376.
KÖSTLIN, K. R., cited, 1, 46, 156, 189, 373.

Lamb of God, meaning of, in John, 168 sq.
LANGE, J. P., cited, 160, 190, 199, 201, 308, 331, 332, 334, 335, 337, 355, 375.
LECHLER, G. V., cited, 46, 127, 201, 241, 336, 355, 375.
LIAS, J. J., cited, 46, 74, 373.
LIDDON, H. P., cited, 74, 76, 102.
Life, God the giver of, 59, 60; laying down of, by Christ, for men, 171 sq.; the spiritual, 241 sq.; "eternal," doctrine of, 312 sq.
Light, its meaning in John, 6; as a

name for God's nature, 60-62; contrasted with darkness in John, 128 sq.
LIGHTFOOT, J., on the meaning of "eating the flesh and drinking the blood of the Son of man," 163.
LIGHTFOOT, J. B., cited, viii, 292.
LIPSIUS, R. A., cited, 74.
Logos, John's doctrine of the, 74 sq.; Jewish or Alexandrian in origin, 76 sq.; roots of, in the O. T., 77-79; in Apocryphal books, 79 sq.; doctrine of, in the Targums, 82, 83; in Philo, 83 sq.; John's and Philo's doctrine of, compared, 96 sq.; purpose of, in John, historical and practical, 100 sq.
Love, its place in John's teaching, 4, 5; synonymous with light, 5; considered as the ethical nature of God, 52-55; John's doctrine of, 266 sq.; words denoting, 266-272; subjects and objects of, 272-274; as the ethical nature of God, 274 sq.; characteristics of, 276 sq.; whether a subordinate attribute of God and optional as to its exercise, 282-287; doctrine of, in Paul and in John, compared, 368 sq.
LÜCKE, F., cited, 67, 69, 74-76, 91, 92, 152, 167, 178, 199, 201, 256, 257, 308, 332, 334, 338, 342, 344.
LUTHARDT, C. E., cited, 76, 107, 256, 332, 334, 337, 344.
LUTHER, cited, 256, 336, 352.

Man, a unit in all his powers, 8, 9; "man of sin" in Paul, how different from "antichrist," in John, 147.
MAURICE, F. D., on the true basis of Christian fellowship, 21; cited, 189, 374.
Memra, the doctrine of, in the Targums, 82, 83.
Mercy, the divine, its relation to justice, 53, 54.

MESSNER, H., cited, 34, 127, 189, 266, 328, 355, 374.
MEYER, H. A. W, on John ii. 21, 38 sq.; cited, 75, 76, 90, 107, 114, 140, 160, 168, 172, 173, 178, 199, 201, 205, 250, 256, 257, 262, 269, 270, 308, 325, 332, 334, 338, 342, 344, 345, 351.
MÜLLER, J., on the nature of love, 275.
MURPHY, J. J., cited, 355.

Name, prayer in Christ's, 298, 302-305.
NEANDER, A., cited, 1, 69, 179, 201, 218; his view of faith in John, 231; cited, 328, 332, 375.
NITZSCH, K. I., on the doctrine of love, 275.

Old Testament, John's teaching concerning, 22 sq.; preparatory to the Gospel, 22, 23; the necessity that its prophecies be fulfilled, 24-29; its unity and inspiration, 25; John's method of interpreting it, 29, 30; its Messianic import, 30 sq.; John's alleged hostility to, 34 sq.; contrast, according to John, between Jesus' views of, and the popular opinions, 37, 38; the Jews' real ignorance of, 43, 44; Jesus, the fulfilment of, 44, 45; basis of the Logos-doctrine in, 77-79.
OLSHAUSEN, H., cited, 201, 337, 342.

Paraclete, Christ represented as, 170, 171, see also Spirit.
PARK, E. A., cited, 266, 286.
Parousia, doctrine of, in John, 329 sq.
PATTON, F. L., on the relation of justice and benevolence in God, 53.
PAUL, his legalism compared with John's type of thought, 15 sq.; his theology and that of John compared, 355 sq.

GENERAL INDEX

Pauline Apocalypse, the (2 Thess. ii. 1–12), 147.
PEABODY, A. P., cited, viii; on the meaning of xxi. 17 *sq.*, 338.
PEYTON, W. W., cited, 374.
PFLEIDERER, O., cited, 75, 159, 375.
PHILO, his philosophy, 76, 77; his doctrine of the Logos, 83 *sq.*
PLUMMER, A., cited, 67, 76, 86, 127, 159, 168, 199, 246, 250, 256, 257, 268, 270, 308, 325, 332, 334, 342, 352.
Prayer, the doctrine of, 290 *sq.*; words used by John to express idea of, 291 *sq.*; the prayers of Christ, 298 *sq.*; of the disciples, 302 *sq.*; assurances of answer to, 310, 311.
Pre-existence, of Christ, doctrine of, in John, 89 *sq.*, 115 *sq.*
Prologue, of John's Gospel, doctrine of the Logos in, 88 *sq.*
Prophecy, as viewed in John, 24, 26–29; necessary to distinguish its original sense from its applications, 29, 30; its Messianic element pervading in the O. T., 30–32; Jesus' appeal to, 32 *sq.*
Propitiation, doctrine of, in John, 181–188.

Religion, its nature and demands, 6, 10, 12; its inward spiritual character, 14, 15; its relation to theology, 18, 19; the Christian, in relation to the O. T., 22; its connection with Jewish history, 24; John's practical conceptions of, 262–265.
Resurrection, doctrine of, in John, 340 *sq.*
REUSS, E., cited, 1, 46, 74, 76, 89, 127, 133, 156; on John's doctrine of atonement, 185; cited, 189; on John's doctrine of the Spirit, 193, 197, 198, 201–203; cited, 218, 266, 312; on the meaning of "eternal life," 327; cited, 328; on John's eschatology, 329 *sq.*; cited, 331; on the resurrection, 341, 343, 345; cited, 355.
REYNOLDS, H. R., cited, 332, 334.
Righteousness, doctrine of, in John, 10; of God, 63–65.
RITSCHL, A., cited, 92.
ROBERTSON, F. W., cited, 290.
ROTHE, R. cited, 67.

SALMOND, S. D. F., cited, 76.
Salvation, the work of, according to John, 156 *sq.*; doctrine of, in chs. v. and vi., 156–164; the use of terms denoting, 164–167; represented as cleansing from sin, 166, 167; represented as the taking away of sin, 167 *sq.*; appropriation of, according to John, 218 *sq.*; doctrine of, in Paul and in John, compared, 360 *sq.*
SANDAY, W., cited, viii, 74.
SARTORIUS, E., on the divine love, 57; cited, 278.
Satan, reference of sin to agency of, in John, 139 *sq.*; in what sense sinned "from the beginning," 140 *sq.*; supposed doctrine of the fall of, in the New Test., 142 *sq.*
SCHAFF, P., cited, 272, 355, 373.
SCHILLER, cited, 354.
SCHMID, C. F., cited, 241, 374.
SCHOLTEN, J. H., cited, 201, 374.
SCHÜRER, E., cited, viii, 74.
SEARS, E. H., cited, 1; on Christian unity, 20, 21; on John's idea of atonement, 185; cited, 373.
SHEDD, W. G. T., on the divine mercy, 53, 54; on the nature of justice and of mercy, 285, 286.
Sheep, other, "not of this [Jewish] fold." 266, 267.
SIEGFRIED, C., cited, 74, 99.
Sin, incompatibility of, with Christian life, 13; John's doctrine of, 127 *sq.*; definition of, 127; represented as darkness, 129; how re-

lated to "the world," 133 *sq.*; considered as bondage, 135 *sq.*; usage of the words denoting, 136 *sq.*; sense in which all Christians do sin, and yet "cannot sin," 137 *sq.*; its relation to demoniacal agencies, 138 *sq.*; referred to Satan's agency, 139 *sq.*; represented as "antichrist," 145 *sq.*; "sin unto death," meaning of, 149 *sq.*; salvation from, 156 *sq.*; the cleansing from, etc., 166 *sq.*; doctrine of, in Paul and in John, compared, 364 *sq.*

Son of God, see Christ.

Spirit, contrasted with flesh in John, 129 *sq.*; the Holy, doctrine of, 189 *sq.*; designations of, in John, 190–193; whether distinct from Christ, 193 *sq.*; whether or not, a person, 195 *sq.*; his mission and work, 203 *sq.*; is sent "in Christ's name," 204 *sq.*; his work in the apostolic age, 209; his relation to unbelievers, 210 *sq.*

STIER, R., cited, 332.

STRONG, A. H., on the divine love and justice, 53, 285, 286.

Targums, doctrine of the *Word* in, 82, 83.

Temple, meaning of reference to in the words, "Destroy this temple," &c., 38–42.

Thayer's Lexicon, cited, 267.

Theology, John's contribution to, 15 *sq.*; its relation to religion, 18, 19; of Paul and John, compared, 355.

Theology, Biblical, its aim and method, 1, 2.

THOLUCK, A., cited, 108, 193, 199, 201, 250, 256, 308, 331, 342.

THOMPSON, J. P., cited, 376.

TISCHENDORF, C., cited, 140, 246.

TOY, C. H., cited, 28.

TREGELLES, S. P., cited, 246.

TRENCH, R. C., on the words meaning *to pray* in John, 292 *sq.*; cited, 307, 308.

Unity, Christian, bearing of John's teaching upon, 20, 21.

VAN OOSTERZEE, J. J., cited, 241; on the significance of "God is love," 275; cited, 355, 375.

WASHBURN, E. A., his translation of Adam of St. Victor's hymn to John, cited, 211.

WATKINS, H. W., cited, viii, 373.

WEBER, F., cited, 82.

WEISS, B., cited, 1, 22; on John ii. 21, 41; cited, 46; on the knowledge of God, 66; cited, 74, 76, 88, 90, 102; on the meaning of *Son of God* in John, 103 *sq.*; cited, 107, 127, 140, 154, 156; on the meaning of Christ's flesh and blood in ch. vi. 162; cited, 167, 168, 173, 178, 189, 199, 201, 218; his view of John's doctrine of faith, 228 *sq.*; cited, 241, 246; on faith, 252, 253; cited, 256, 257, 259, 262, 269–271, 290, 308, 312, 316, 318, 325, 328, 332, 334, 336, 338, 342, 344, 352, 373.

WENDT, H. H., cited, 22, 32; on John x. 8, 36; on John ii. 21, 41; cited, 46, 72, 102, 104; on the preexistence and sonship of Christ, 115–122; cited, 127; cited, 156; on the meaning of Christ's *flesh and blood* in ch. vi., 162; cited, 218; his view of John's doctrine of faith, 230; cited, 241, 266, 312, 316, 328, 332, 374.

WEIZSÄCKER, K., cited, 76, 88, 99, 308.

WESTCOTT, B. F., cited, 1, 22, 46 67, 69, 70, 75, 91, 108, 127, 149, 151; on "Sin unto death," 150 *sq.*; on the meaning of Christ's *flesh and blood* in ch. vi., 162; cited, 168, 179, 182, 190, 199, 204; on the conviction of the world by the Spirit, 214; cited, 241, 246, 250; on childship in John, 253; cited, 256, 257, 262, 266, 270; on the doctrine of love, 275; cited, 290, 292, 308, 312; on the meaning of "eternal life," 320; cited, 325; on the parousia, 332; cited, 336, 337, 342; on the judgment, 352; cited, 376.

WESTCOTT AND HORT, cited, 108, 246.

WHITTIER, J. G., his poem *Palestine*, cited, 225, 226.

Wisdom, Book of, doctrine of wisdom in, 81 *sq*.

Word, see Logos.

WORDSWORTH, C., cited, 292.

World, John's doctrine of the, 133 *sq*.

ZELLER, E., cited, 75.

www.ingramcontent.com/pod-product-compliance
Lightning Source LLC
Chambersburg PA
CBHW070008010526
44117CB00011B/1468